Love of Friendship
in the Christian Life

Love of Friendship in the Christian Life

Jonathan Sammut

Foreword by Nadia Delicata

WIPF & STOCK · Eugene, Oregon

LOVE OF FRIENDSHIP IN THE CHRISTIAN LIFE

Copyright © 2019 Jonathan Sammut. All rights reserved. Except for brief quotations in critical publications or reviews, no part of this book may be reproduced in any manner without prior written permission from the publisher. Write: Permissions, Wipf and Stock Publishers, 199 W. 8th Ave., Suite 3, Eugene, OR 97401.

Wipf & Stock
An Imprint of Wipf and Stock Publishers
199 W. 8th Ave., Suite 3
Eugene, OR 97401

www.wipfandstock.com

PAPERBACK ISBN: 978-1-5326-7325-2
HARDCOVER ISBN: 978-1-5326-7326-9
EBOOK ISBN: 978-1-5326-7327-6

Manufactured in the U.S.A.   NOVEMBER 19, 2019

To the glory of God, Eternal Friend, and to all my friends.

To know someone only from the outside is not really to know the person: we do not know the nucleus of the person, even if we see him many times and recognise him in the way he looks, acts, speaks, moves. Only with the heart are we able to truly know a person . . . We substantially understand and get to know more about a person only through the heart, in friendship . . . Heart speaks to heart in coming to know a person essentially, in his truth.

—BENEDICT XVI, GENERAL AUDIENCE, OCTOBER 8, 2008

Contents

Foreword by Nadia Delicata | ix

Introduction | xiii

Chapter 1　Elements of Friendship in the Classical and Christian Tradition | 1

Chapter 2　Characteristics of "Love" and "Friendship" in the Fourth Gospel | 48

Chapter 3　*Caritas* as "*Amicitia* with God" in Thomas Aquinas | 77

Chapter 4　Friendship in the Process of Renewal of the Theology of the Christian Life | 108

Chapter 5　Conclusion | 138

Bibliography | 143

Index | 155

Foreword

A LONG TIME AGO, when I was still pondering what should be the focus of my PhD dissertation, my mentor in Christian ethics, Rev. Dr Ron Mercier, SJ, suggested quite evocatively: "The Christian life is nothing without friendship; why not consider the long deep history of what it means to be a 'friend' as focus of your study?"

Back then, I had already been toying with the idea how the Johannine Gospel is the quintessential manifesto of the Christian life and the suggestion was very tempting indeed. But as these things go, friendship was not to be the focus of my work, even if it remained the highest principle around which I sought to organize my theological reflection. So, when Mr Jonathan Sammut expressed his own fundamental conviction that "the love of friendship" was the anchor of the Christian life and that his desire was to ponder the heights of this conviction, I was more than thrilled.

As the reader, who has the privilege to read this book will soon note, however, Mr Sammut did more than study friendship, its historical significance or even theological depths. With much elegance, he takes us on a powerful journey to the true source of the Christian heart, pondering the true "best" of the tradition. The Fourth Gospel and its exegesis through the times—indeed, culminating with that of the Angelic Doctor—is a testament of the Christian heart that beats powerfully through the ages, like salt that enriches our taste buds, or the flicker of light that makes the world come alive amidst darkness.

When Mr Sammut argues for the retrieval of "the love of friendship" as the foundation of the Christian life, he prophetically reminds us of what is at stake in the world today. Not just in a world on the brink of political wars, but even more poignantly—or ironically!—in the smaller enclaves of our churches and Christian communities called to be salt and light of the earth who witness to peace. For, amidst the Christian culture wars, amidst our petty divisions about what should have ethical priority (whether social ethics or private ethics), we realize that our deeper crisis is that Christians are forgetting what their true mission is: "love of God and neighbor" that always begins with the gracious love of the Father to be his friends. Peace, reconciliation, the Christian life, are nothing without "the love of friendship" that is God in Godself.

Thus, only God elevates us to return his love as friends; for it is God alone who perfects us to become creatures imbued with love who overflow with his joy. Friendship is the quintessential experience of "joy"—the good news of the gospel as our salvation and friendship in Christ—and as such it is the gift of abundant mercy that, over time, matures to the true mutuality that will transform the world.

Pondering this work should not just open the depths of our collective memory of salvation; it should also shake us to an examination of conscience of how much, each one of us, truly *seeks* to be "friend" with our neighbors (whoever they might be), in our social circles, at our workplaces, in our professional networks, on social media, and even in our churches. We might want to ask ourselves how our society is schooling in "friending," or whether, as we increasingly take our "friendships" online and dissolve in face-to-face anonymity, we merely continue to succumb to the temptation of the tribalistic tendencies of the digital age driven by existential angst and fear. When all is said and done, what is it that makes my heart burn? Is it a spirit that seeks to reach out to embrace the other, because I am truly attuned to how in the flesh flickers the light of God? Or is it an instinct of self-preservation that overrides all my good "moral" intentions? Ultimately, we must ask ourselves how open are we to the long, rigorous training in asceticism and self-restraint? Or in the purification of our desire for justice (even when it hurts oneself most)? This training and purifying are the only efforts demanded of us to be sufficiently open to the grace of seeing the other as "another self" and of loving him or her in return with love joyfully received.

Mr Sammut's work is thus also balm for the soul and not just food for the mind. As both healing and enriching, may it also be another instance of that ongoing post Vatican II journey in the Catholic tradition especially, of renewing moral theology from the limiting legalistic frameworks that for centuries were imposed as "structure" over the much more fundamental truth of the ongoing need of personal conversion and transformation. Friendship, as a holistic experience that perfects body, mind and spirit, is the essence of the Christian moral message. And friendship is what the church is called to "gift" as witness in a world that desperately needs to be restitched from existential wounds, intellectual doubts, and ultimately, fear about the future.

Thank you, Mr Sammut, for your "friendship" to the world in cultivating such a precious work that all can ponder and be touched by.

—Dr Nadia Delicata
University of Malta
September 28, 2019

Introduction

AS A CHRISTIAN AND member of a long-established lay order—the Society of Christian Doctrine—founded by Saint George Preca in 1907, I have glimpsed the transcendental character and the divine beauty of the "love of friendship" from Holy Scripture, the Founder's prolific writings, and friendships with members of the Society. This book is both record of and tribute to the "love of friendship." What began as my dissertation for the Master of Arts in Theology Degree from the University of Malta progressed in later revision to writing that emanated out of the love for God and the Catholic Church.

During the years studying theology at the University of Malta and at the University of Notre Dame, USA, I discovered that "love of friendship" is highly praised by Holy Scripture and that the language of friendship has been used relatively freely by the patristic writers of the early centuries and some later systematic and mystical theologians. Nevertheless, I also noticed, particularly as one moved through the Reformation and towards the present day, the inhibition of its use in philosophical and theological circles.

In my studies, I found that the problems were varied, and sometimes contradictory. There was the overarching influence of the classical tradition of Greco-Roman friendship, which in its final Ciceronian form reserves true friendship for a tiny minority of educated and virtuous males who enjoyed and depend on each other's character. Such friendship elects with great care whom it will love and is partial, exclusive and contingent on worthiness. How unlike the universal love commanded by Christ!

Nevertheless, classical friendship was sufficiently broad that New Testament writers, especially the Fourth Evangelist, drew on its language, and

Introduction

the great theologians of the fourth century, including Saint Augustine, who were still steeped in its tradition, integrated them into their understanding of love in Christ. Long afterwards, in the Cistercian abbey of Rievaulx in twelfth-century England, Aelred Christianised Cicero's *On Friendship*, and Aristotle's philosophy of friendship served as basis for Saint Thomas Aquinas as he explored the Christian doctrine of the theological virtue of *caritas* as "friendship with God". Unfortunately, neither Aelred, nor Saint Thomas on this subject, came to have a wide impact until the late twentieth century. In later Medieval Period, "friendship with God"—which for Saint Thomas was the foundation of all our understanding of love, both for God and neighbor—became little more than a stock synonym for "being in a state of grace".

With the rise of Modernism, classical friendship became for a time the preserve of scholars with pagan leanings, who thought that Christianity— with its emphasis on the universal and disinterested character of love of neighbor—had little or nothing to contribute to the subject, rooted as it was in antiquity. By the eighteenth century, friendship somewhat lost the aura of manly strength and virtue, which had graced it since the classical period; it began to be understood quite differently, as a sentimental attachment that was the product of irrational feeling but not of rational choice. It was merely a feeling of affection, engendered by liking (but having nothing in common with the Christian command to love), and as such it could be excluded from the sphere of ethics in both philosophy and theology. Friendship and Christian love had drifted very far apart, although there were always a few spiritual writers who continued to revive the link between them; and in the nineteenth century there was some *rapprochement,* especially in the writings of Saint John Henry Newman and the Oxford Movement, of which he was a central figure.

At the dawn of the twentieth century, the shadow over "love of friendship" appeared in a new form in the study of biblical language. Protestant scholarship made a sharp distinction between the revealed Judaeo-Christian religion of the Bible and natural pagan Hellenism. One focus of this distinction was found in the Greek of the Bible, and especially in its different words for love. This trend of thought reached its zenith in the 1930s in Anders Nygren's highly influential work, *Agape and Eros*. In his book Nygren argued that the term *agapē*, generally translated as *caritas* in Latin, is to be identified with the biblical thought-world and therefore considered a revealed and divine kind of love, while *eros* is selfish, possessive, desiring

Introduction

love. In his theory Nygren simply dismissed *philía* (loosely translated as friendship) as a subsidiary of *eros*, as love that seeks reward. More recently, friendship has come to the fore as a key paradigm of community and renewed human society, while the concept of friendship has been steadily evolving through the interest on personalism and virtue in Christian ethics. This renewed interest in friendship has prompted me to reflect more about it from a theological perspective and not merely a philosophical view.

Friendship is commonly used in two senses, on the one hand to denote a reciprocal relationship and, on the other, to convey the kind of love one associates with a friend. This book is more inclined towards and interested in the latter sense, while keeping in mind the former sense. It seeks to explore the meaning of "love of friendship," the love of a friend. It also seeks to explore how the retrieval of a proper theology of friendship, rooted in Holy Scripture and Christian Tradition, can enrich the life of an authentic Christian and contribute to the ongoing renewal of the theology of the Christian life (Christian ethics, theological ethics or moral theology), both in its fundamental and practical aspect.

This book is divided into five chapters. Although the approach of this book is fundamentally theological, I found it necessary to begin with a philosophical-historical study of the roots of the classical Greco-Roman understanding of friendship in moral reflection prior to Christianity and how (and to what extent) this was appropriated in the Christian Tradition. Chapter 2 illustrates the transcendental character and the novelty of the Christian understanding of friendship found in Holy Scripture, focusing particularly on the most relevant texts in the Fourth Gospel where "love" and "friendship" stand to be important themes. Chapter 3 shows how Saint Thomas Aquinas, through his exegesis of the Fourth Gospel, his synthesis of the Christian Tradition and his ability to rearticulate Christian theology through Aristotelian philosophy, inimitably defines the theological virtue of *caritas*, fully and in every respect, as "friendship with God"; in so doing he depicts friendship as the finality, the *telos* of the Christian life. Chapter 4 shows how the retrieval of a proper theology of friendship, rooted in Holy Scripture and Christian Tradition, can enrich the life of an authentic Christian and contribute to the ongoing renewal of moral theology called for by the Second Vatican Council (see *Optatam Totius*, par. 16). The final chapter consists of some concluding remarks.

Many people have contributed to this project through their scholarly guidance, spiritual encouragement, friendship, and support (both physical

Introduction

and emotional). My dissertation tutor, Dr Nadia Delicata, and co-tutor, Rev. Dr Martin Micallef, OFM CAP, provided guidance and encouragement throughout the course of this project at the University of Malta. Of a more enduring legacy, they made my time far more profitable than it would have been through their willingness to relate to me as a friend as well as mentors. I am also grateful to my parents, the first teachers who taught me the meaning of true love, to my adorable niece, Aaliyah, who nourished within me a sense of fatherhood, and to all my friends for their support. A special tribute to my American friend, Mrs Ruth D. Lasseter, without whom the book could neither have been begun nor ended. Working with me from the other side of "the pond" through electronic communication, Ruth has been a constant source of encouragement and help, and she continues to play the role of friend to perfection.

The limitations and errors are mine, since love reflects God's own nature, forever remaining above and transcending our human grasp. Love is nevertheless our calling, and in the end, it is a matter of grace. The love revealed in Jesus Christ is God's love, given to us to practice in the power of the Holy Spirit. The love of Christ on the Cross is that of a friend, who wills to draw all—through forgiveness and reconciliation—into friendship. Hence, divine love can rightfully be described in terms of the "love of friendship."

—Jonathan Sammut
   September 29, 2019
   Feast of Archangels Michael, Raphael and Gabriel

Chapter 1

Elements of Friendship in the Classical and Christian Tradition

FRIENDSHIP'S EARLIEST THEMES

THE DIMENSIONS OF FRIENDSHIP have been experienced and discussed since the beginning of recorded history. Indeed, if the Stone Age cave paintings of Lascaux and elsewhere of friends hunting are included, the depictions of friendship have been a reality since the dawn of time. It is both simple and complex at the same time; it is the relationship sought by all people, who tend to undertake friendship in one of two ways: true or false, in loyalty or for betrayal. Friendship is one of the oldest themes of epic poetry, storytelling, fables and myth, as well as central to Classical Antiquity and the Judeo-Christian tradition. While there are many words for the variety of emotions and qualities of friendship, which come to us in the rich heritage of classical writings on friendship, which will be explored in these pages, the most perfect and beautiful consideration of friendship is found in the wisdom tradition of Christianity. Unlike other creation myths of the ancient world, there is an emphasis on goodness, even gentleness, in the Genesis narrative that points to a Creator who takes delight in his creation. There is a charming portrait of prelapsarian friendship with Adam, when God creates the animals, but wants to know what his "man-creation" will call the creatures. Then, after the Fall, sacred scripture relates how God and Moses spoke "man to man" in their discussions about how the "Chosen People" would *live as friends* in their newly granted freedom from

Egyptian enslavement; so the short list of divine commands were given to safe-guard love in the community. The Judeo-Christian tradition proclaims that all creation itself reflects the glory of God, but it is human people who can gratefully come to know all of humanity's sacred origins as part of the divine revelation that culminated in Jesus Christ, the incarnate word of God, who alone taught his followers how to be friends with him, with one another and even with his Father, the God of Abraham, Isaac and Jacob.

The desire for friendship can be seen as parallel to and dependent on the desire for God because all people long for this loving relationship with other people and with a transcendent creator: "In many ways, throughout history down to the present day, men have given expression to their quest for God in their religious beliefs and behavior: in their prayers, sacrifices, rituals, meditations, and so forth. These forms of religious expression, despite the ambiguities they often bring with them, are so universal that one may well call man a religious being."[1]

There is a prelapsarian harmony in the friendship of the first people with God and with one another and all creation. The mystery of that friendship continues from the ancient Genesis account of humanity's sacred origins, where the shattered trust between Adam and God joined with the resentful blame between Adam and his wife in bewailing the seemingly eternal loss of their happiness in friendship. Theologians have explained "the Fall" as the broken community among people and the enmity with God as a reality, not just a concept; it can be recognized simply by looking into the earliest art and cultures, as well as our own relationships, even today.

Sociologists declare that we are social animals; anthropologists note that all humans, everywhere, and at all times have had tribes and social structure. However, faith seeking understanding through the arts and sciences has found no adequate explanation for that ancient tragedy of the loss of friendship with God and others, nor adequately given account as to why there should be evil, violence, passion, lies and hatred among peoples and cultures. Where theologians, historians, and scientists have been able to agree is in acknowledging that there have been times, both preceding and throughout recorded history, that have been marked by amazing inspirations and inventions, such as the wheel, the screw pump and larger team-work creations, like the Egyptian pyramids or gigantic standing

---

1. Catechism, I.1.28.

Elements of Friendship in the Classical and Christian Tradition

stone-sculptures, like Stonehenge or Ħaġar Qim, a megalithic temple complex on the Mediterranean island of Malta.

There have been moments in invisible realities, too, such as friendship, which have also been marked by amazing inspirations and distinctions from other forms of human enterprise and relationships through the long roll of history and cultures. The Bible records these moments of such "grace-filled change" in the Judeo-Christian tradition. Through Moses, God sent a Law to give human beings a guide for friendship, but few would listen. God sent prophets and raised up kings, both good and bad, but all concerned with the human life form and its relationship to the God of Abraham, Isaac, and Jacob. Then, came the greatest change that happened to the world, to humanity since the creation of Adam and Eve themselves, and for all human beings that came after them. God revealed himself through Jesus in the event called the Incarnation; God's word itself came to the world and was made possible by the cooperation of a human woman, Mary. With the birth of Jesus Christ, the Incarnation changed history; it changed humanity; it changed friendship. All that came afterwards is seen as a response to the event of the Incarnation, and all the thousands of years that came before Jesus are seen as a preparation for receiving what the coming of the divine revelation would make known to those who come to him. The divine revelation of Jesus Christ, his coming into the world of people, is the greatest event in all of human history, where friendship has played so illustrious and essential a part, and which is still evolving.

Can we think of such times of Grace-filled evolution as so vast that the new creature can hardly be recognized as the same life-form or being? In-depth study of the philosophical, theological, and historical overview of friendship indicates that the concept and understanding of friendship preceded and has undergone a vast change through recorded history, and especially since the final revelation of God in the Incarnation. However, due to many conflicting forces and conventions, friendship has continued to evolve as a particular type of Christian love in the tradition, which, despite some beautiful blossoms, has even yet to yield the mature fruit that was taught by the Son of Man himself who taught his disciples that they were the branches, but he was the life-giving vine, the *sine qua non*. The "love of friendship" has yet to be realized, even among Christians, as the treasure that it can be.

By no means, theological understanding and appreciation for friendship itself has not been a straight, smooth highway through the centuries.

At times "Christian friendship" has been excluded, overshadowed, and even opposed by other classical-based understandings of "Christian love," expressed by the Greek *agápē* and the Latin *caritas*. Even though "friendly relationships" were deemed important from the beginning of Christianity, there has been no clear "theology of friendship" itself—known as *philía* in Greek and *amicitia* in Latin.[2]

Even though "friendship" often had to struggle against classical templates in order to justify its unique and significant importance in Christianity for human flourishing, friendship (*philía/amicitia*) is the essential ingredient by which Christians grow in virtue, moral character, and holiness. The uniqueness can be found in the distinctive dimension of friendship that is generated and sustained by divine revelation. Without Grace, it would not be possible for humans to sustain the "love of friendship" in its unique dimension, which is the subject of this book.

Any contemporary moral theological discussion on friendship must begin with the foundational writings of the classical era, since friendship's moral nature and social application were first considered fully here. Indeed, before it emerges in a Christian context, a wealth of exploration into friendship's nature extending over a significant period of time is found in classical literature. The philosophers of antiquity are perhaps the first to come to mind, as they are the most studied in scholarly pursuits, but even the Greek storytellers, such as Aesop, have given earthy examples of distinctions and unequal friendships through animal stories, such as "The Mouse and the Lion" from which came the adage: "A friend's kindness is never wasted." The three great contemporary Greek dramatists—Sophocles, Euripides, and Aeschylus—all dealt with the theme of friendship, usually treachery and betrayal of friends, but "Antigone" stands out for its poignancy of loyalty in familial friendship and duty. This abundant heritage from antiquity forms a foundational discourse for later Christian writers, especially Saint Augustine and Saint Thomas Aquinas. Each saw God's love reflected in friendship itself; however, each drew significantly different conclusions regarding what they had envisioned.

However, scholars generally agree: the first systematic treatment of friendship began with Aristotle, but he was certainly not the first to reflect on friendship. In Ancient Greece, from the seventh to the fourth century BC, discussions on friendship were already held (sometimes emotionally

---

2. For an historical treatment of the tension between *agápē* and *philía*, see Carmichael, *Friendship*, 35–39.

and tumultuously) as recorded in Homer, Hesiod, Theognis, the Pythagoreans, the Greek playwrights and, famously, in Socrates and Plato.

"The Iliad" and "The Odyssey," Homer's two great epic poems, are foundational to classical culture. They date back to the eighth century BC but reveal the mindset of a more ancient pre-literate Greece. They include reflection of friendship through the example of friends in stories and narratives, rather than through philosophy and abstract concepts. Thus, while the classical form *philía* does not feature in Homer, terms like *philéō*, *philos* and *philótēs* can be found. The verb *philéō* is the verb "to love" or "to be friendly to one," while *philos* is a reflexive possessive pronoun in the sense of one's "own" and is used as an emotive adjective, usually in the passive sense of "dear," "beloved," and occasionally in the active sense of "loving," or "friendly."[3] The closest to our understanding of "love" or "friendship" is *philótēs*, a term having two strands of meaning: the first is that of "affection" and "obligation," initially brought together in Homer as he describes the commitment that a virtuous man has to love those within his household. The second strand is that evidenced in the "heroic friendship" of the Homeric poems, such as that between Achilles and Patroclus.[4]

In "Theogony," a methodical poem of primeval history, Hesiod explains the structure of the world and gives speculative information about the gods who rule it and the powers that are at work in it, often violently, passionately, and vindictively. Hesiod uses the word *philótēs* exclusively for sexual love between the many pairs of divinities whose unions create the cosmos.[5] Hesiod's view of friendship is narrow and rather pessimistic, partly because of his own situation at the time of writing, around 700 BC, when he had a quarrel with his brother Perses over a legacy. At the death of their father, the two brothers divided the inheritance. The division was supposed to be final, but Perses later appropriated additional portions which belonged to Hesiod's share. In the poem, Hesiod hopes and urges that the conflict may find a speedy and just decision which will put an end to all doubts.

A work attributed to Theognis is a loosely connected sequence of poems or sayings, probably complied at the end of the sixth and beginning of the fifth century BC in Megara, a small town to the southeast of Athens.

---

3. For more on friendship terminology in Homer, see Fitzgerald, "Friendship in the Greek World," 13–34.

4. See Fränkel, *Early Greek Poetry*, 1.

5. See Carmichael, *Friendship*, 8–9.

The content of the poems and sayings may be described as a threefold commentary: on contemporary events, philosophy of life, and personal affairs. Their tone is partly utilitarian, and to a certain extent passionately intemperate. He aimed to be less philosophical and speculative; his intention was more as practical and realistic. It is in Theognis[6] that the classical word for "friendship" (*philía*) first makes its appearance: "In its Iconic form *philiē*, when the author claims that the wicked are not wicked from birth but learn wickedness through *philiē* with the vile (1.305–6)."[7]

However, it is in the fifth century BC that the concept of friendship as *philía* is amplified through the Ionian philosopher Pythagoras and his followers, who were strongly associated with friendship. Pythagoras founded a community and imparted therein the ideals of temperance, courage and friendship. Two hundred years later, Diogenes Laertius wrote in the third century BC that "friends have all things in common," and he attributed to Pythagoras this principle. Within the Pythagorean community, friendship was seen as having not only a unifying relationship with other human beings but also the possibility of a higher dimension; the Pythagoreans envisioned friendship as a bringing about communion between the divine and the human. "Friends are as companions on a journey, who ought to aid each other to persevere in the road to a happier life," Pythagoras wrote. In the same Pythagorean community, there was an extraordinary understanding of friendship with a god, which was the greatest of all friendships and was considered as a "partnership in divine goods." The Pythagorean way of life was so imbued by this intense concept of friendship that "*philos*" itself became a technical term for any member of a close community.[8]

By the fourth century BC, reflection on the nature and value of friendship was arriving at its culmination in Hellenic[9] culture, and it would continue in far-reaching effect into the Hellenistic[10] and "Roman Greece" era

---

6. See Fränkel, *Early Greek Poetry*, 413–24.

7. Carmichael, *Friendship*, 9.

8. See Dillon and Hershbell, *Iamblichus*, 167.

9. "Hellenic" (510 BC–323 BC) is the term used for the period when so many of the influential scholars, writers, scientists, and philosophers were born in Athens; it is known as "Ancient Greece," or more generally, "Classical Greece." It also refers to the impact of Hellenic civilization and culture on later time periods in the West—the Middle Ages, the Renaissance, and Modernity.

10. "Hellenistic" (323 BC–146 BC) begins with the death of Alexander the Great, who conquered and assimilated the Asian cultures, particularly Macedonia, into his empire, which changed under the presence of foreign ideas, religions, and cultures;

and beyond to the rising of the Middle Ages and Renaissance in the West. Plato opted for a narrative approach in his analysis of friendship. In the "Lysis," he avoids an all-encompassing definition of friendship, taking a view of friendship that is not just self-oriented, but which focuses on the good of the other person. In a key statement, Plato defines love for someone as wishing them to be "as happy as possible."[11] By wishing happiness for another, Plato places friendship in the domain of non-possessive love, a relationship that seeks the well-being of another. Persons are seen as friends when they are alike in goodness. For Plato, therefore, friendship is reserved only for the good.

Indeed, a key feature in his thought is that friendship is consistent with "the pursuit of the Good." By "the Good" Plato means that which characterizes the best possible life. The "best possible life" consists of the effort to attain and be part of that which is aligned with the ideal form of the "Goodness." Friendship, with these goals of ideal goodness and best possible life, was seen to be superior even to love. The interpersonal characteristics of stability and faithfulness seemed better guaranteed in friendship, which gave confidence that one could trust the friend who was nigh in all one's circumstances. Friendship required that one should be willing to die for a friend, as in Alcestis' willingness to die for Patroclus.[12] Hence, in the "Phaedo"—the pre-mortem speech of Socrates—we see that philosophers "should be ready and willing to die."

The third century BC marks the inauguration of the Hellenistic Age. Two major empires collapsed in the second half of the third century BC: the first was political and the second was philosophical. The first found its culmination in Plato and Aristotle; the second in Athens and Sparta. The philosophical empire crumbled when Aristotle died in 322 BC. The political empire came to an end when King Philip of Macedon defeated the armies of Thebes and Athens in 388 BC. The first marked the end of the metaphysical speculation that had dominated philosophy for three hundred years, from the seventh to the fourth century BC. The second marked the end of the Greek city-states in all their diversity of government—whether ruled by king, tyrant, oligarchy, or democracy (Athens).

---

ultimately, the Athenian republic was compromised and finally ended when the Romans began conquering the entire Mediterranean world and assimilated the Greek culture as "Roman Greece."

11. Plato, *Lysis*, 207e.
12. See Plato, *Symposium*, 179–80.

The end of these eras, and other politico-social changes, brought about a change in the basic moral beliefs and values that upheld the structure of Hellenic culture—and also, therefore, in the understanding of friendship. While the Hellenic people realized their destiny as human beings in their *polis*—that is, as members of the "community"—the Hellenistic people realized their destiny in the cosmopolis as "individuals." Despite their differing worldviews and moral outlooks, both Hellenic people and Hellenistic philosophers gave a prominent place to friendship in their moral reflections. They considered friendship an essential ingredient, and—in some cases—deemed it a *sine qua non* for the good life. Both the Hellenic and the Hellenistic philosophers subscribed to the view that, in the scheme of things, human life was the most distinctive type of reality, and that the highest good was to be found in the realization of this good. Hence, as a modern historian of the Hellenistic era claims: "The history of Greek friendship is thus intertwined with Greek political history, and one cannot be written without knowledge of the other."[13]

The examples, although briefly given in some areas of the classical period, are important in setting the stage for the Christian understanding, which grew out of the classical era. Thus, foundationally, it is important to show the importance that friendship had in ancient times; it was fundamental in ethical discourse and illustriously central in philosophy. The classical era embraces both the Hellenic and Hellenistic phases, with Aristotle and Cicero as prime representatives of these two phases. Other contributions of this era (i.e., Seneca's "Of Happy Life" and Lucian's "Toxaris") are significant for a strictly philosophical study, but they are not included for the sake of brevity and focus of this book on the uniquely Christian form of friendship, which was instituted by Jesus.

Aristotle can be understood as the culmination of the Hellenic understanding of friendship. Cicero, who was probably the most important Roman jurist and rhetorician, had a strong influence on Latin Christianity.[14] Both Aristotle and Cicero offer a detailed and structured analysis of the concept of friendship, and their descriptions are pivotal to subsequent theological analysis of friendship in the Christian tradition. In conjunction with the views of these towering figures from ancient Greece and Rome, there is an all-embracing "logic" which underlies the inclusion of friendship in their moral reflection.

13. Fitzgerald, "Friendship in the Greek World Prior to Aristotle," 27.
14. See McLuhan, *Classical Trivium*, 13–78.

Elements of Friendship in the Classical and Christian Tradition

Aristotle's View of Friendship

Aristotle's treatment on friendship is found in the *Nicomachean Ethics* (*NE*), where he considers *philía* as a kind of "love" or "affection." The kind of affection that friendship is depends on the three objects of the affection, or "lovable" (*philētá*): "the advantageous" (*khrḗsimon*), "the pleasant" (*ḗdú*), and "the good" (*ágathón*). According to Aristotle, only human beings meet the criteria of "lovable objects" with whom one can establish a relation of friendship (*philētá*) in one of its three dimensions. (Love for inanimate things, such as wine, cannot be called *philía* because one cannot wish for the "well-being"—*eudaimonía*—of an inanimate object and reciprocate "good-will"—*eúnoia*—with it.)

The three objects of love are the basis for three kinds of friendship: first, friendships based on advantage or utility (which are necessary when one is not economically self-sufficient); second, friendships based on pleasure (where one enjoys the company of others and is stimulated by their presence); and third, friendships based on goodness or excellence (the most highly developed relationships where the good of the other is the primary motivation).

In the first kind, friends love each other not for each other's sake—the intellectual, moral, and artistic qualities they possess and by virtue of which they are lovable—but for the sake of some advantage. Hence, the friendship that exists between them is external, not internal, in the sense that the human bond between them is only an "accidental" bond. For this reason, a friendship based on utility lasts only as long as the advantage lasts. Consequently, the termination of this kind of friendship does not generate a feeling of severe pain or regret; this is why one can establish this kind of friendship with as many people as possible. Even today as in Aristotle's time, we usually encounter this kind of friendship, for example, among the elderly, amid people with different backgrounds, or between poor and rich people.

The second kind of friendship is based on pleasure. Unlike the first, this kind of friendship is more common among younger people, whose lives are in a period dominated by pleasure-seeking and opportunities of the moment. One of the strongest feelings that impels them to action is sexual attraction, but when their libido declines as they age and their practical responsibilities increase, these feelings change—along with other youthful interests. Hence, this kind of friendship does not last, because it is based on passing interests and as such is accidental. Like friendships based on utility, friendships based on pleasure cannot be claimed as being true friendships.

Aristotle insists that true friendship is not possible without equality in virtue as its basis and motive. He goes on to argue that complete or "perfect friendship" (*téleia philía*) is possible only when it was between men "who are good, and alike in virtue" because such friends are attracted to each other because of the good qualities they possess.[15] These qualities, in turn, arouse the affection needed for the bond of friendship to grow between them and give rise to their "good-will" (*eúnoia*). However, there the limitations of the classical understanding begin to appear; the classical distinction limits "goodwill" to the personal, not the impersonal. In Christian understanding, friends are supposed to have goodwill towards all people, whether they know them or not.

In developing their friendships, friends are not prompted by goodwill alone, but by the goodness they show to each other and because they wish each other good. As Aristotle put it: "It is those who desire the good of their friends for the friend's sake that are most truly friends, because each loves the other for what he is, and not for any accidental quality." Possessing the desire of good for the other's sake is, for Aristotle, what distinguishes friendship as "a virtue or implies virtue."[16] Friendship, as defining a relation, does not arise merely from a "friendly feeling" (*philēsis*), although it necessarily involves affection or an emotion of some kind. Rather, it is "a state of character."[17] It is a state, a disposition, that exists as an integral quality of the character of the one who befriends another. "This is why when a good man becomes a friend to another," as Aristotle explains, "he becomes that other's good; so, each loves his own good, and repays what he receives by wishing the good of the other and giving him pleasure."[18] This affirmation implies that friendship becomes "actual" in the activity of practicing it. Complete, or perfect, friendship requires a truly virtuous character, a character cultivated in justice, compassion, generosity, courage, honesty, honor, temperance, and practical wisdom. It also requires a culture in which both education and growth of good character are possible.

Although Aristotle admits that such conditions appear to be rare among men, he is convinced that the lofty place accorded to friendship is

---

15. Aristotle, *NE*, 1156b7.
16. Aristotle, *NE*, 1155a4.
17. Aristotle, *NE*, 1157b21.
18. Aristotle, *NE*, 1158a7.

Elements of Friendship in the Classical and Christian Tradition

attainable and realistic. The American classicist, David Konstan, who has written and taught extensively about the experience of beauty and human emotion in the classical world, offers an analysis of Aristotle's work as identifying the specifically personal nature of virtuous friendship: "Friendship does not exist between virtues but between people, in whom virtues are instantiated; all instantiations are particular."[19]

Friendship's interactive nature implies a reciprocity with both the community, which enables it, and also with the individuals, who are affected by it, in how they live and choose. This view is reinforced by the theologian Paul J. Wadell who writes, "Friendship is a practical implication of what the moral life requires . . . virtue cannot be attained in solitude."[20]

While the treatment of friendship from Aristotle to modern scholars (such as Konstan and Wadell) covers thousands of years, there is agreement on certain foundational qualities of friendship. To be precise: one needs friends to provide the means to execute good habits and good deeds, which—according to Aristotle—are the marks of the virtuous life and the expression of *eudaimonía*, which is often translated as happiness, well-being or good fortune. Wadell renders *eudaimonía* as "the best possible life."[21] He calls upon this ancient truth, which has its origins in classical training for friendship and which was picked up in Christian formation, so that people may love the good and seek it in everything they do.

Thus, *eudaimonía* may be thought of as describing a life of activity aligned with the ultimate good; we can draw on a very long tradition in order to understand that *eudaimonía* is more than happiness, because it is not limited to an emotional state. It is an activity that is associated with a pleasurable result, and Aristotle considered this outcome as being fulfilled and expressed as "living the best possible life." This state of well-being is active, valuable, and desirable in its own right. It exceeds happiness, comfort, or even pleasure; it is "the good for the sake of which everything else is done."[22] Aristotle comes to this conclusion after reflecting that the individual life is good, or happy, inasmuch as it is a rational life, since the essence of mankind is "rational being," one who can choose rational activity. This implies that human beings are not rational simply by virtue of possessing the faculty of intellect, but by exercising it properly as Right Reason. In

19. Konstan, *Friendship*, 76.
20. Wadell, *Friendship*, 64.
21. Wadell, *Friendship*, 31.
22. Aristotle, *NE*, 1097a19.

Aristotle's system, *aretē* is the word that indicates a standard of excellence for judging whether an action is performed rationally and rightly. In turn, the habitual exercise of such right action, guided by Right Reason, builds the virtuous character.

Along these lines, virtue is a condition of true friendship, and it goes beyond itself to the greater human community. Aristotle claims that "the supremely happy, too, although not needing useful friends do need agreeable ones; for they want companions of some kind."[23] They need true friends, the sort that are trustworthy and loyal, with whom they can share their lives. Friends are needed in times of adversity and prosperity. In times of prosperity, friends are needed in order to share the fruits of success, wealth, honor, pleasure, or knowledge. In time of adversity, friends offer shelter and consolation. Moreover, the young as well as the old need the help of friends: "To the young, in keeping them from mistakes; and to the old, in caring for them and doing for them what through frailty they cannot do for themselves; and to those in the prime of life, by enabling them to carry out fine achievement."[24] Hence, society at large is enhanced by friendship, since it forms a framework that indirectly benefits others, who are apart from the friends—it engenders true community.

Simply and universally, human beings are by nature social beings and are naturally inclined to lead a social life. Aristotle pointed out that the desire, even need, for friendship is inherent to human beings: "Nobody would choose to have all the good things in the world by himself, because man is social by nature and naturally constituted to live in company."[25] Moreover, the need for friends arises from the fact that, by its very nature, friendship is an active, productive relationship. It is an ongoing process of growth. It develops in the process of sharing and pursing worthwhile ends. It is virtuous in modelling the highest to which humanity can aspire.

The point to stress is that if we define friendship as an activity, as Aristotle does, the quality of goodness that characterizes friendship resides primarily in the activity itself. Thus, the love that is peculiar to friendship characterizes the one who loves, more than the one who receives love.[26] This line of reasoning is based on two assumptions. First, even among people

---

23. Aristotle, *NE*, 1158a3.
24. Aristotle, *NE*, 1155a3.
25. Aristotle, *NE*, 1169b11.
26. See Aristotle, *NE*, 1159a27.

of different station, for example parent and child, husband and wife[27] or teacher and student, where one can give more than the other, the friendship is not possible if it is not based on some kind of equality and similarity in goodness. But in such asymmetrical cases the equality intended is proportional, not mathematical.[28] Second, friends are united by their good character, their desire to promote the good of each other, and their choice to share their lives together.[29]

For Aristotle, equality and similarity in goodness are necessary conditions that establish between the friends the "concord" (*harmonía*) that is crucial for friendship. By *harmonía* Aristotle does not mean "agreement of opinion" between the friends; rather, he points to harmony or agreement between their characters and in their outlook about themselves and life in general.[30] Insofar as friendship is a kind of concord, it holds together the members of society or community under the conditions of cooperation, peace, and amiability; it casts away enmity, faction, and disorder. For Aristotle, friendship is more desirable than justice: "Between friends there is no need for justice, but people who are just still need the quality of friendship; and, indeed, friendliness is considered to be justice in the fullest sense. It is not only a necessary thing but a splendid one."[31] Underpinning Aristotle's reasoning on friendship is the assumption that friendship depends on *koinonía* between two human beings and, as such, it is a part of the

---

27. Aristotle does not mention friendship between men and women apart from marriage, nor does he explicitly touch on friendship between women. He asserts that true friendship can exist also between husband and wife of good character. See Aristotle, *NE*, 1162a25–27. Yet, he sees the nature, function and proper goodness of man and woman as being so different that they exclude the equality and similarity demanded for perfect friendship. See Aristotle, *NE*, 1158b11–28; Tracy, *Physiological Theory*, 318–28.

28. Konstan has discussed this apparent inconsistency which seems to potentially violate the equality in friendship Aristotle so insisted upon in *NE*, 1157b36: *philotēs isotēs* (friendship is equality). He argues that the problem is derived not from any inconsistency in Aristotle, but rather from a misapprehension concerning the Greek terminology for friendship. Konstan claims that by the fourth century BC the verb *phileīn* had already began to give way to *agapān* as the ordinary word for "love." According to Konstan, Aristotle employs *phileīn* frequently in *NE*, 8 and 9, but this reflects the continued use of the word as a technical term in philosophical discussion. While *philía* and *philos* retain their currency in post-classical Greek, *phileīn* tends to be restricted to the sense of "kiss," which is first attested in the fifth century BC and appears gradually to have displaced the more general significance of the verb. See Konstan, "Greek Friendship," 74–75.

29. See Aristotle, *NE*, 1168b7.

30. See Aristotle, *NE*, 1167b4.

31. Aristotle, *NE*, 1155a24.

larger political community;[32] it derives its being and possibility from this community.

It appears that for Aristotle the greater the commonality and sharing the greater is the potential for friendship. He recognizes that the basic requirement for friendship to occur is the *koinonía* of humanity. So, in relationships that do exhibit friendship, Aristotle recognizes a sense of communion, through shared preferences and tastes, which allow compatibility between individuals; *koinonía* acquires fresh significance in Christianity and is a key concept in Saint Thomas Aquinas's treatment of the theological virtue of *caritas* as *amicitia*.

The end of Aristotle's life marks the inauguration of the Hellenistic period, which brought a transition in Greek politics. From an era in which the city-state was the center of power, the Greek world became one in which Alexander the Great's Empire was divided into large swaths of land under rule by kings. Politico-cultural changes also brought about a change in the concept of friendship. The emphasis shifted from the Athenian ideal (friendship between equals) to formal associations between individuals of unequal rank, which fell under the rubric of patron-client relationships.[33]

Nevertheless, following their predecessors, both Hellenic and Hellenistic philosophers interpreted the highest good in terms of happiness; the philosophers of the Hellenistic period were convinced that an adequate answer to the question of the highest good would meet all the inner demands—desires, capacities, potentialities, and urges—of human nature. Despite their distinctive anthropology (and so, diverse opinion of what the highest good really is) both Hellenic and Hellenistic philosophers were convinced that human nature was ordered by laws proper to it. They believed that what defined human nature was not given at birth as a ready-made reality. Instead, it was a potentiality to be realized in the process of choices, training, and instruction in daily activity. Thus, the natural law is "natural" because it conforms to the order of the flourishing of human "nature" or "essence."

Two important systems of philosophy during the Hellenistic period are Epicureanism and Stoicism. Epicureanism was founded around 307 BC; it was based upon the teaching of Epicurus, who held that the primary impulse of human nature was an impulse for pleasure, and not merely physical but ethereal. The Epicurian philosophers claimed that the

---

32. See Aristotle, *NE*, 1159b31.
33. See O'Neil, "Plutarch on Friendship," 105–22.

highest good consisted in meeting the demands of the pleasure-seeking impulse, primarily through invisible pleasures of the mind, such as beauty and harmony (rather than limited to the physical "creature-comforts"). For the Epicureans, virtue was the means to attain happiness. They also emphasized friendship as being integral for the pleasure of happiness.

Also, founded in the early third century BC, Stoicism was established in Athens by Zeno, a pre-Socratic philosopher. The followers of Zeno, called Stoics, argued that the distinctive quality of human nature is reason: people are human by virtue of possessing the faculty of reason. A later Stoic philosopher and Roman statesman, Seneca, would ask: "What quality is best in man? By virtue of reason he surpasses the animals and is surpassed only by the Gods. Perfect reason is therefore the good peculiar to man."[34] This conviction prompted the equating of virtue with happiness in the school of Stoicism, which reasoned that—if virtue is said to be happiness, and happiness is man's supreme end—one should seek virtue as its own reward, as an end for itself. Thus, the Stoics held that the virtuous person was self-sufficient because he could attain the highest good without the indulgences of the body, without the possession of material objects, and without the expectation of immortality. Virtue in itself was the one and only thing the Stoics deemed important for the attainment of the highest good. By their understanding, the only path that lead to virtue was sagaciousness. This enshrining of virtue as itself the goal and the highest good served as the basis for Cicero's view of friendship.

Cicero's View of Friendship

Cicero was a Roman statesman and practical philosopher who transmitted the Greek schools of thought to the Latin-speaking West; his teaching efforts and erudition towered above all others. He hammered out his understanding of friendship and its duties in the midst of an active political life. "I can only urge you," wrote Cicero in his dialogue *Laelius de Amicitia* ("Laelius on Friendship"), "to prefer friendship to everything else in life; for there is nothing else so fitted to nature—so well suited both to prosperity and to adversity."[35] Seeking a life of social harmony, he praises virtue as having another dimension beyond the Stoic's "end in itself"; Cicero saw virtue as the way to achieve harmony among friends:

34. Seneca, *Letters from a Stoic*, 185–86.
35. Cicero, *On Friendship*, 28.

> Friendship is nothing else than harmony of opinion and sentiment about all things human and divine, with good-will and affection: and no better thing than this, it seems to me—unless we except wisdom—has been given to man by the immortal gods . . . [Whereas those who] regard virtue as the highest good, and their opinion is noble and true one; but it is this very virtue that begets and preserves friendship, for without virtue there can be no friendship at all.[36]

Cicero distinguishes between two types of friendship: one that depends solely on advantage, and the other that is based on virtue or goodness. The first is untrue because it is fleeting, uncertain, and conditional; therefore, it does not last. Furthermore, in this kind of friendship the friends remain external to each other; a spiritual bond of friendship does not exist between them. Cicero insisted that such a bond was the foundation of true human friendship; he affirmed that the "affection" of love *(caritas)* created the bond of friendship between friends. Thus, those who formed friendships based on mutual advantage (but devoid of *caritas* or affection), were not true friends because they cared only for the personal gain and material advantage, which could result from the association and develop for the mutual advantage of all concerned.[37] This was a different experience from that of true friendship, even though authentic friendship was impossible, he insisted, in the absence of virtue.

While Cicero considered virtue as the basis and the motive of all sorts of successful partnerships, it was also the source and origin of true friendship. In true friendship, the person loves the friend for the friend's sake, because the friend is lovable, and he is lovable because he is virtuous—worthy of love. Thus, a true friendship was to be experienced as a preferential relationship of mutual affection; because it was mutual, it created a "union" *(societas)* between friends. "The clear perception of a virtuous character to which a kindred can attach and devote itself produces friendship," declared Cicero, "and when this happens love necessarily springs into being."[38] For Cicero, the bond of love between the friends was not an abstract affection or sentimental feeling, but instead the sort of fondness that results from the interchange of the friends themselves, and this exchange takes place

---

36. Cicero, *On Friendship*, 33–34.
37. See Cicero, *On Friendship*, 49–51.
38. Cicero, *On Friendship*, 76–77.

Elements of Friendship in the Classical and Christian Tradition

through the medium of sharing their material and spiritual lives.[39] This kind of spiritual union between two people can only be achieved by meeting certain essential criteria and fulfilling some basic conditions, beginning with "equality in virtue," or goodness, as an essential condition of true friendship.

Equality in virtue, Cicero insisted, was a level of goodness that created the conditions of "harmony" (*concordia*) between friends, without which the bond of love was impossible to forge between them. The equality that Cicero has in mind here is proportional in nature, since it is impossible for any two human beings to be identically equal in every respect—a character trait, a talent, or some material or physical aspect—there are differences that are unavoidable. What matters is that the two friends reciprocate their "goodwill" (*benevolentia*) in such a way that they are fair in whatever they do for each other.[40] This kind of reasoning is based on the assumption that human beings are not born virtuous, but they have the capacity to become virtuous and the ability to choose to do so. Therefore, a circular reinforcement of goodness could be established.

If one person was loftier or more accomplished than another in some way, then the "superior" person, as a friend, should try to raise up the lesser of the two. This elevation to a higher level of goodness or excellence was to be accomplished without arrogance or condescension, which was itself an attitude deprived of virtue. The virtuous life was seen as an on-going process of growth and development; it became the very signature characteristic of both the aristocratic Roman as well as his later counterpart, the English gentleman, which migrated to the English colonies worldwide, including the eastern seaboard of the young United States. The Turkish-born philosopher and immigrant to the USA, Michael Mitias wrote: "Although friendship is an offspring of virtue, it becomes, once established, a community, and we can say a school, for its cultivation."[41]

Thus, as a community of virtuous persons, friendship can be experienced and promoted as "a condition, indeed an element, of happiness."[42] It is a condition in the sense that virtuous persons cannot acquire virtue on their own, but everyone needs the company and cooperation of a true friend. Cicero's understanding parallels that of the Vatican II fathers, who

---

39. See Cicero, *On Friendship*, 94–95.
40. See Mitias, *Friendship*, 81.
41. Mitias, *Friendship*, 81.
42. Mitias, *Friendship*, 81.

began with the assumption, shared with the ancient world, that alone and unaided by a good and virtuous friend, an individual cannot arrive at the highest attainments, which it might be able to do when united and associated with another.[43]

If such an honorable society or community, even between just two persons, either exists or has existed, or is likely to do so, their companionship is to be esteemed ... most excellent and most happy. The good things in life—including pleasure, social respect, tranquility of mind, and material success—are only achieved and enjoyed through friendship. This leads us to conclude that, as Cicero understands it, friendship is an essential condition and ingredient in the pursuit of happiness and for the attainment of virtue. Thus, Cicero ends his dialogue on friendship with the following appeal: "This is what I had to say to you about friendship; and I beg you to give to virtue so high a place in your esteem that it shall be the only thing that you prefer to friendship, without which virtue cannot exist."[44]

Cicero's *Laelius de Amicitia* has profoundly influenced Latin Christian thought on friendship and not necessarily in the service of authentic faith; later generations of Christians have found philosophy an obstacle to following the Christ of the Gospels. The nature of Cicero's approach, and the passion he conveys, may be the reason why his treatise was appropriated so extensively by the Latin Fathers of the Church, particularly by Saint Augustine, and by the monastic tradition a thousand years later, notably by Aelred of Rievaulx in his treatise on love.

There is a limit to the assertions of Cicero, however noble and impassioned his sentiments. The nineteenth century convert to the Catholic faith, Saint John Henry Newman, was extremely well-educated in the classics, and he saw their limitations, as earlier writers, such as Saint Augustine, tended to overlook. Newman wrote extensively about the church, spiritual life, human nature, education, philosophy, and the importance of friendship, which was a constant and important theme of his profusive writings.[45]

---

43. A key document of Vatican II, *Gaudium et Spes*, shares what is natural to humankind beginning in Chapter 1, "The Dignity of the Human Person," in the opening discussion about communion and friendship: "God did not create men and women as solitary beings ... For by their innermost nature men and women are social beings; and if they do not enter into relationships with others, they can neither live nor develop their gifts." Vatican II, *Gaudium et Spes*, par. 12.

44. Cicero, *On Friendship*, 150–51.

45. See for example, Newman, *Letter Addressed to His Grace the Duke of Norfolk*; "Love of Relations and Friends," Sermon 5.

Elements of Friendship in the Classical and Christian Tradition

Newman understood that there was a perverse darkness inherent in human nature, wounded by sin, which could not achieve the lofty goals desired by the noble Cicero, who himself died, betrayed, and under horrific circumstances.[46]

FRIENDSHIP IN THE FATHERS OF THE CHURCH

In the first centuries of Christianity, the saintly Church Fathers wrote in an area of four prerogatives: sanctity, antiquity, orthodoxy and church approval. Usually, the Church Fathers are divided in two: the Latin and Greek Fathers. It is commonly held that the last western Father was Saint Isidore of Seville (AD 560–636) while the last eastern Father was Saint John Damascene (AD 675–749). With their writings, the Church Fathers serve as great witness and contributors to the Christian faith. Early Christians readily made use of the philosophical world of the dominant Greco-Roman culture in which they lived; this included the conceptual field of friendship. However, Christianity provided a new paradigm for classical ideals of friendship; it was a new pattern that transcended the pleasures and sentiments of this world. During the first four centuries of Christianity, while early Christians (including the New Testament writers) tended to describe their relationships with one another in kinship terms (brothers/sons), rather than in terms of friendship, the new paradigm was beginning to emerge; the language of friendship makes an appearance and the *topos* of friendship continued alongside the familial imagery.[47]

Although they did not often use "friendship language," the Apostolic Fathers used such references with ease. For instance, they present friendship as embodied in the relationship between Jesus and his disciples.[48] Justin Martyr (AD 100–165) wrote about the friendship between God and people in his *Dialogue with Trypho*, where Christians are described as "friends of Christ" and "friends of God." Saint Clement of Alexandria (c. AD 150–215) placed Aristotle's division of friendship into three classes and argues that

---

46. After the assassination of Julius Caesar, Rome was in chaos, and Cicero was in despair; he was betrayed and murdered on the orders of Marc Anthony, against whom he had spoken. He was murdered, by a man whom he had once befriended; his severed head and hand were dishonored and put on public display at the place where he had once spoken so eloquently.

47. See Harnach, "'Friends,'" 421.

48. See Mews and Chiavaroli, "Latin West," 79.

friendship based on virtue is *agápē*. He also regularly used the expression "friend of God." Origen, a prolific early Christian writer and theologian, reflected that Christ-the-shepherd once led his sheep to pasture, but now, as Christ-the-friend, he calls us to the eternal table. Origen made it a practice to accept his students as friends.

In the late fourth century, when Christianity became the religion of the Roman Empire, theologians like Saint Basil of Caesarea, his brother Saint Gregory of Nyssa, Saint Gregory of Nazianzus, Saint John Chrysostom, Saint Ambrose, Saint Jerome, Saint Augustine, and Saint John Cassian all made important contributions to the Christian consideration of friendship.[49] They started to redefine classical ideals of friendship within the framework of the newly established religion.

Gregory of Nyssa considers Christ as our friend, wounded with love yet loving those who wounded him. Gregory claims that, like Moses, we are called to be known by God and become his friend.[50] In his description of his relationship with Saint Basil, Saint John Chrysostom emphasizes this foundation: "Classical assumptions regarding friendship's demand for equality of circumstances and similarity of interests."[51]

Saint Ambrose, Bishop of Milan, views friendship as an important component in spiritual unity among his clergy. Ambrose's focus on relationships among clergy suggests the profound influence monastic life had on Christian social thought in late antiquity.[52] He places a strong emphasis on self-disclosure between friends. He specifically links the importance of such self-disclosure within a friendship to the teaching and example of Jesus, as found in John 15:14, "You are my friends if you do what I command."

Ambrose considers friendship as a virtue for it consists in freely showing honor and kindness, which may not necessarily be reciprocated; it does not consist in a desire for material gain.[53] Ambrose teaches that Christians should manifest the virtue of friendship by being potential friends to all. Ambrose reflects that we are like Abraham—all are called to become friends of God through obeying him. Consequently, we obey God as a friend out of

---

49. For a comprehensive study about Christian friendship in the fourth century, see White, *Christian Friendship in the Fourth Century*.

50. See Gregory of Nyssa, *The Life of Moses*, 320.

51. Clark, *Jerome, Chrysostom, and Friends*, 42–43.

52. See Konstan, *Friendship*, 149.

53. See Ambrose, *On the Duties of the Clergy*; cf. Newman: "In a Christian view, it is not quite this [that friendship is a virtue]; but it is often accidentally a special *test* of our virtue." Newman, "Love of Relations and Friends," Sermon 5.

love, not out of fear, like a servant. At first, "Obedience is the condition for divine friendship, and then becomes consequential upon it."[54]

Augustine's Theology of Friendship

Joseph Lienhard identifies Saint Augustine (AD 354–431) as the first Christian author to offer a theology of friendship.[55] As Augustine's writings give testimony, friendship was central to his personality. His theology of friendship is definitely experiential, which can be seen in three distinct phases of his life. Before his religious conversion, Augustine had several friendly relationships; after his conversion he insisted on living in community with friends; as a bishop in northern Africa, he drew other clergy around him to live a form of monastic life at the cathedral. He seems to have been naturally and culturally gregarious; he valued and cultivated friendships all his life. In practice, Augustine's writings are a rich resource for the legacy of friendship in the Christian tradition, and yet his doctrine of divine love is not wholly hospitable to friendship itself.

Rather than a merely human relationship, Augustine claims in his *Confessions* that true friendship is a bond (between souls that cleave to each other through charity) that is established by the Holy Spirit, a gift of God's grace.[56] The novelty in Augustine is that it is divine grace—not human nature—which creates friendship.[57] In the *Confessions*, after his grief over his friend's death at Thagaste, Augustine came to realize that his problem was loving his friend as if he would never die. Augustine concludes that, instead, he should have loved God in that everlasting way and then loved his friend in God: "Blessed is he who loves you, and loves his friend in you and his enemy for your sake."[58] Indeed, this is Augustine's basic view of friendship. We need, first, to love God and then to love our friends in God, who himself brings friends together as a grace of the Holy Spirit working within us.

Saint Augustine makes love a central theme of his theology and anthropology.[59] In Augustine's doctrine of God, love is the key to the

---

54. Anderson, "Abraham: The Friend of God," 353–66.
55. See Lienhard, "Friendship, Friends," 372–73.
56. See Augustine, *Confessions*, 4.4.7.
57. See Carmichael, *Friendship*, 60.
58. Augustine, *Confessions*, 4.9.14.
59. See Leinhard, "Friendship, Friends," 372–73.

understanding of the Trinity: The Father loves the Son, the Son receives and returns this love to the Father, and the Holy Spirit simply is that love. In his *City of God*, Augustine interprets all of human history through the contrast between two loves: there is the "city of God," which is grounded on love of God to the contempt of self; and the "city of man," which is grounded on love of self to the contempt of God. Hence, the justification for Augustine's putting the love for God at the center of his theological anthropology. Through Jesus Christ, each human person is made to love God, a love that animates everything we do and that can be satisfied by God himself alone.[60] Augustine recognizes in friendship a powerful expression of "love of God," but his challenge was to advance a specifically Christian understanding of friendship without abandoning the traditional understanding of friendship: associating friendship with virtue and recognizing it in the society at large.

Affirming that humans have the *imago Dei* within them, Augustine recognizes friendship as a means of expressing this image of God, allowing it to be realized within the context of love and forgiveness, desiring the very best for the other in Christ. Augustine describes his stance most clearly in a letter to his old friend, Marcianus, in which he expresses his delight at Marcianus's conversion to Christianity. "Although you seemed to love me greatly," Augustine wrote to Marcianus, "you were not yet my friend."[61] Having previously been friends based on attraction and seeking the good of the other (following the classical tradition), they now share a foundation of mutual love of Christ. Only when Marcianus became a Christian do these two achieve Christian friendship; they "have a united devotion to a shared vision of the good in which they would journey together and assist each other in the acquisition of virtues."[62]

Saint Augustine is convinced that the character of Christian friendship is something unique and essentially different from any other form of friendship. Christian friendship for him was of another order altogether, not merely a higher order of secular friendship, but an exclusive variant accessible to a certain group. Those in this group are not socially defined, but are Christians experiencing interpersonal relationship, essentially mirroring their "love of God." This love will not reach its highest point until it

---

60. See Augustine, *Confessions*, 1.1.1.

61. Augustine, *Epistles*, 258.3; see Crouse, "Love and Friendship in Medieval Theology," 140–41.

62. Thorne, "Friendship," 55.

is fulfilled in the next life. Meanwhile, all human experience of it is incomplete or flawed by the human condition.[63]

Augustine still defines genuine friendship as: "Desire for good things for someone for his own sake, together with a reciprocal desire on his part."[64] While this appears at first to be in line with the classical tradition, it is not quite so. Augustine maintained that this friendship can only be fully realized when its locus is the mutual "love of God" between two friends: "No friends are true friends," Augustine wrote, "unless you, my God, bind them fast to one another through that love which is sown in our hearts by the Holy Spirit."[65] The presence of God through the Holy Spirit is the core of Augustine's understanding of friendship: ultimately, there can be no true friendship without God being in the center. Just as in the Trinity the Holy Spirit is the bond of love between the Father and the Son, the Holy Spirit is also the bond of love between and among human beings.

Marie Aquinas McNamara explores this redefinition of friendship and outlines four areas in which Augustine's distinctive definition of friendship is evident: (i) God is the author and giver of friendship; without his presence and action, true friendship cannot exist; (ii) God brings stability to friendship and provides the means for perseverance; (iii) Christian friendship is transfigured by grace to go beyond wishing natural virtue for the friend, to wishing supernatural virtue for life and eternal joy in heaven; and (iv) friendship reaches its completion only in heaven, in the "City of God."[66]

McNamara also notes that it is important to recognize that the notion of *totus Christus* is foundational for Saint Augustine, who cannot conceive of a completion of communion and unity for the Church until the eschaton. It is held together in Christ and will be recovered through final unity with him; in the eschaton, the unity of the human race, lost through original sin, will be restored. This has obvious implications for how enthusiastically Augustine could embrace earthly friendship, and what status he might accord it in the Church; in this world, friendship must always be incomplete and partial.[67]

In McNamara's definition of Augustine's stance—the crucial elements of divine enabling and eschatological hope—are evident. These together

---

63. See Summers, *Friendship*, 80.
64. Augustine, *Eighty-Three Different Questions*, 31.3.
65. Augustine, *Confessions*, 4.4.7.
66. See McNamara, *Friends and Friendship for St. Augustine*, 215–16.
67. See McNamara, *Friends and Friendship for St. Augustine*, 215–16.

lend a dimension and an edge to the Christian relationship that is bound to be absent in secular friendships. Nevertheless, this theological understanding of friendship must not be allowed to skew Augustine's generally positive view of human virtuous friendship, in itself. Although believing that human friendship is inferior to that springing from Christian love, Augustine admits that even earthly friendship can be inspired by Christian disinterested love. Still, from his experience, Augustine knew that human friendship could also be problematic. He described his anguish when reflecting on an adolescent misdemeanor: accompanied by a group of friends, his theft of pears from a neighbor's tree. In the *Confessions*, he initially stated that "friendship is also a nest of love and gentleness because of the unity it brings about between many souls."[68] Then, a little further on, in describing the crime, he wrote this qualifying circumstance: "Had I been alone, it would have given me absolutely no pleasure, nor would I have committed it. Friendship can be a dangerous enemy, a seduction of the mind lying beyond the reach of investigation."[69]

Having witnessed Augustine's struggles with friendship, and the potential problems that it could bring, it should follow that the only way he can accept its true value and trust its merit is by considering it to be a relationship transformed by God's redeeming love. At least in this interpretation, Augustine can justify the failings of friendship in the present life without degrading its value in principle; he deemed it as a relationship that could only reach its peak after bodily life. In the *City of God* Augustine wrote that heaven would provide, "a perfectly ordered and perfectly harmonious fellowship in the enjoyment of God and a mutual fellowship in God."[70]

Indeed, Augustine's view of friendship provides a secure place for human friendship, but it is at the cost of relegating friendship to a second-class "citizen" in the City of God! His belief that all things, even friendship, are for the sake of God is very different from the ideal of Aristotle and Cicero that true friendship is offered for the sake of the other person, but also reciprocated among those equal in virtue. The love for God, in Augustine's view, seems to be uni-directional, unlike the love for friends. And yet to love a friend in God might result in its own uni-directionality, a love toward the friend, a love that promotes the good of the friend, and so forth, without being a reciprocal love—which also receives from the friend. Here,

---

68. Augustine, *Confessions*, 2.5.10.
69. Augustine, *Confessions*, 2.9.17.
70. Augustine, *City of God*, 19.13.

Elements of Friendship in the Classical and Christian Tradition

Augustine seems to be setting up defenses against the inconstancy, frivolity, and weakness—indeed, against the ongoing sinfulness—of actual friends, and against the chances of disease and war, but there is something more fundamental in the trajectory of Augustine's position:

> Augustine's formal doctrine of love subsumes human friendship within the ordered love that effectively draws all our powers into a strongly one-way for God. Good so far as it goes, this is not yet an adequate account of our love-relationship with God as known in Christ. Nor does it do justice to love of neighbor . . . [I]t will be little surprise if loving God through the neighbor, or even effectively bypassing the neighbor, will tend to eclipse loving our neighbor or friend in God, let alone with or from God.[71]

FRIENDSHIP IN MEDIEVAL MONASTIC THEOLOGY

"Medieval" was the name chosen by the Italian poet and scholar, Francesco Petrarch (1304–1374), one of the earliest humanist fathers of the Renaissance, to denote what he saw as the gulf separating his time from a world in which life in the flesh was regarded as a vale of tears, a dark and dangerous antechamber, to the felicity promised for those who could endure it with as little stain of sin on their souls as possible. In the medieval period, which dates from the fifth to the sixteenth century, classical ideals of friendship never disappeared completely.[72]

Yet, there are also profound shifts in the understanding of friendship, provoked not least by the encounter between the elitism of classical culture and the universalizing aspirations of the Christian religion. Christianity offers a radically different set of ideals from those that prevailed in the political structures of the Roman Empire. Above all, we see, at least in the context of formal religious life, "An apparent tendency to subordinate the ideal of friendship to that of union with God in the life to come."[73]

The medieval world was not a peaceful world, but a terribly difficult one. The loss of Roman technology, the hardships of deteriorating roads, effects of weather and devasting outbreaks of disease made for a harsh and comfortless existence, in which life was not only short but full of misery.

---

71. Carmichael, *Friendship*, 66–67.

72. For an excellent overview of the transmission of Ciceronian ideals in the medieval period, see McEvoy, "The Theory of Friendship in the Latin Middle Ages," 3–36.

73. Mews and Chiavaroli, "Latin West," 73.

From a theological perspective, the reality of sin was very palpable and manifested itself in fragmentation and human atrocities. Together with other factors, this situation led to personal devotions and individual piety wherein people became more concerned with their own salvation and human relationships were pushed back, becoming less important.

Furthermore, during the late medieval period friendship was sometimes seen to pose peculiar challenges and threats to theology. The theology that had developed was clear: Jesus came into the world to save all humanity from the consequences of sin. He revealed to humanity not only absolute obedience to the Father, but also that the kind of love that brings the person closer to the love of God, is the love of neighbor, including enemies and sinners. The fountain of one's love for God flows more and more abundantly the more one loves the neighbor in the way Jesus loves them (see John 15:12). To love God is defined by leading a good life, and to lead a good life is to observe the commandments—especially, to love God above everything else and the neighbor as oneself (see Mark 12:30–31; Matthew 22:27–29; Luke 10:27). In loving our neighbor, we discover what it means to love God: the love of neighbor is itself the way to love God and, consequently, to eternal salvation.

Thus, it seemed obvious that Christian love of neighbor ought to be universal and all-inclusive. In contrast, the "love of friendship" as a preferential kind of love, seemed of a lower caliber; one cannot "be a friend" with all humanity. From a theological perspective, therefore, during the late medieval period "love of friendship" was sometimes considered to be incompatible with Christian charity because it was seen to impinge on the commandment to love the neighbor as oneself. The discussion about this incompatibility intensified with Protestant thinkers after the Reformation in the sixteenth century.[74]

Nevertheless, love as friendship survived in the medieval Christian tradition, even if between the fifth and late eleventh century, friendship was more of a literary paradigm, eclipsed by the values of monasticism. The first literary appearance in monastic tradition of *spiritalis amicitia* should be credited to Paulinus of Nola (c. AD 353–431). In a letter to Pammachius, his "brother in Christ," Paulinus made it clear that their friendship was not *secularis* (of this world), but *spiritalis*, born of God and uniting them in the mysterious brotherhood of "spirits."[75]

---

74. See Carmichael, *Friendship*, 136.
75. See White, *Christian Friendship in the Fourth Century*, 164–84.

Elements of Friendship in the Classical and Christian Tradition

The Church, and particularly its monasteries, preserved the classical Latin learning in which its early scholars had been steeped. From the ninth century onward, there was a fresh flowering of the literature of friendship in letters, poems, and prayers in monastic and ecclesiastical circles. By the mid-eleventh century, political stability and a new economic prosperity encouraged a subtle transformation in ideals of *amicitia*, taking it beyond purely political function to a more personal role, that of expressing individual identity. The rising of a whole spectrum of friendship can indeed be traced in the lives and correspondence of monks, and ecclesiastical ministers throughout the Middle Ages.[76]

The whole history of friendship in the monastic tradition cannot be here outlined in full.[77] The summary of that history reveals a consistent theme of suspicion, which emerges in some early monastic authors. The recurring theme (which probably was mutually reinforcing of the idea) was that friendship, as a preferential love, would likely lead to community factions and even sexual temptations. The result within the monastic tradition of this era was that friendship was ignored or seen as a diversion, if not an overt temptation. The "love of friendship," as a value in itself, simply did not resonate as having a particular worth within the monastic setting.[78] The monks did not train themselves to the "love of friendship" and did not expect it as such in their avowed lifestyle. A few voices, however, such as John Cassian (c. AD 360–433), recognized the complexity of relationships in the community, and he saw the need for a broader, more well-rounded approach.[79] Cassian showed how friendship could exist between spiritual father and disciple, especially among people of prayer. However, he warns against less ideal friendship or emotional entanglements, either with other religious or with those outside the monastic walls, as they "could threaten the monk's . . . inner tranquility and devotional orientation and lessen equality of regard among the community."[80] Cassian's observations show how friendship was habitually understood (and always treated) within the context of the community: dismissive as irrelevant to a controlled society

---

76. See McGuire, *Friendship and Community*.

77. For a fuller treatment of the history of friendship in the monastic tradition, see Fiske, *Friends and Friendship in the Monastic Tradition*; see also, McGuire, *Friendship and Community*; White, *Christian Friendship in the Fourth Century*, 164–84.

78. See Summers, *Friendship*, 133.

79. See John Cassian, *The Conferences*.

80. Carmichael, *Friendship*, 71.

where the prime concern was that the monastic community be preserved and its spirituality maintained with steady zeal and obedience. Simply, friendship was not a private matter between individuals, but considered only within the monastic framework of "the common good."

Recent theological studies and the widely copied letter collections of Saint Anselm (1033-1108) and Saint Bernard of Clairvaux (1090-1153) enable us to see how Ciceronian ideals of *amicitia* could be integrated into a Christian and, indeed, specifically monastic milieu.[81] Saint Anselm, and even more Saint Bernard of Clairvaux, had waxed eloquent about their enthusiasm for personal friends within the monastic life; the language of both might easily be perceived as homoerotic. For Bernard, the erotic imagery of the Song of Songs provided a rich medium through which to explore his enthusiasm for love for God as emerging out of love of self and neighbor.[82]

A generation later, Aelred of Rievalux (1109-1166), who became abbot of the Cistercian Rievaulx Abbey, in the Benedict tradition, addressed friendship systematically. In the Latin West the Rule of Benedict established a working constitution for a stable, all-male community under the authority of an abbot elected in theory by his monks. There was no place for special friendship in the monastery, which Benedict defined as *schola caritatis*. The abbot must love no monk more than another, unless he finds someone advanced in good actions or obedience (Rule 2.16-17). Special friendship might therefore exist between virtuous monks and their abbot. Benedict neither explicitly instructs monks to love one another equally, nor mentions particular affection, although he forbids anyone defending another for any reason.[83] Aelred's *Spiritual Friendship*, written in the 1120s, kept alive the classical understanding of friendship and drew extensively upon Cicero's *On Friendship*.[84] He is content to adapt Cicero and apply what he can of his thought to the life of his monastery. His approach will emerge in later considerations of friendship in the Christian tradition that

---

81. McGuire has written extensively on monastic friendship in the twelfth century. See for example, "Love," 111-52; also "Cistercians," 1-63; "Monastic Friendship," 147-60; "Looking Back on Friendship," 123-42.

82. See Bernard of Clairvaux, *Sermo* 83, 4-6.

83. In *Rule* 69 he states, "Every precaution must be taken that one monk does not presume in any circumstance to defend another in the monastery or to be his champion, even if they are related by the closest ties of blood. In no way whatsoever shall the monks presume to do this, because it can be a most serious source and occasion of contention."

84. See White, *Christian Friendship in the Fourth Century*, 146-63.

borrow from the classical era, yet acknowledge points of difference as well as similarities.

In the three "books," or sections, of *Spiritual Friendship*, Aelred reworks Cicero's *On Friendship* into a specifically Christian discussion on monastic friendship. Aelred's style of writing is experiential, practical and dialogical, seeking to raise and then solve questions about the propriety and challenges of being a Christian friend in a monastic community. For example, Aelred believes the absolute commitment of friends to each other is exemplified in the sharing of common property. He acknowledges that corruption of true friendship can occur by the incursion of sin that debases its virtue into acquisitive love.[85]

In the first section of the treatise, Aelred envisions the "love of friendship" as being rooted in the God who loves all. He expands a great deal on the consequences of God-as-love. The most interesting part is Aelred's portrayal of a conversation with his fellow monk, Ivo, who wonders if he should say of friendship what the author of the first letter of John said of *caritas* (1 John 4:16): "Shall I say . . . 'God is friendship' (*Deus amicitia est*)?" Aelred responds positively but with circumspection: "That would be unusual, but still what is true of charity, I surely do not hesitate to grant to friendship," because, he concludes, "he that abides in friendship, abides in God, and God in him."[86] This conciliatory tone and the ability to develop a theology by extrapolating from what is known to what might be experienced (so that his community will be drawn deeper and more intimately into the knowledge of God) is typical of Aelred's literary approach, which is not unlike the approach famously taken by Plato and Xenophon in the discourses of their Socratic dialogues.

In the second part of the treatise, Aelred discusses the thorny dimension of physical expression of love, and he affirms that a certain physicality is not only appropriate but necessary; the spiritual kiss between friends can be physical, yet it denotes the "mingling of spirits."[87] This implies that the kiss is given almost by proxy, from the (invisibly present) Jesus Christ through the (physically present) Christian brother. In this section, Aelred's conversation partner is Gratian, who expresses surprise at the easy expression of friendship being suggested, and, with it, surprise at the lack of prohibition against physical contact. Although he seemed very much aware of

---

85. See Carmichael, *Friendship*, 70–100.
86. Aelred, *Spiritual Friendship*, 1.69–70.
87. Aelred, *Spiritual Friendship*, 2.26.

the risk he was taking, Aelred's approach is typically controlled, advocating reasoned permission rather than outright prohibition. Aelred offers the following guidance for choosing the purity of course and action; paramount is the convicted agreement that the foundation of friendship is the love of God. After this foundation, he writes: "You see therefore, the four stages by which one climbs to the perfection of friendship: the first is selection, the second probations, the third admission, and the fourth perfect harmony in matters human and divine with charity and benevolence."[88] For Aelred, a friendship that has passed through a period of discernment and has been subjected to his four stages of "clearance," need not be feared as a "near occasion of sin." On the contrary, the appropriate expression of chaste friendship will be mutually beneficial to the spiritual well-being of the friends and also to the community. In the third section, Aelred locates the particularity of friendship within the matrix of a loving community.[89] He sees no conflict with the love of many and the love of particular friends. In order to love a friend, Aelred contends, one must chastise oneself, "allowing nothing which is unbecoming and refusing nothing which is profitable."[90] This rule applies not only to those who are known friends, but also is expanded to those who are neighbors and even strangers.[91]

In an age when great interest was taken in setting religious goals and analyzing the states of spiritual progress, Aelred was apparently unique in teaching that true friendship, which essentially is "spiritual," can be the highest stage leading to perfection, "a stage toward the love and knowledge of God."[92] However, his writings did not endure as a major voice or influence in monasticism. His writing and reflection on the "love of friendship" formed part of an extensive collection of twelfth-century literature on love, which, unfortunately, did not survive much beyond its own era.[93]

Nevertheless, Aelred's work has persisted, doggedly resurfacing to offer his profoundly human treatment of this subtle and delicate subject matter through practical example for its appropriate expressions.[94] Perhaps only an exceptionally wise and holy abbot, and with Aelred's interpersonal skills,

---

88. Aelred, *Spiritual Friendship*, 3.8.
89. See Aelred, *Spiritual Friendship*, 3.82–83.
90. Aelred, *Spiritual Friendship*, 3.129.
91. See Aelred, *Spiritual Friendship*, 3.129–30.
92. Aelred, *Spiritual Friendship*, 2.18.
93. See Carmichael, *Friendship*, 97.
94. See Summers, *Friendship*, 135.

would be capable of leading such a community. Such an abbot would need to be aware of both the danger and the treasure for the community and the individual friends; he would also need, as well, to possess a patient and loving gentleness, both in his own interiority and in his exterior authority of being able to hold in tension the advantages and risks of such open friendship. Although sin and grace grow together—and grace can do more—such abbots rarely have exhibited such a necessary combination of attributes. Aelred himself was treated with suspicion by the Cistercian General Chapter, and "[h]is interest in friendship and his provision of opportunities of it, were probably seen as laxity."[95] Close friendship was neither an expected nor intended feature of monastic life. "No duties of friendship appeared in manuals of self-examination, suggesting that friendships somehow fell outside the realm of morality, or were non-existent or unreal."[96]

So far, we have been following friendship in monastic medieval theology, but that is only part of the story. Undeniably, the Middle Ages cannot be discussed without referring to Scholasticism, where the culmination of Scholastic theological reflection on friendship can be seen in Saint Thomas Aquinas (1225–1274), who studied friendship in the context of man's relationship with God and spoke of friendship as a kind of love.

Although the "love of friendship" is seldom remembered in connection with his other teachings, Saint Thomas Aquinas declared that *caritas* is simply *amicitia* with God. The "love of friendship," Aquinas taught, is essentially spiritual; it, therefore, serves well to explain the relationship that unites man to God—namely, *caritas*! However, after his sudden death, although Aquinas was highly esteemed, his voice on friendship was scarcely heard. It was his teaching of Christian doctrine, assailed as it was by the threat of Islam's expansion and the destabilization of Europe, that has been remembered in the ensuing centuries and taught in all Catholic seminaries. "By 1286 all Dominicans were required to promote his teaching, in 1323 he was canonized, and in the sixteenth century his *Summa Theologiae* replaced Lombard's *Sentences* as the basic Catholic theological text."[97]

Only four years before Pope Pius V declared Aquinas a Doctor of the Church in 1567, a powerful statement, which reflected Aquinas's writings, came out of the decrees of the Council of Trent (1545–1563) featured this statement: "We are changed, by justification, from an enemy into a friend

---

95. Carmichael, *Friendship*, 97.
96. Carmichael, *Friendship*, 97.
97. Carmichael, *Friendship*, 126.

of God."⁹⁸ After the Council of Trent, moral theology became a matter of drawing up detailed manuals for the use of priests in their task of hearing confessions. These so-called "confession manuals" were consequently dominated by degrees of sinful actions, common peccadilloes, transgressions, and ordinary legal obligations, based on the Ten Commandments. Henceforward, during this time and in the following centuries, "friendship with God" was either incorporated as a technical term. "Friendship with God" came into moral theology's definitions to mean specifically "being in a state of grace"; under much more rare instances, "friendship with God" came to be assimilated into the theologically specialized realm of mystical theology, associated with the heights of contemplative life. The specific and inclusive "love of friendship" as such was simply overlooked theologically (as the still untapped experience of romantic love has been similarly discounted as a theological reality) and, as Carmichael notes, "this did far less than justice to Thomas."⁹⁹

After the Council of Trent, Aquinas's original imagery of "friendship with God" is found discreetly tucked away in the writings of the mystics, but it did not become an integral part of catechesis. The "love of friendship" can still be discovered, however; the mystic tradition has some excellent examples of the beauty inherent to the "love of friendship." The English anchorite and mystic writer, Dame Julian of Norwich (who wrote *Revelations of Divine Love*, the earliest surviving book in English by a woman), hails God as "our friend" who has overpowered the devil; Mother Julian embraces Jesus Christ as our "highest sovereign friend," who wants us to keep close to him, however sinful we may be, and to follow his will and counsel.¹⁰⁰ Similarly, in another passage on friendship with God, the great Spanish mystic, Saint Teresa of Avila (1515–1582), wrote that God is the one that, "No one has ever taken for a Friend without being rewarded; and mental prayer, in my view, is nothing but friendly intercourse, and frequent solitary converse, with him who we know loves us."¹⁰¹

Unfortunately, there is a theological tendency to channel such writings among the mystics into the form of individualist piety or moral imperatives. *The Imitation of Christ* was written in the Netherlands in the early fifteenth century (c. 1420), and it became the most popular devotional

---

98. See Trent, Session 6 Cap. 7 and 10; Carmichael, *Friendship*, 126–27.
99. Carmichael, *Friendship*, 127.
100. Julian of Norwich, *Showings*, 329.
101. Teresa of Avila, *Complete Works*, 50.

booklet ever written, next only to the Bible (which came off the Guttenberg printing press in 1455, the first book to be printed with moveable metal type). Although it was written anonymously in Latin, *The Imitation of Christ* is attributed to a mystic, Thomas à Kempis, and it exemplifies the search for an affective relationship with Jesus through meditation on his life and particularly on his Passion. *The Imitation of Christ* teaches a very individualistic, inward devotion, arising in the interior life. It is, indeed, a devotional guide, a spiritual comfort, and a way to holiness; however, it falls significantly short of "friendship with God," as envisioned by Aquinas. It is more about the inner life of the individual (almost a precursor to psychology) than a guide book of positive outward extension in friendship for all whom God has made. This early intimation of the eclipse of friendship in theological discourse will only enter a colder period in the centuries that followed, darkening into Modernity.

FRIENDSHIP IN MODERNITY

In the four hundred years that followed the sixteenth-century Reformation, theologians and philosophers of the West gave scant philosophical and theological consideration to friendship as an essential force in the shaping of culture, community, moral life, as well as individual human flourishing. During this period, the rich heritage of friendship was simply ignored, intentionally or otherwise.[102] According to Gilbert C. Meilaender (a Lutheran theologian, teacher, writer, and critic), the reason for the neglect of the "love of friendship" (as well as a complete absence of any theology of romantic love) was that "Christian thought displaced *agápē*, and it is impossible to think theologically about love without giving that simple fact careful consideration."[103]

Although European society is deeply rooted in the Hellenic, Hellenistic and medieval cultures, a general mistrust and malaise—even rejection, of these traditional origins—denotes Modernism, which prevails in the West. The reasons for this long change as the centuries of the first millennium evolved towards modernity are many: warfare among the nations, the spread of Islam, the Fall of Constantinople, the obliteration of a third to half of the population of Europe due to plague, the Protestant revolt, religious persecutions between Protestants and Catholics, the discovery of

102. See Thorne, "Friendship," 49.
103. Meilaender, *Friendship*, 2.

the New World, the rise of global trade, technological advances (such as the printing press), and global missionary vigor, due to the Catholic Counter Reformation and the rise of new religious orders, such as the Society of Jesus. The many new ideas that began to ferment into a kind of cultural energy impelled Europe into a change of identity in the Renaissance of the seventeenth century. It was a time in which modern European society began to break away from the late medieval period and cultivate a different cultural identity, characterized by nationalism, rationalism, and humanism. While these features are certainly not absent from the cultures of classical antiquity and medieval Europe, the novelty of the modern age is its disenchantment with the mystery and manners of Christendom, and its radical reliance on human technological accomplishment.[104] The idea of an earthly utopia through power and might, as well as other non-Christian or anti-Christian ideas features, have continued to foment change, for better or worse, over centuries and have contributed to the wholesale relegation of the "love of friendship" away from modern moral reflection, which has long been dominated by utilitarian thinking and deontological ethics.

The eighteenth century was the age of the Enlightenment, when the Christian faith was exiled as irrelevant from public discourse; human reason became the new measure of reality, and usefulness became the value of modernist living. The world was less and less seen with reference to God and revealed truth, but it was culturally shaped by "intellectuals" from the standpoint of what can be known by the scientific method and human reason alone. The Beatific Vision—indeed, all contemplation of divine revelation—had no place of worth in modernism. All authority was suspect, including both clergy and monarch. The deductive method, once so useful in theology, was seen as limiting, especially when explaining natural events. This rejection did not necessarily mean a denial of the existence of a supreme being, but it did make impossible any empirical knowledge of transcendent truth or a living relationship with any kind of deity—beyond oneself. It did not mean, at least initially (until the French Revolution), the need to overthrow the church as an institution, but it made such an institution irrelevant; the church was thought of as one more power structure among others. What it did mean was that only human reason (working on the natural and visible world) and not faith in any unseen reality, was a reliable faculty in humanity's attempt to understand the world and the nature of the human life-form on earth. Through the process of secularity,

---

104. See Taylor, *Secular Age*.

faith became increasingly a private affair, a sentiment of religion, while only science could be verifiable—and therefore useful—in public discourse.

In fact, during this time the classical assumption that human beings are by nature social beings and form communities to assist one another was challenged by the opposite supposition that human beings are fundamentally self-interested, isolated and competitive individuals. The English philosopher of materialism, Thomas Hobbes (1588–1679), offered a new conception of human nature. He argued in his book, *Leviathan*, that all human beings are by nature equal in faculties of body and mind. From this equality and other causes in human nature, everyone is naturally willing to fight one another: "During the time men live without a common power to keep them all in awe, they are in that condition which is called war; and such a war as is of every man against every man." In this state, Hobbs contended, every person had a natural right or liberty to do anything necessary for preserving one's own life; yet, a culturally deprived and an impoverished life, which was the lot of most people, was, according to Hobbs: "Solitary, poor, nasty, brutish, and short."[105]

The individual as subjective thinker took prominence among the Enlightenment thinkers, even though some recognized that it was in the best interest of individuals to form associations within a greater society. However, these clubs and associations were based mostly on utility and elitism; each had its own rules of conduct and requirements for membership; often these were secret regulations. Thus, under the influence of many modernist thinkers, friendship faced relegation from the realm of ethics and politics to that of private sentiment, taste, culture and leisure.[106]

This does not mean that friendship was viewed as something trivial; nor does it mean that people who had bonds of friendship, and derived satisfaction from them, were seen as acting improperly. It just means that modernist thinkers did not appreciate friendship as a moral value; nor did the philosophers have the "love of friendship" as the sort of moral value the pursuit of which necessarily brings human beings closer to happiness, fulfillment, and human flourishing.[107] This is exemplified in the strikingly different understandings of friendship in the writings of the German Enlightenment philosopher, Immanuel Kant, and that a century later of the Danish philosopher, Søren Kierkegaard. Kant's understanding of friendship

105. Hobbes, *Leviathan*, XIII.9.
106. See Carmichael, *Friendship*, 156.
107. See Mitias, *Friendship*, 158.

serves to highlight the reasons why friendship faced relegation from the realm of ethics in modern moral reflection, while in Kierkegaard we can notice a novel understanding of friendship that points beyond the contemporary impasse.

Although he was a theist, Immanuel Kant (1724–1804) sought to base morality on reason alone. Kant makes a clear distinction between the concept of morality and the concept of happiness, but he recognizes a unity between them. According to Kant, the "right" is above the "good"; that which is "good" he saw as morally irrelevant; however, for Kant the supreme good was a synthesis of both virtue and happiness. Interestingly, in Kant's quest for the higher good, happiness is subordinated to virtue. In fact, Kant does not include in the moral sphere actions conducive to happiness, mainly because they are subsumed under the governance of the "categorical imperative."[108] In his *Groundwork of the Metaphysics of Morals* (or *Fundamental Principles of the Metaphysics of Morals*), Kant defined what he meant by a categorical imperative: "Act only according to that maxim whereby you can, at the same time, will that it should become a universal law." Put more simply, a "categorical imperative" is when, ethically, one sees that there is a fundamental moral imperative that is binding for all people in all circumstances and does not depend upon an individual's immediate circumstance. In his *Groundwork of the Metaphysics of Morals*, Kant makes it amply clear that respect for the moral law is the ultimate ground for the human action that promotes the highest good. For Kant, therefore, being moral is simply understood as fulfilling the obligations that come from the categorical imperative.[109]

However, in Kant's understanding, happiness is not merely subordinated to virtue, but there is a dividing wall between them. Kant argued that an imperative of happiness is not possible. There could be no imperative because the concept of happiness is indefinite, indeterminate, and because it is empirical.[110] The pursuit of happiness, Kant contends, depends on prudence, precepts, and counsels derived from experience; it is impossible to determine the occurrence and occasion of happiness, which is always subjective, relative, and changing. By creating a dividing wall between virtue and happiness, Kant omits friendship from the moral sphere; he writes:

---

108. See MacIntyre, *Short History of Ethics*, 193–94.
109. See Kant, *Groundwork*, 38.
110. See Kant, *Groundwork*, 35.

Elements of Friendship in the Classical and Christian Tradition

> Friendship is a union of two persons through equal mutual love and respect. One easily sees that it is an ideal in which a morally good will unites both parties in sympathy and shared well-being . . . so that friendship among men is our duty, as a maximum of good sentiment toward one another, is no ordinary duty but rather an honourable one proposed by reason, yet perfect friendship is a mere idea, unattainable in every attempt to realize it.[111]

This short passage calls for some response and commentary. First, Kant treats friendship as part of his ethical law of perfection, the law to "love thy neighbor as thyself." Yet, the oddity of treating friendship in terms of perfection is that the general basis of the division between duties to oneself and duties to others is that the former are based on cultivation of one's own perfection, while the latter on the happiness of others.[112] Second, friendship involves the union of two persons through equal love and respect. The basis of the union which unites friends is twofold: sympathy and shared well-being. Accordingly, it is a practical, personal, intimate, and subjective relationship. People seek to establish such a relationship not as a moral imperative *per se*, but as a result of inclination—or they seek it as the motivation of their happiness. So, in reality, friendship cannot be forced or created as a duty. In fact, by the term "love" Kant does not mean aesthetic feeling, although that may follow, but as the maxim of benevolence that results in magnanimity. It is this type of "love of others" (called benevolence) which is a duty. Respect, on the other hand, is courtesy to another, not imposing on others; it is allowing them their own space.

In the case of friendship, the equality of love and respect ensures that the "love of the other" does not degrade them by a lack of respect.[113] Yet, perfect friendship is unattainable in the real life, mainly because "love" ought to be reciprocal. However, according to this "calculative" mindset, it cannot be reciprocal because it is impossible for a person to know exactly whether the disposition to benevolence is equal to that of the friend. Nor can one know whether the feeling of duty to love the friend is equal to the feeling of duty to respect all persons. Even though friendship is unattainable in practice, as Kant concluded, striving for it is nonetheless a duty. Thus, although it is a duty to seek friendship (because conducive to

---

111. Kant, *The Doctrine of Virtue*, 140–44.
112. See Banham, "Kantian Friendship," 172–73.
113. See Wennemann, "The Role of Love in the Thought of Kant and Kierkegaard," 417–24.

happiness), it is not an ordinary duty but an "honorable duty," because it cannot be subsumed under the categorical imperative.[114]

A rare but possible reality is what Kant calls "moral friendship," which he defines as, "Complete confidence of two persons in revealing their secret judgments and feelings to each other, as far as such disclosures are consistent with mutual respect."[115] Hence, in Kant's view on moral friendship there is a tension between upholding self-disclosure (and thus honesty) on the one hand and avoiding intimacy on the other. This kind of friendship is not dependent upon feelings that can become inconsistent over time.[116] For Kant, this seems to suggest that moral friendship is primarily based on respect rather than love.[117] What is actually possible for Kant is to be a "friend of man" in the moral sense, (i.e., to take an affective interest in all men with a view to their equality). Because he is willing to humble himself, this kind of friend is able to act as a benefactor for others; however, the benefactor does not place himself in a superior position. As Kant puts it, "Taking to heart the duty of being benevolent as a friend of man, serves to guard against pride that usually comes over those fortunate enough to have the means of beneficence."[118] Kant deliberately chooses the idiom "friend," as connoting more than mere "philanthropy." The choice of the term "friend" carries the avoidance of condescension and patronage, and implies equality among all, "As if all men are brothers under one universal father who wills the happiness of all."[119] However, in no way did Kant's understanding reflect morality as it was known in classical times; Kant was a man of his time, and his attempt to make friendship a "duty" is within his familiarity of the moral domain, and grows out of it.

The role that friendship plays in modern ethical reflection influenced by Kant is minimal, and it is even seen as a hindrance to the ethical life. The moral agent is no longer considered in terms of a person who develops a good and worthy moral character, but as a rational person who is able to act on abstract and universal principles of justice and duty. To put it more

---

114. See Wennemann, "The Role of Love in the Thought of Kant and Kierkegaard," 417–24.

115. Kant, *Lectures on Ethics*, 471.

116. See Wennemann, "The Role of Love in the Thought of Kant and Kierkegaard," 417–24.

117. See Van Impe, "Kant on Friendship," 135–37.

118. Kant, *Lectures on Ethics*, 473.

119. Kant, *Lectures on Ethics*, 473.

Elements of Friendship in the Classical and Christian Tradition

simply: The Kantian approach of duty asks: "What shall I do?" or "How should I act?" Thus, the Kantian approach suggests that the task of becoming a good person is independent from the development of virtues that will help the person to the good life, a life worth living. The view of the moral self as purely rational would imply that the "emotional intimacy of particular friendships can provide no significance insight into one's moral self."[120]

The main problem associated with "love of friendship" during the late medieval period, and even more in era of Modernism, is that it is such a unique expression of love—inimitable, particular, and even exclusive. This is especially the case when *philía* is contrasted with the Christian universal love, often represented by *agápē/caritas*.

In fact, the Danish philosopher and theologian Søren Kierkegaard (1813–1855) saw in *philía* the possibility to subvert the Christian command to love all people. According to Kierkegaard, Christianity inaugurates a very different type of relationship to the other person, with a love that does not arise from within our natural possibilities, but from the command of God in and through Jesus Christ. Accordingly, friendship is not, and cannot be, considered as a moral value because it is not viewed as an avenue that leads to the "love of God." In his *Works of Love* Kierkegaard states: "If anyone thinks that a man by falling in love, or by having found a friend, has learned to know the Christian love, then he is seriously mistaken."[121]

Kierkegaard insisted that Friendship and Christian love are not only essentially different, but that they may even be radically opposed. According to Kierkegaard, this is an either-or situation; he does not grasp that both *philía* and *agápē* are possible. Kierkegaard claimed that if one chooses to make *philía* the love of his life, then *agápē*—the love that makes the person like God—will stand eternally out of reach. On the other hand, if one chooses to model one's love on God, the person must abandon the preferential "love of friendship."

Kierkegaard holds that Christian charity (*agápē/caritas*) must leave the preferential "love of friendship" behind. According to Kierkegaard, the power of *agápē* comes from the fact that it teaches us that every person is our neighbor and that we are called to love all. However, in a Kierkegaardian paradox, it teaches us this commandment by abandoning our friendships, not by enlarging and expanding them. He also links erotic love with friendship and labels them as passionate:

120. Thorne, "Friendship," 53.
121. Kierkegaard, *Works of Love*, 47.

> Christianity has thrust erotic love [*Elskov*] and friendship [*Venskab*] from the throne, the love based on drives and inclination, preferential love, in order to place the spirit's love [*Kjerlighed*] in its place, love for the neighbor, a love that in earnestness and truth is more tender in inwardness than erotic love in the union and more faithful in the sincerity than the most celebrated friendship in the alliance . . . the praise of erotic love and friendship belong to paganism, that the poet really belongs to paganism since his task belongs to it—in order with the sure spirit of conviction to give to Christianity what belongs to Christianity, love to one's neighbor, of which not a trace is found in paganism.[122]

Kierkegaard also takes the classic description of a friend as "another self" and turns it on its head.[123] It is a proof, he argues, not of friendship's nobility, but of its selfishness.[124] According to Kierkegaard, in friendship the person loves the friend not for the friend's sake, not for the goodness the person sees in the friend, not even for the friend's individuality or uniqueness, but as a reflection and extension of oneself.[125] In this narcissistic comprehension, friendship is selfishness disguised because the person loves the friend not for who the friend is, but only insofar as the person can see oneself in the friend.[126] The irony, as well as the tragedy of friendship, as Kierkegaard sees it, "is that the greater the union of love we think we have with our friends, the greater the imprisonment we have within ourselves."[127]

---

122. Kierkegaard, *Works of Love*, 44.
123. Cf. Aristotle, *NE*, 1170b6–7.
124. See Blum, *Friendship*, 70–75.
125. Blum holds that what Kierkegaard calls friendship is more aptly to be called a relationship of exploitation and manipulation. While Blum does not deny friendship's particularity, he claims that preferential love is not necessarily selfish. If it is the preferential love of friendship, then it is a love that not only prefers the friend, but prefers the interests, concerns, and cares of the friend. In this sense, friendship can school us in the virtues as it demands developing a horizon of interests and concerns beyond the confines of the self. According to Blum's description then, learning to love and care for a friend can be a means of learning to love and care for many more. In this way, the Christian neighbor-love, and preferential love are not mutually exclusive but intrinsically connected; friendship is the love in which Christian love of the neighbor is learned. See Blum, *Friendship, Altruism, and Morality*, 70–75.
126. See Kierkegaard, *Works of Love*, 53.
127. Wadell, *Friendship and the Moral Life*, 76. Wadell also notes that the problem in Kierkegaard's treatment of friendship is that he presumed so much that needs to be proven. See Wadell, *Friendship and the Moral Life*, 77.

Kierkegaard's contribution to the conversation on friendship comes in the form of a challenge. The temptation may be to reject his extreme stance on the grounds that he may be emotionally stunted and therefore suspicious, or even incapable of, friendship.

However, taken as a whole, Kierkegaard is not an enemy of friendship. In the end, despite his concerns about friendship, Kierkegaard does not set "love of friendship" and "love of neighbor" in strict opposition. "Far from it,"[128] as he himself wrote; but without doubt, Kierkegaard esteems "love of neighbor" more. However, Kierkegaard contends that "love of friendship" is to be "transformed by neighbor–love, rather than existing in simple opposition to it; it is not simply to be abolished."[129] For this reason, some critics even go so far as to suggest that Kierkegaard upholds friendship just as positively as Aristotle and Aquinas.[130] Kierkegaard's intention is not to attack friendship, but rather to "warn against the limitation inherent in relations based on preference."[131] Inclination and preference are not necessarily found in "love of neighbor."

Thus, love must begin with a command, the point of which is to dethrone the self-love at the heart of such preferential love, but not to eliminate preferential love altogether.[132] This command is intended to teach people to love themselves in the proper way. The refusal, or unwillingness, to love oneself in the right way can itself be a selfish, even sinful, act; self-loathing is not Christian! If the self is unwilling to be taught by Christianity how to love itself, Kierkegaard insisted, then it will be impossible to love the neighbor.[133] To be taught proper self-love means to be told the truth about oneself: to recognize oneself as a sinner before God, but to gratefully acknowledge that, nevertheless, one is loved by God and offered forgiveness.[134] If anyone is unwilling to believe that God loves in this way, or refuses to do so, that person will not be able to show this love to a neighbor, for God is love, and proper self-love originates in God's love. Christianity not only teaches what proper self-love is, but also what genuine love for a friend is. According to Kierkegaard, Christianity demands that "love of friendship" is not simply

---

128. Kierkegaard, *Works of Love*, 61.
129. Gregor, "Friends and Neighbors," 926.
130. See Ferreira, *Love's Grateful Striving*, 46.
131. Ferreira, *Love's Grateful Striving*, 46.
132. See Ferreira, *Love's Grateful Striving*, 46.
133. See Kierkegaard, *Works of Love*, 22.
134. See Kierkegaard, *Works of Love*, 280–99.

abolished but transformed to "love of neighbor." In light of this transformation, all expressions of love have their true and proper situation in relation to God.[135] In Kierkegaard's words: "No love and no expression of love may merely humanly and in a worldly way be withdrawn from the relationship to God."[136] As Kierkegaard continues to elaborate: "In love for the neighbor God is the middle term. Love God above all else; then you also love the neighbor, and in the neighbor, every human being."[137]

Kierkegaard concludes that through Christ's love for humanity, "Friendship can be transformed from a self-seeking, preferential love into a love that actually loves the other."[138] Since every relationship is rooted in the God-relationship, and because God stands between the self and the other, it is only in the God-relationship that the person can learn how to love; thus, Kierkegaard abolishes "The entire distinction between the many different kinds of love."[139] This can be understood as an existential ethic of subjective love, poured forth from the transformed individual, standing before God. For Kierkegaard, "love of neighbor" focuses on the distinct person of the other, and when it is mutual it is inter-subjective, between ongoing independent existents. For him, there is no question of friends being welded into a single self. Therefore, his thought: "Also leads in quite another direction, towards existentialism and personalism: Love for one's neighbor is love between two beings eternally and independently determined as spirit."[140]

In the early twentieth century, the tension between *agápē/caritas* (as the distinctive term for Christian love) and *philía* (as the preferential kind of love), once again becomes a theological issue, when German theology perceives a sharp dichotomy between the Hebraic and Hellenistic thought-worlds, and the Greek words for love were placed either on one or on the other side of this divide. The term *agápē* together with its related verb *agapān* (to love) are identified with the biblical, Hebrew thought-world, and the words are considered to have been deliberately chosen by the Septuagint[141] translators to denote God's strong, revealed divine love, which

---

135. See Gregor, "Friends and Neighbors," 928.
136. Kierkegaard, *Works of Love*, 112.
137. Kierkegaard, *Works of Love*, 58.
138. Gregor, "Friends and Neighbors," 928.
139. Kierkegaard, *Works of Love*, 143.
140. Carmichael, *Friendship*, 159. See Kierkegaard, *Works of Love*, 56.
141. The term "Septuagint" (derived from Latin meaning seventy) refers to the Greek

is wholly generous and unmotivated. By contrast, *philein* and its cognate words were often considered to denote a weak, motivated, earthly love.

The quarrel that arose among the theologians may not have been so much with the concept of friendship or with its relationship to Christian love as it has often been construed. No matter what apology for friendship might be made, it could never satisfy the demands of *agápē* because it was assumed that *agápē* and *philía* were autonomous and self-sufficient;[142] not only was one defined independently of the other, but it could be understood without reference to the other.

In fact, it was precisely in *agápē* being something other than *philía*, and vice versa, that each was secured by one being defined against the other.[143] Another possible reason as to why *agápē* and *philía* are often seen to be at odds is that, in concrete terms, *agápē* is seen as that love which makes one like God. In contrast, this description is seldom applied to *philía* because it is often forgotten that the "love of friendship" is not an abstraction but a whole way of life, based upon tradition. In other words, what shape a friendship takes—as well as what it achieves and what becomes of it—depends on what friends choose as the purpose of their friendship. In the language of contemporary ethics, understanding friendship requires understanding the narrative or story in which it is situated and according to which it is explained. Indeed, as Wadell writes: "Part of the reason *philía* is often overruled by *agápē* is that it is interpreted apart from the narrative that allows it to be integral to the Christian life."[144]

Thus, if one is to understand and evaluate the "love of friendship" and Christian love, one must first note the narrative which forms the lives of the friends. By so doing, one may discover that it is not friendship's particularity that leaves the "love of friendship" in tension with *agápē*, which may be nothing more than learning to love the people God loves. Rather, the tension may well come from a friendship that seeks something other than the "Kingdom of God" or between people who desire to be outside the community of the "People of God."

A contemporary Lutheran critic, Gilbert Meilaender, attributes the tension between *philía* and *agápē* to friendship's exacting particularity.

Old Testament translations. See Brown and O'Connell, "Texts and Versions," 1092.

142. Wadell, *Friendship and the Moral Life*, 72.

143. For an account of how our understanding of certain concepts depends on the narrative and tradition in which they are placed, see MacIntryre, *After Virtue*, 190–209.

144. Wadell, *Friendship and the Moral Life*, 72.

While Meilaender values the place of "love of friendship" in the Christian life, he argues that there is an inherent and enduring incompatibility between the two expressions of love. Meilaender perfectly agrees with the seventeenth century Anglican theologian Jeremy Taylor, who wrote: "When friendships were the noblest things in the world, charity was little."[145]

Given this description of "love of friendship" and Christian love, a description that, subsequently influences mainstream Christian understanding (and misunderstanding), it is not surprising that their relationship is often seen to be problematic at best, and at worst, irreconcilable. Once *agápē* is chosen as the love proper to Christianity and defined as both unconditional and universal, the "love of friendship" is unavoidably judged as a lesser, indeed, a secondary love; by its very essence, it lacks what is required by the Christian understanding of love. Yet, this does not imply that "love of friendship" is something to be avoided; it simply means that, from a theological perspective, it is deficient (as from a medical perspective, a doctor might diagnose a patient as deficient who might be lacking in red blood cells or adequate insulin receptors).

C. S. Lewis's famous treatment of friendship in *The Four Loves* has been a significant influence since its radio debut in 1958 and book publication in 1960. Lewis set out to expound the implications of the four Greek words for love (*storgē, philía, érōs* and *agápē*). Lewis's central argument is that there exists "Need-Love" and "Gift-Love," of which the latter is the higher form, exhibited most fully in God's love for humanity. However, rather than discount human love as being weak and sentimental, Lewis intended to show reflections of the divine love within human love. Lewis's reaction is an attempt to steer a middle course between the excessive idolatry of erotic love in the nineteenth-century writing of Browning, Kingsley and Patmore, and the reaction to them in the twentieth century, at a time that was altogether skeptical about erotic love's having any virtuous value at all. Hence, Lewis wrote, "the human loves can be glorious images of Divine love. No less than that: but also no more;"[146] and he defines the following terms: (i) *storgē* (affection, such as that between parent and child), (ii) *philía* (friendship, but only between those of the same gender), (iii) *érōs*, (the state of "being passionately in love"), and (iv) *agápē* (charity, the love that has parallels with the divine love, as held by Christian doctrine).

---

145. Taylor, "Discourse," 72.
146. Lewis, *The Four Loves*, 18.

Elements of Friendship in the Classical and Christian Tradition

Lewis's work has been influential in discussions of love and friendship in Christianity because he succeeds in showing the importance of different terminology used to describe human relationships. However, his work also reveals the danger of trying to compartmentalize human feelings and emotions into easy categories. Indeed, although Lewis was a great scholar, writer, teacher, and Christian apologist in the Anglican tradition, his approach in treating friendship has definite shortcomings. By defining relational terms as inflexibly spiritual and by squeezing experiential relationship into linguistic categories, Lewis sets up unrealistic descriptions, which emerge throughout his book. Writing from a Christian perspective, Lewis already acknowledges the supremacy of *agápē/caritas*. He esteems *philía/amicitia*, first, on the basis of it being the most closely aligned to divine love and, secondly, because it does not involve a physical dimension.[147] Indeed, for Lewis the measure of purity is the absence of physicality; the purer the love, he implied, the less it has to do with the body.[148] This seems to suggest that, for Lewis, while friendship continues to be valued in the Christian tradition, it nevertheless has a certain deficiency, which categorizes it as a "less-than" because of the ambiguities associated with the valuation of friendship. More to the point, in Lewis's understanding—which was undoubtedly influenced by his participation in the Inklings group which met regularly at the "Eagle and Child" pub to converse with one another—friendship itself was a "good" human love (because allied to divine love and without physical expression), but the "love of friendship" was ambiguous. It remained unclear to Lewis whether friendship itself could be considered as essential to the Christian life.[149] Thus, even to the present, the theology of friendship has yet to be taken up in the conversation across the ages of Christian theologians and sages of the cultures. With C. S. Lewis, the tension between *agápē/caritas* and *philía/amicitia* might have been partially rehabilitated, but not as foundational to the Christian life and therefore not crucial to the theology of the Christian life.

---

147. See Lewis, *The Four Loves*, 71.

148. See Summers, *Friendship*, 55.

149. The group of Oxford Christians that formed the "Inklings" included both C. S. Lewis and J. R. R. Tolkien, who was the sole Catholic in the group of scholars and writers; Tolkien expressed a much deeper understanding of friendship and the value of the "love of friendship" in his great fictional trilogy, *The Lord of the Rings*. It may be that this difference of understanding became one of the factors that separated Lewis and Tolkien in their final years.

While the first buds of theological possibility for the "love of friendship" can be seen, the full blossom and ripening fruit are still to be generally realized. The recovery of friendship as a moral category and the establishment of the "love of friendship" as foundational of the Christian life may have well begun, but there have been many detours and obstacles, and it remains in the future to be fully realized, even now.

We have now explored how the Hellenic and Hellenistic cultures considered friendship as essential for the perfection of human nature and, in some cases, a necessary condition of the good life. These cultures of classical Greece and Rome considered friendship to be an offspring of virtue, which, once established, became the crown of life and a school of virtue in itself.

Early Christianity readily made use of the conceptual world—including that of the friendship world—of the dominant Greco-Roman culture into which it was being assimilated, and against which it was defining itself. The Fathers of the Church used the language of friendship alongside the familial imagery of Holy Scripture. In the fourth century, Saint Augustine offered the first theological treatment of friendship. Despite his warnings about the potential dangers of friendship, Augustine acknowledged its value in the life of the Christians by considering it a relationship that was being transformed by God's salvific workings.

In early medieval monasticism there was a consistent theme of suspicion about friendship, which was feared as it might lead to community factions and sexual temptation. Yet, others recognized the complexity of relationships in the community and the need for an easier, more rounded approach. The apex of the monastic treatment of friendship was reached by Aelred of Rievalux in his twelfth-century treatise, *Spiritual Friendship*. Despite its great contribution, Aelred's work did not survive much beyond its own era, and his dialogical conciliatory approach was sometimes seen as moral laxity.

The task of medieval systematic theology was to formulate as clearly as possible an orderly, rational and coherent account of the Christian faith and beliefs. In a strictly theological context, friendship was becoming a subject deemed irrelevant by the theologians. During this period, friendship's particularity was often put in opposition with the universality demanded by Christian love. However, the apparent eternal opposition between the two kinds of love was questioned and opposed by Saint Thomas Aquinas with his understanding of *caritas* as *amicitia* with God. Yet, after Saint Thomas's death, his theological synthesis collapsed, in particular through the great new division between moral and spiritual theology. Friendship with God could be understood as a spiritual reality, but it seemed irrelevant to a moral theology mostly concerned with the adherence to laws and precepts.

Furthermore, the wariness about friendship's particularity intensified after the sixteenth century, in particular in Protestant theology. In reaction against a Christianity that had grown superficial, the Danish Lutheran, Søren Kierkegaard, saw in friendship the possibility to challenge the Christian command to love all people. The dialogue among the Oxford Christians, including C. S. Lewis, may have turned often to the friendship and fellowship that the Inklings enjoyed; yet, it was only a partial rehabilitation, with many challenges and distractions that have been raised in the last throes of Modernism's gender confusion and the redefinition of marriage.

The element of "choice" in what constitutes the moral dimensions of a friendship remains in the future to be fully realized, while the "love of friendship" as foundational of the Christian life may yet remain in a transcendent realm, despite the clear directives to be found in the Johannine Gospel.

Chapter 2

Characteristics of "Love" and "Friendship" in the Fourth Gospel

DESPITE THE ROCKY DEVELOPMENT that "love of friendship" has historically managed, and despite its often being misunderstood, this conception has secured a precarious place in the life of the church. From a theological perspective, this misunderstanding stems from the fact that "love of friendship" is a preferential kind of love, and, if taken on face value in the hierarchy of loves, seems to contradict the biblical command to love all people.

What has been so repeated overlooked in theological debate over more weighty dogmatic material is that a Christian understanding of "love of friendship" is deeply embedded in scripture and emerges only shyly, without trumpet blasts, from the biblical texts. Of course, it is obvious that in the Fourth Gospel, "love" and "friendship" are important themes. However, only a limited number of studies have focused on friendship in the Fourth Gospel, or friendship in Johannine literature as a whole. Even so, there is a long tradition linking friendship with the Fourth Gospel. What especially comes to mind is the image of the Beloved Disciple reclining next to Jesus at the Last Supper, which came to be viewed as the prototypical example of friendship during the medieval period.[1] Moreover, in John 15:13–15, the Fourth Gospel explicitly "gives the 'love of friendship' a central place."[2]

---

1. See McGuire, *Friendship & Community*, 219.
2. Carmichael, *Friendship*, 39.

Characteristics of "Love" and "Friendship" in the Fourth Gospel

Here, the Johannine author presents a monumental change of status for Jesus's disciples: they are no longer regarded as slaves or servants but are called friends. Finally, in the history of theology, the Fourth Gospel has a special role. As Origen wrote, it is "the first fruits of the gospel."[3] Thus, it is a natural and logical progression from the central theme of friendship in the Bible to the acknowledgement of the "love of friendship" as having importance in Christian theologizing. There is, indeed, a central role of friendship for Christian theology, and the theology of the Christian life more specifically. In fact, this will be precisely the role that Thomas Aquinas will grant friendship in his *magnum opus*, the *Summa Theologiae*.

In recent years, the theme of friendship has returned to become the subject of discussion and discernment among biblical scholars, who have naturally focused on Jesus and regarded him as the ideal friend, especially through his laying down his life for his friends (John 15:13). Such was a commonplace sentiment of ancient friendship, but the scholarly concern rarely goes beyond a Christological use of friendship discussion. In the following pages, Greco-Roman friendship customs and standards are applied to the Johannine presentation of Jesus and to other characters in the Fourth Gospel—namely, John the Baptist, the three friends from Bethany, and the disciple whom Jesus loved (an unnamed disciple introduced at John 13:23, often called the Beloved Disciple). A sensitive interpretation of the relationships (especially in the case of the disciple whom Jesus loved) by readers of John's Gospel might bring to light that this Beloved Disciple's behavior would have been those of a friend of Jesus. The properties of a friend are discernible during the Last Supper (John 13:1–17:26); it becomes even more evident that the Jesus of Saint John's Gospel came among people not only with the mandate to save the world, but also with an invitation to a relationship that Greco-Roman philosophers only dreamed of and Jews probably found preposterous: a friendship with the Lord is offered to those who want to follow him and even with his God the Father, who dwells in unapproachable light.

The classical writers offered a description of human friendship which Christian writers have drawn on. What made ancient friendships exemplary was their embodying the various commonplaces of friendship, whether it was their virtue, the harmony of their views and values, or their willingness to share their lives and fortunes with one another. The first systematic study of friendship goes back to Aristotle who proposed a tri-partite analysis of

---

3. Elowsky, *John 1–10*, 1.

friendship in which friendship arose because of utility, pleasure or virtue, as opposed to those based on virtue being genuine friendships.⁴ Cicero constantly underscores the importance of virtue or goodness in friendship, going so far as to say that friendship cannot exist in any way without virtue (*sine virtute amicitia esse ullo pacto potest*)⁵ or that friendship exists only among good men (*in bonis*),⁶ whom he describes shortly afterwards with a virtue list: loyalty (*fides*), integrity (*integritas*), fairness (*aequitas*), and generosity (*liberalitas*). Among these good men Laelius places his friend Scipio.

The second commonplace—friends enjoying a harmony of views or being of one mind—is also characteristic of friendship,⁷ and again Cicero emphasizes this quality when he defines friendship in part as being nothing else than an agreement in all matters, human and divine.⁸ Indeed, Laelius sees his own friendship with Scipio in this light, saying that their friendship consisted *inter alia* of agreement and consensus in public matters.⁹

Perhaps it is the third commonplace mentioned above—that of sharing a friend's life and fortunes—that most often characterizes these exemplary friendships. Plutarch speaks of the pleasure that friends have from simply spending their days together.¹⁰ Cicero elaborates these daily activities, saying that Laelius and Scipio share one home, ate the same food, went on military tours together, visited foreign sites together, and vacationed together in the country.¹¹

However, friendship means more than daily association. Fortunes change, for the good or ill. Thus, Aristotle speaks of friends sharing their joys and sorrows¹² or of the need for a friend in both prosperity and misfortune, and this sentiment is repeated in general terms by Cicero¹³ and Seneca.¹⁴

---

4. See Aristotle, *NE*, 1155b17–1156b32; Schroeder, "Friendship in Aristotle," 35–45.
5. See Cicero, *On Friendship*, 6.20.
6. See Cicero, *On Friendship*, 5.18; cf. 8.26; 9.32; 22.82; 27.100.
7. See e.g. Dio, *Orat.*, 38.15: "What is friendship except unanimity among friends?"
8. See Cicero, *On Friendship*, 6.20.
9. See Cicero, *On Friendship*, 27.101.
10. See Plutarch, *De amic mult.*, 94F.
11. See Cicero, *On Friendship*, 27.103.
12. See Aristotle, *NE*, 1166a8.
13. See Cicero, *On Friendship*, 5.17 and 6.22.
14. See Seneca, *Ep.*, 9.8.

Characteristics of "Love" and "Friendship" in the Fourth Gospel

Although discussions about friendship are not as commonly found in Jewish literature as in Greco-Roman literature, certain traditions (particularly within the Wisdom literature) highlight important features of friendship. In the Old Testament there are many accounts of different kinds of friendship, from Moses and Abraham through the Prophets, in the Proverbs and the Psalms, and through the allegorical lover/beloved poem, Solomon's Song of Songs. In the Book of Exodus, it is recorded that: "The LORD used to speak to Moses face to face, as one speaks to a friend" (Exodus 33:11). Here is an explicit reference to friendship with the divine when God and Moses are seen conversing "man to man," just as friends do.

Likewise, in 2 Chronicles 20:7 there is a reminder of this relationship between them: "Did you not, O our God, drive out the inhabitants of this land before your people Israel and give it forever to the descendants of your friend Abraham?" In addition to these references to friendship with God, there are also scriptural references to intimate personal friendships (Deuteronomy 13:6), family friendships (Proverbs 27:10), and political friendships (Esther 6:13). A good example of an intimate personal friendship is the relationship between David and Jonathan, who is said to have loved David "as his own soul" (1 Samuel 18:1–3) and "as his own life" (1 Samuel 20:17). One critic even describes the friendship between David and Jonathan as "the Bible's lengthiest and most complex narrative reflection on friendship."[15] Jonathan's friendship with David transcended his relationship with his own father, leading him to act in the best interest of his friend when Saul was threatening David's life. Their relationship included the sharing of knowledge (1 Samuel 19:1–7). After Jonathan's death, David lamented and expressed his love for his lost friend in these words: "I am distressed for you, my brother Jonathan; greatly beloved were you to me; your love to me was wonderful, passing the love of women" (2 Samuel 1:26). The absolute devotion of Ruth and Naomi, though not expressed using friendship conventions, nevertheless reflect ideals, such as loyalty and respect, which are associated with genuine friendship (Ruth 1:16–17).

The most extensive treatment of friendship in the Old Testament is found in the Book of Ben Sirach (Ecclesiasticus).[16] Ben Sirach provides practical guidance for making friends, being a faithful friend, and dealing

---

15. Tull, "Jonathan's Gift of Friendship," 130. She goes on to provide a helpful treatment of the ambiguity inherent in the narrator's account of David's friendship towards Jonathan. See Tull, "Jonathan's Gift of Friendship," 130–43.

16. See Corley, "Caution, Fidelity, and the Fear of God," 313.

with threats to friendships; in his writing, he concentrated his teaching in 6:5–17; 22:1–36 and 37:1–6.[17] He views faithful friends as an invaluable treasure (Sirach 6:14–15) that should not be easily abandoned or betrayed (Sirach 7:18; 9:10; 27:17a). A similar emphasis on loyalty is found in Proverbs, where friends are said to love at all times (Proverbs 17:17) and it is noted that "a true friend sticks closer than one's nearest kin" (Proverbs 18:24). Loyalty toward friends is also enjoined: "Do not forsake your friend or the friend of your parent" (Proverbs 27:10). As in the Greco-Roman tradition, Ben Sirach noted that friends are an important ingredient in a happy life: "Faithful friends are life-saving medicine" (Sirach 6:16).[18] Like Greco-Roman writers, he also emphasized the need for caution in choosing friends (Sirach 6: 5–13). Friends were only to be chosen after careful testing (Sirach 6:7), for apparent friends could easily turn out to be enemies (Sirach 6:8–10). Ben Sirach warned that "every friend says, 'I too am a friend'; but some friends are friends only in name" (Sirach 37:1). Consequently, he urged his readers to "keep away from your enemies and be on guard with your friends" (Sirach 6:13).

In contrast to Greco-Roman writers, Ben Sirach drew a firm link between piety and the possibility of genuine friendship. Finding true friends was directly dependent upon fearing God (Sirach 6:16), since only a God-fearing man could act as a friend ought to act, and those who fear God associate with others who do the same (Sirach 6:17).[19]

In the New Testament the term *phílos* (friend) occurs twenty-nine times. It is found eight times in the Johannine corpus,[20] eighteen times in Luke/Acts,[21] once in Matthew,[22] and twice in James.[23] The term *philía* (friendship) occurs only in James 4:4. It is notable that even though Saint Paul never uses the terms *phílos* or *philía*, his letters contain a significant amount of friendship language, particularly his letter to the Philippians; his emphasis on likeness and equality in Philippians 1:30; 2:2. 6 gives a hint of friendship language.

17. See Harrington, "Sage Advice About Friendship," 80.
18. Cf. Plutarch, *Adul. Amic.*, 49F.
19. See Irwin, "Fear of God," 553.
20. See John 3:29; 11:11; 15:13. 14. 15; 19:12; 3 John 1:15.
21. See Luke 7:6. 34; 11:5. 6. 8; 12:4; 14:10. 12; 15:6. 9. 29; 16:9; 21:16; 23:12; Acts 10:24; 19:31; 27:3.
22. See Matthew 11:19.
23. See James 2:23; 4:4.

Characteristics of "Love" and "Friendship" in the Fourth Gospel

However, it is in the Gospel of John that the truly glorious paradigm is found, and there is a long tradition linking friendship with the Fourth Gospel. In the history of theology, the Fourth Gospel has a special role in "Love and Friendship." As stated above, Origen claims in his Commentary on John that it is "the first fruits of the gospel."[24] These ripe fruits—friendship and love—arise from the very depths of the mystery of the Incarnation of the Word of God. Moreover, the Fourth Gospel explicitly gives "love of friendship" a central place:

> No one has greater love than this, to lay down one's life for one's friends. You are my friends if you do what I command you. I do not call you servants any longer, because the servant does not know what the master is doing; but I have called you friends, because I have made known to you everything that I have heard from my Father.[25]

Here, the author presents a sweeping change of status for Jesus's disciples: they are no longer regarded as slaves or servants but are called friends. The author of the Fourth Gospel proclaims Jesus as the one who came not only to save the world, but also to offer those who want to follow him a privileged relationship that the Greco-Roman philosophers despaired of realizing and Judaism probably found absurd: a friendship with none other than the Incarnate Divine Lord himself.

Before proceeding with our exposition of the friendship between Jesus and a number of Johannine characters (together with that of Jesus and the whole group of disciples during the Last Supper), it is important to make an etymological detour and speak briefly about the terminology used for "love" in the Fourth Gospel.

The Johannine envisioning of the words "love" and "friendship" span two word groups: *agapān* and *phileīn*; the verbal form, *agapáō*, is used thirty-seven times in John, whereas *philéō* occurs twelve times.[26] Most of this usage congregates around the "farewell discourse" (John 13:31–17:26) where love and friendship are major themes and where (according to the vast majority of Johannine scholars) the two verbs, together with their respective cognate groups, are interchangeable with no distinction in

---

24. Origen, *Commentary on the Gospel of John*, 31–36.

25. John 15:13–15.

26. For references of the occurrences of these verbs, see Gignac, "The Use of Verbal Variety in the Fourth Gospel," 193–95.

meaning.²⁷ Francis T. Gignac holds that with the possible exception of John 13:1 and John 15:19, where a contrast might be drawn between the love (*agapēsas . . . ēgápēsen*) of Jesus for his own and that of the world loving (*ephílei*) its own, together with Jesus's final dialogue with Simon Peter in John 21:15–23, the two verbs seem to be used interchangeably with no distinction in meaning.²⁸ The consensus of those Johannine scholars who conclude that this alternation represents John's stylistic preference for using different but synonymous words, is based on their insistence that all attempts to draw a semantic distinction between *agapáō* and *philéō* are doomed to failure, whether in Greek literature generally, the Septuagint, the New Testament, or John's Gospel itself. One of these scholars, James Barr, wrote in his essay, "Words for Love in Biblical Greek" the following:

> There is a difference of stylistic level, of associations, and of nuances. But within any one individual passage these differences do not amount to a distinction of real theological reference: they do not specify a difference in the kind of love referred to.²⁹

This conclusion, held by the majority of Johannine scholarship, was challenged by a number of nineteenth century British scholars including R. C. Trench, B. F. Westcott and A. Plummer, who tended to see the alternation of verbal forms in John 21:15–17 as not merely one of style but of substance.³⁰ However, support to this archaic position dwindled in front of apparently irrefutable evidence that the Fourth Gospel regularly deploys synonyms for the exclusive purpose of stylistic variation. For example, besides the two words for "love" (*agapáō* and *philéō*), in John 21:15–17 there are two verbs for "feed" or "tend" (*bóskō* and *poimaínō*), two nouns for "sheep" (*arnía* and *próbata*), and two verbs for "know" (*oīda* and *ginōskō*).³¹

The imagery of friendship is present in the first half of John's narrative, but it comes into its sharpest focus in the second half of the Gospel,

---

27. See Popkes, *Die Theologie der Liebe Gottes in den johanneischen Schriften*. Biblical scholars who hold that the two verbs, together with their respective cognate groups, are used interchangeably in the Fourth Gospel include Schnackenburg, *John*, 362–63 ("used synonymously"), Moloney, *The Gospel of John*, 559 ("the Johannine practice of using synonymous verbs for stylistic variety") and Beutler, *Gospel of John*, 536 ("the difference in meaning is of little significance).

28. See Gignac, "Verbal Variety in the Fourth Gospel," 194.

29. Barr, "Words for Love," 15.

30. For a fuller list of defenders of this position, see Shepherd, "'Do You Love Me?,'" 777–92.

31. See Potterie, "Oèda et ginÎskw: Les deux modes," 709–25.

particularly during the Last Supper, when Jesus refers to his disciples as "friends" in John 15:15.

The reference to friendship that precedes John 15:15 prepares the way for this astounding transformation of relationship with Jesus. Specifically, this reference appears in the pericopes concerning John the Baptist, Jesus's three friends from Bethany, and the Beloved Disciple. In these different characters and three distinct relationships, the author of the Fourth Gospel makes use of the conceptual field of friendship, relationships which, in some ways, mirror the reciprocal immanence and love between Jesus and the Father.

"THE FRIEND OF THE BRIDEGROOM"

The noun *phílos* (friend/beloved) appears for the first time in John 3:29 when John the Baptist identifies himself as "the friend of the bridegroom" (*paranúmphios*). While the Baptist's role is secondary, there is an intimacy between the groom and his "best man," who had the role of preparing and presenting the bride to the bridegroom.[32] In his book, *Imaginative Love in John*, Sjef van Tilborg suggests that, in a way, the reference to "the friend of the groom" in John 3:29 is more akin to the Hellenistic and Roman understanding of the friendship between groom and groomsman. In the classical world custom, there is only one *paranúmphios*, in contradiction to the Jewish customs where there are always two "best men": one for the bride (*sjosjbin*) and one for the groom.[33] To be a *paranúmphios* is an honor which expresses the bond of friendship between the groom and his best friend, who is chosen as the "one and only" from among the groom's circle of friends.

Moreover, while a special and mutual relationship existed between Jesus and John the Baptist, as written in the Fourth Gospel, the focus is more on the contrasts between them. Throughout John 3:27–36, the superiority of Jesus is repeatedly emphasized: Jesus's divine origin; Jesus's permanent endowment with the Spirit; and Jesus's distinctive role as judge. Jesus's status must increase (v. 30), since he is the one who has come from above (v. 31), and he is above all (v. 31). John the Baptist is not himself the Messiah, but only the one sent by him to prepare the Messiah's way (v. 28; cf. 1:20–23). While the Baptist is merely one from the earth (v. 31), Jesus bears first-hand

32. See Coloe, "Witness and Friend," 319–32.
33. See van Tilborg, *Imaginative Love*, 76–77.

knowledge from above (v. 32). Jesus is sent from God and possesses the fullness of God's Spirit (v. 34); thus, he is perfectly able to speak the words of God (v. 34). Moreover, God has given Jesus authority over everything (v. 35), including the right and ability to convey eternal life (vv. 35–36).

Though there is a clear distinction in status between Jesus and his kinsman, John, the latter is not reluctant to describe himself as the friend of the bridegroom; he is the one who stands and hears him and "rejoices greatly at the bridegroom's voice" (v. 29). In this "rejoicing," where the emotional state of one is shared by his friend, there is a hearkening into the past, which draws onto the friendship dimension characterized by the pre-Christian world of classical Greece and Rome friendship, where ideal friends shared in all of life's experiences, whether good or ill. In this way, John the Baptist can be understood as the precursor and bridge between pagan friendship, built on natural virtue and affinity, and the Christian understanding of friendship, built on grace. The joy that the friend of the bridegroom experiences is now felt by the Baptist in his last testimony on behalf of Jesus. It is a perfect joy in which the readers are also to share.

THE BETHANY FAMILY AS JESUS'S FRIENDS

John the Baptist is not the only Johannine character described as Jesus's friend. Another is also given this title in John 11:11 where Jesus says enigmatically: "Our friend Lazarus has fallen asleep, but I am going there to awaken him." Lazarus is the only individual character in the Fourth Gospel explicitly identified by name as Jesus's friend.[34]

The two pericopes where Lazarus is mentioned (John 11: 1–46 and 12: 1–8) take place in Bethany, which recalls the Bethany on the other side of the Jordan where John the Baptist began his mission (see John 1:28; cf. 10:40). Perhaps here, as Johannes Beutler notes, "an arc is being registered deliberately. A new cycle opens. Lazarus now enters instead of the Baptist."[35] He is someone whom Jesus loves (v. 3) and so prepares the transition to the Beloved Disciple, who appears at Jesus's side from John 13 and becomes his witness thereafter.

Jesus's love for Lazarus needs to be considered within the context of Jesus's relationship with Lazarus's sisters, Mary and Martha, as well. Using

---

34. For this reason, some Johannine scholars associated Lazarus with the "Beloved Disciple." See Charlesworth, *The Beloved Disciple*, 185–92.

35. Beutler, *John*, 297.

Characteristics of "Love" and "Friendship" in the Fourth Gospel

an imperfect tense of the verb "to love" (*ēgápa*) in John 11:5, the Gospel writer suggests the extended and continuing nature of Jesus's love: he loves Martha and Mary, as well as Lazarus, who has the bonus reference as being Jesus's friend. In this pericope, Jesus is depicted as a friend of the family, but not as a blood relative. The nature of this friendship, however, is one that has made him effectively like one of the family;[36] this friendship between Jesus and the three siblings of Bethany lends itself to being equated with a familial relationship. The relationships are treated in this exchange with great finesse by the Johannine author. It is remarkable that in the verbs used throughout his account, love itself and the action of loving always originates and come from Jesus himself. This can be seen even within their summoning message to Jesus stating that their brother is ill. In the sisters's appeal to Jesus for help based on his affection for their brother (v. 3)—"Lord, he whom you love is ill"—"whom you love" is written using the verb *phileīn*, with the root that expresses rather a relationship of friendship (see John 15:13–15).

Jesus's love for Lazarus seems to be a source of tension in the narrative: love as absent and love as present. On the one hand, Jesus is ready to risk his life for his friend; on the other hand, he deliberately stays away for two more days before taking any action (John 11:6). This seems to suggest that, although Lazarus may well be Jesus's friend, Jesus is the one who works entirely by the Father's will. The fact that Jesus expects his disciples to accompany him to the Bethany family is based on the friendship which they also enjoyed with Lazarus. Jesus's reference to Lazarus as "our friend" (v. 11) highlights the disciples' responsibility as friends and serves to motivate them to accompany him. Some theologians interpret Jesus's sharing the information with his disciples that Lazarus has fallen asleep in verse 11 as an expression of friendship between Jesus and his disciples as well.[37]

In John 11:14, the narrator describes the speech—"then Jesus told them plainly"—by which Jesus corrects the disciples' misunderstanding about the truth of Lazarus's situation as speaking frankly, *parrhēsía*. One of the primary distinguishing marks of a true friend in the Greco-Roman culture was being able to use "frank speech," *parrhēsía*. Unlike elsewhere in the Fourth Gospel (cf. John 4), where the writer uses misunderstanding, irony, and metaphor as intentional literary strategies to move characters to deepening levels of theological understanding, the misunderstanding in

---

36. See Esler and Piper, *Lazarus, Mary and Martha*, 84.
37. See Puthenkandathil, *Philos*, 100–101.

this instance is explicitly corrected as soon as Jesus realizes it has occurred.[38] Thus, it can be noted that Jesus is affirming the friendly relationship with his disciples by speaking *parrhēsía*—frankly and plainly—to them.

After the initial misunderstanding on the part of the disciples regarding Lazarus's death, they give voice through Thomas to their willingness to die for a friend: "Let us also go, that we may die with him" (John 11:16). It has occasionally been doubted whether to take Thomas's words seriously; after all, they sound similar to the boastful words of Peter in John 13:37, which are followed immediately not by deeds, but by the triple denial. However, in this instance, everything speaks for the fact that Thomas's words should be taken seriously. In other places too, Jesus commands the disciples to be faithful to him until death[39] and predicts for them a coming persecution to the death.[40] Thomas's words contain a clear message: to be ready to go with Jesus even to death in order to find life. This declaration by Thomas could also be taken as an illustration of the classical distinction between the true and the false friend, which arises again at the Last Supper; the false friend is not around in a time of crisis, but the true friend will be. Thomas's response may be understood as his being willing to act in accord with the expected responsibilities of friendship; he is willing to play the part of a genuine friend.

Ironically, by going to Bethany in concern and friendship towards Lazarus, Jesus set in motion the actions that led to his own arrest, suffering, and death. The illness and subsequent death of Lazarus was the means through which the glory of God would be manifested (John 11:4). Hence, it may be suggested that the glorification of Jesus on the Cross is ultimately reached "through the sickness of his friend."[41]

Jesus's prayer before raising Lazarus makes use of the conventions of classical friendship: unity, mutuality, and equality. Yet, it is in Jesus's friendship with the Father that the prayer draws its profound revelation of true friendship—that of the perfect love between Jesus and the Father. Addressing the Father aloud, Jesus affirms that the Father "always listens" to the Son and that the Father loves the Son (John 11:42). In the awesome proclamation that "the Father and I are one," the full mutual and reciprocal nature of the divine friendship is revealed (John 10:30). When Jesus exemplifies

---

38. See O'Day, "Jesus as Friend in the Gospel of John," 88.
39. See John 12:25–26; 21:18–19.
40. See John 15:26–27; 16:1–3.
41. Puthenkandathil, *Philos*, 99.

Characteristics of "Love" and "Friendship" in the Fourth Gospel

divine power and calls Lazarus back, it is as if he is addressing a still-living person, and this might be read as an expression of their friendship. For his part, Lazarus may be seen as responding in a personal way to his friendship with Jesus when at Jesus's command he returns from beyond death and walks out of the tomb. He acts as one of the sheep that hears the voice of the Good Shepherd and follows (see John 10:16).

The fourth Gospel narrative also makes clear reference to a relationship of friends in that Jesus's love was not restricted to Lazarus alone but equally towards his sisters, Martha and Mary, as well. The bold address and content of the message sent by them to Jesus is based on the friendship already present between Jesus and Lazarus (John 11:3). Jesus's intervention in response to Martha's request also demonstrates his friendship with her (vv. 21–26). Traditionally, in the Synoptic Gospels, Martha is understood as type for the active life, and Mary is considered as the contemplative. Gradually, however, in the Johannine version, Jesus leads Martha to a fully Christological confession, thus exemplifying the ideal of faith, which is the ultimate message of the Fourth Gospel itself (see John 20:31).[42] Indeed, it is in the Gospel of John that the closest parallel to Peter's famous confession of faith is to be found on the lips of Martha: "Yes, Lord, I believe that you are the Messiah, the Son of God, the one coming into the world" (John 11:27). Through its positioning in the center of John's Gospel, this confession gains extra weight.[43]

Likewise, in the next passage, Jesus's friendship with Lazarus's sister, Mary, is evident in his calling for her to come: "She [Martha] went back and called her sister Mary, and told her privately, 'The Teacher is here and is calling for you'" (John 11:28). Acting as a sheep which comes at the voice of the Good Shepherd, Mary goes outside her house to where Jesus was standing. Her immediate actions demonstrate clearly her attachment to him; hers is both a response of faith and at the same time one of deep frustration—if Jesus had not tarried overlong, Lazarus would not have died. It is this disappointment of his friends which gives way to Jesus's weeping over Lazarus's death.

The use of the Greek verb for "weeping" (*dakrúō*) in John 11:35 might portray Jesus as crying serenely while showing the genuine tears of an ordinary man at the death of his friend.[44] In the narrative, this is the conclusion

---

42. See Smith and Williams, *John*, 109.
43. See Beutler, *John*, 302.
44. See Westcott, *John*, 171.

of a group of Judeans who interpreted Jesus's crying as an expression of the depth of Jesus's love towards Lazarus: "So the Jews said, 'see how he loved him'" (v. 36).

Yet, Jesus's sentiments at a human level for his friend must also be seen in its immediate context. Jesus sees Mary weeping along with those who had come with her, and "he was greatly disturbed in spirit and deeply moved" (v. 33). In John 11:38, the emotional emphasis is again repeated: "Then Jesus, again greatly disturbed, came to the tomb." In John 11:33 Jesus's strong emotional response to the situation is described with the verbs *tarássō* (greatly disturbed) and *embrimáomai* (deeply moved). The verb *tarássō* occurs six times in the Fourth Gospel,[45] but the rare verb *embrimáomai* for "deeply moved" is unique; *embrimáomai* denotes an angry feeling or action stirred up by a feeling of ire. Was this feeling of indignation provoked by the tears of the mourners, because their tears indicated a lack of faith on their part? Or was it simply wrath against the very power of death? Or, possibly, is the anger directed against the final rejection of Jesus himself, even by the people he loves?

Soon after the raising of Lazarus, in John 12:1-8, we find Martha "serving" (*diēkónei*) during the dinner given in honor of Jesus at the house of Lazarus in Bethany, the place of Jesus's "friends" (see John 11:1, 18). The imperfect form of the verb *diēkónei* suggests a habitual action on the part of Martha, thus showing the familiar relationship and the friendship that exist between Jesus and Martha. The same could be said in the ensuing scene where Mary's returned love towards Jesus is seen in the act of her anointing him. Here, the wastefulness of her gesture is underlined: a pound of fine oil signified a fortune, and, moreover, it is unalloyed—pure and precious oil of spikenard (v. 3). Jesus allows Mary to anoint his feet, and in this is revealed that aspect of friendship that not only gives, but also receives.

To share with one another is a characteristic of friendship; a genuine friend not only gives but also receives. Otherwise, it would seem to be a relation between a benefactor (one who gives or dispenses his bounty) and beneficiary (one who receives the largesse). In the Fourth Gospel, there follows a protest, which was raised not by an anonymous "some" (Mark 14:4), but by an individual, namely Judas. His objection is to the wastefulness of anointing the Lord's "beautiful feet"[46] because the nard could have been sold and the proceeds given to the poor. This concern stems from tradition,

---

45. See John 5:7; 11:33; 12:27; 13:21; 14:1. 27.
46. See Isaiah 52:7.

but in what follows it is characterized as hypocritical since, according to the Fourth Gospel writer, Judas was a thief and used to misappropriate donations from the common purse.

In friendship terms, here Mary is depicted as a true friend of Jesus while Judas acts as an anti-friend. As a loyal friend of Jesus Mary acts in a loving and munificent gesture; Judas only speaks. She takes the precious oil and anoints Jesus's feet with it, wiping his feet with her hair—a grand gesture of a grateful heart! Judas grumbles only of what could have been done for the faceless poor. Mary shows extravagant devotion to Jesus; Judas shows his true colors as a self-centered man, who diverts contributions to the common purse for his own use (vv. 4–6).

Moreover, Mary has anointed Jesus, who makes reference to its being for his imminent death and burial (after his death, in fact, this anointing was not carried out). Furthermore, Mary sensed that her loving act was a matter of urgency. While she has understood that haste is required, Judas sees no urgency (vv. 7–8). Through these antitheses, the evangelist is offering role models of the true and false friends, and the sincerity—or lack thereof—is seen in the intention of Mary and of Judas Iscariot; one was giving thanks for Jesus's gift of life returned, while the other was indifferent to both Jesus and to the liberality of friendship.

Indeed, the element of friendship in the anointing of his feet can be seen if we take into consideration the already-existing friendship between Jesus and the family at Bethany.[47] The interaction between the characters in the narrative of the raising of Lazarus and what follows—the meal with Lazarus, Martha's serving without complaint, and the anointing of Jesus's feet by Mary—can best be understood within the framework and against the background of genuine friendship.

THE DISCIPLE WHOM JESUS LOVED

In the Fourth Gospel, the nameless disciple reclining at Jesus's breast is introduced at the Last Supper as "the one whom Jesus loved" (John 13:23). As a character, he comes into the second part of John's Gospel almost in the place of Lazarus whom Jesus had loved, along with his sisters; the friendship of the three siblings of Bethany is surpassed by the one who is a faithful friend to the end.

---

47. See Varghese, *Imagery*, 239.

The Beloved Disciple is explicitly named again under the Cross (John 19:26), at the empty tomb (John 20:2), and post-resurrection on the lakeshore in Galilee (John 21:7–20). Apart from these explicit mention of the Beloved Disciple, there are three other passages which mention anonymous disciples who may be identified with the Beloved Disciple: John 1:35–42; 18:15; 19:35. However, especially with reference John 1:35–42, Beutler argues that "to want to find him [the Beloved Disciple] earlier in the 'other disciple' who remains nameless in John 1:40 has no convincing basis in the text."[48] Thus Beutler concludes that "it is more probable that this disciple is introduced first in the passion narrative."[49] Although we will not be dealing with these three texts, the passage concerning the arrest and trial of Jesus (John 18:1–27) is worth mentioning because it is explicit in the use of one of the linguistic friendship conventions. In this pericope the disciples are present in the garden when Jesus is arrested (vv. 1–14), and while only Peter is explicitly mentioned in this context (vv. 10–11), the Beloved Disciple is presumed to be present as well, for after the arrest he and Peter are described as following a bound Jesus to Annas, the father-in-law of the high priest Caiaphas (vv. 12–14). While much attention has been paid to the remark that the Beloved Disciple was known to the high priest and the implications of this relationship for the disciple's identity, the following verb *suneisẽlthen* (he entered with) has been all but ignored. And yet, this Greek verb has the prepositional prefix *sun-*, which is one of the linguistic conventions for describing the closest of friends.[50]

While Peter followed Jesus after the arrest as far as the gate, only the presumed Beloved Disciple entered the high priest palace together with Jesus (v. 15) for his interrogation (vv. 19–24). Clearly, readers familiar with friendship conventions would have picked up on this linguistic clue and recognized the Beloved Disciple as acting as Jesus's friend when he enters together with him into the palace.[51] Something which has to be stressed is that each time this Beloved Disciple appears in the narrative, his friendship with Jesus is defined more fully, both through the context of the scene, as well as in the repetition of his title as "the disciple whom Jesus loved." In any case, whoever this disciple was, he was of huge significance for the Johannine tradition as the close of the Gospel shows (John 21:24).

48. Beutler, *John*, 360.
49. Beutler, *John*, 360–61.
50. See Lucian, *Toxaris*, 18.
51. See Culpepper, *John, The Son of Zebedee*, 61–63.

Characteristics of "Love" and "Friendship" in the Fourth Gospel

From the beginning of the Fourth Gospel, Jesus is depicted as having access to the innermost being and secrets of God. In John 1:18, Jesus's relationship with the Father is translated in several synonymous ways, any one of which conveys that he enjoys the deepest of intimacy, "close to the Father's heart" or, more poetically, "in the bosom of the Father" (*eis tòn kólpon toũ patrós*). A similar portrait is given at the Last Supper when the Beloved Disciple, or the "disciple whom Jesus loved," appears for the first time (John 13:23), "reclining next to him [Jesus]" (*en tõi kólpōi toũ Iēsoũ*). By using the same language that has previously characterized Jesus's relationship with the Father, the Johannine author associates that same relationship as reflected also in the Beloved Disciple's privileged position near the heart of Jesus.[52] Indeed, what makes this passage suggestive is the context in which this disciple is introduced, and that context is filled with content that can be related to conventions of friendship, including the setting of the supper itself.[53]

First, the passage opens with a sharp change in Jesus's situation; the tone is one of crisis. His "hour" (*hṓra*) has come (John 13:1), meaning that Jesus knows that he will soon face betrayal, arrest, and death—a situation that would call for a true friend and is in fact precisely when the Beloved Disciple, previously unidentified among the disciples, is introduced into the narrative. In addition, Jesus himself is characterized here as a true friend in that it is said that, having loved his own in the past, he would also love them *eis telos*—meaning both "to the end" (of life) and "to the utmost" (v. 1),[54] a phrase that points forward to Jesus's death on the cross and so to the convention of dying for one's friends.[55]

The reciprocal dimension of their friendship is revealed in the second incident where the Beloved Disciple stands near the mother of the crucified Jesus (John 19:25–27). In his last earthly action, Jesus entrusts the care of his mother to this Beloved Disciple, and the Beloved Disciple receives her. Indeed, here Jesus simply and confidently assigns his mother to the Beloved Disciple's care, and the latter accepts the responsibility immediately. All this conforms to one of the duties of friendship that was found in the

---

52. See Beutler, *John*, 361.
53. See Konstan, *Friendship*, 137–40.
54. See Brown, *John*, 550.
55. See Puthenkandathil, *Philos*, 212.

Greco-Roman culture: a man readily assumed filial responsibilities in taking care of a deceased friend's relatives.[56]

Of particular importance for interpreting this passage in classical terms is Lucian's story of the friends Eudamidas, Aretaius and Charixenos.[57] Eudamidas can trust his friends Aretaius and Chrarixenos to care for his mother and daughter after his death and so stipulates this role for them in his will. Although Charixenos dies too soon after Dudamidas's death to carry out his responsibility, Aretaius takes on both posthumous responsibilities. But, as Lucian notes, the credit goes not only to Aretaius for fulfilling both stipulations of the will, but also to Eudamidas for the confidence which he had in his friends to act on his behalf after his death.

However, the Fourth Gospel echoes the language of Jewish family law and so goes even deeper than the classical understanding in a grave responsibility, which is vitally important for both Jesus and the Beloved Disciple. Jesus uses precise words, addressed generically to "woman" and "son": "When Jesus saw his mother and the disciple whom he loved standing beside her, he said to his mother, 'Woman, here is your son.' Then he said to the disciple, 'Here is your mother.' And from that hour the disciple took her into his own home" (John 19:26–27). According to the Israelite Law the mother who loses her last son is no longer in possession of a social network. Thus, she needs a person to take care of her, usually another relation. Here, we see the Beloved Disciple entrusted with this responsibility.[58] It is therefore in the context of the choice of his words that the relationship between Jesus and the Beloved Disciple has to be weighed: to legally fulfil the duty of caring for the dependent of a deceased friend, reveals a level of intimate love reserved for the closest of friends.[59]

Such care of a deceased friend's relatives also occurs in the case of David and Jonathan from Old Testament precedent. In Josephus's fuller account of David's actions in 2 Samuel 9:1–11 (2 Kings 9:1–11 LXX), he says that David (after Jonathan's death) recalled the friendship that Jonathan once had for him and so enquired about any remaining relatives. When he

---

56. See Culy, *Echoes of Friendship*, 134. Culy also refers to a letter from the late second century, from a man who was caring for his friend's daughter and home, which nicely illustrates the sense of commitment that friends shared in this regard: "Have no more anxiety about your household than you would if you were present." Culy, *Echoes of Friendship*, 134.

57. See Lucian, *Toxaris*, 21–22.

58. See Beutler, *John*, 487.

59. See Witherington, *John's Wisdom*, 309.

learned that Jonathan had left a crippled son, David summoned the boy and not only left him the land and slaves of his grandfather, Saul, but also included him at his own table to eat as one of his sons.[60]

The Beloved Disciple appears for the third time in John 20:1–10 when, together with Peter, he races to the tomb on hearing the news from Mary Magdalene that Jesus was alive; as elsewhere, he seems to be superior to Peter.[61] The priority of the Beloved Disciple corresponds to the Johannine perspective. At the Last Supper, he reclines next to Jesus (John 13:23) and is close to Jesus also at the last moment of his earthly life (John 19:26–27). Thus, he also reaches the tomb of Jesus first (John 20:4). Here, the Beloved Disciple's absolute love for Jesus is spotlighted in verse eight (John 20:8) where the Beloved Disciple "saw and believed," even though there is no explicit reference to "what" the Beloved Disciple believed. Was it in the resurrection of Jesus? Or, did he simply believe what Mary Magdalene had reported? Cumulatively, it is the Beloved Disciple's faith, expressed in his belief which is seen throughout this pericope: running to the tomb, waiting outside the tomb, entering the tomb, seeing the linen wrappings rolled up and lying by itself and believing—all these, interpreted theologically, portray him as an ideal disciple who comes to Easter faith, which is itself based on his relationship of friendship with Jesus.[62] Just as he is loved by Jesus, so he too loves his LORD, and so has understanding, i.e., "eyes to see." With his readiness to look for his LORD, the Beloved Disciple recognizes him also in the unimpressive sign of the towel rolled up and lying by itself. His intimate relationship of friendship with Jesus opened his eyes for what remained hidden to others.

The Beloved Disciple appears again in the third manifestation of the risen LORD to a group of disciples on the shore of the Sea of Tiberias[63] on the occasion of a miraculous catch of fish (John 21:1–14). His intimate relation with Jesus allows him to quickly recognize the risen Christ and points it out to the other disciple (v. 7). He is also mentioned in the conversation between the risen LORD and Peter, where he appears only as the object (vv. 15–23); the Beloved Disciple is referenced as "following" (*akolouthoūnta*) Jesus and Peter. The present participle of *akolouthoūnta* indicates an already

---

60. See Josephus, *Ant.*, 7.111–16.
61. See Beutler, *John*, 502.
62. See Varghese, *Imagery*, 269.
63. This lake is called by Mark the "Sea of Galilee" (1:16), by Luke (5:1) the "Sea of Gennesareth." The same expression "Sea of Tiberias" also appears in John 6:1.

started but continuous act of following. Moreover, the fact that in this verse Peter had to "turn" (*epistrapheis*) around to look back at the disciple whom Jesus loved suggests that he was walking ahead of him, possibly in step with Jesus.[64] Siebech contends that, unlike Peter, the Beloved Disciple was (perhaps already since John 1:38) and is still continually a follower.[65] Indeed, whenever the Beloved Disciple is mentioned in the Fourth Gospel, particularly in this pericope, he functions as an "ideal follower, the epitome of what it means to be a believer."[66] Varghese interprets the following of the Beloved Disciple "in terms of love, which is an expression of friendship."[67]

The Beloved Disciple's following of Jesus "remains" (*ménō*) even after Jesus's own death by giving written "testimony" (*marturía*) to what Jesus said and did.[68] Thus, "[t]he Beloved Disciple's following of Jesus in a permanent manner which remains even after his own death is a demonstration of his faithfulness which is one of the characteristic elements of friendship."[69] In the Fourth Gospel *ménō* has a deep theological meaning of remaining true to Jesus and to his teaching, whether in life or in death (see John 15:4–6; 8:31). The present participle *marturõn* (bearing witness) together with the aorist participle *grápsas* (having written) in v. 24 shows the lasting nature of his testimony.

The recurrent theme in the Fourth Gospel of Jesus's relationship with the unnamed character, gives an "everyman" quality to the Beloved Disciple, who becomes a type for all believers in all times and places. Who is the beloved disciple? He is the one who is loved by Jesus, who enjoys a special place next to Jesus, is given the responsibility for the care of Jesus's Mother, believes in the risen LORD, and who follows him. He also has a special role as a witness to Jesus's words and deeds, which he records in detail.

As a genuine friend, the Beloved Disciple thus functions to embody in an exemplary fashion Jesus's command to love one another (John 15:17), that is, he demonstrates what it means to be a friend, particularly when one's friend is facing adversity, danger, or even death. He exemplifies the hopes that such a sublime friendship with Jesus is, in fact, not impossible, even though Jesus's special friendship with the Beloved Disciple is embedded in

---

64. See Puthenkandathil, *Philos*, 298.
65. See Siebeck, *Resurrection*, 325–26.
66. O'Grady, "Role of the Beloved Disciple," 60.
67. Varghese, *Imagery*, 272; see Kragerud, *Der Lieblingsjünger im Johannesevangelium*.
68. See Quast, "Peter and The Beloved Disciple," 151.
69. Varghese, *Imagery*, 273.

Characteristics of "Love" and "Friendship" in the Fourth Gospel

a wider relationship of all-inclusive love: that between Jesus and the whole group of disciples. The setting of the Last Supper reveals the details and terms of Jesus's inclusive love.

FRIENDSHIP AS EXPRESSED BY JESUS DURING THE LAST SUPPER

Johannine scholars have often noted that the theme of the Last Supper is typical of the farewell (or testament) of a hero who is about to die; this is a recurrent theme in biblical, extra-biblical Jewish literature, and Greco-Roman literature.[70] Such discourses are underscored as particularly noteworthy because they typically encapsulate the hero's most significant teachings; the crisis of the moment removes all frivolities and non-essential material. Often, such "last words" are accompanied by passing along items of significance and power, or giving final orders "to the troops." The author of this text, likewise, colors the relation between Jesus and the disciples in a unique and distinctive way, beginning with the washing of the feet.[71]

At first glance, the scene of the washing of the feet (John 13:1–30) may appear to provide little more than background information for the Farewell Discourse that follows (John 13:31–17:26). However, when read through the lens of Greco-Roman notion of friendship the connection to what follows becomes more apparent. The actions of Jesus in this pericope are given new significance as they are reinterpreted in light of his audacious statements in his Farewell Discourse. The scene opens and is introduced using friendship language: "Having loved his own who were in the world, he loved them to the end" (John 13:1). The ambiguity in the prepositional phrase "to the end" (*eis telos*) serves a dual purpose and meaning. First, Jesus's love for his disciples is the extreme offering of his life on their behalf; second, "to the end" demonstrates the extent and nature of Jesus's love; he loved them "completely." The emphasis on complete love places Jesus's relationship with his disciples within the context of his completion in relationship with the Father. That is, Jesus's act of friendship in the scene that follows and his declarations of friendship in the Farewell Discourse both originate in and flow from his unity, mutuality, and equality with the Father.

---

70. See Segovia, *Farewell*, 5.
71. See Stevick, *Jesus and His Own*, 1–4.

Finally, the setting of the foot-washing as prelude to a shared meal is itself significant. It not only fulfils the custom of the time, it goes beyond it toward a new dimension. It was a sign of genuine friendship in the Roman period (as well customary in the rest of the Judeo and classical world) to have friends attend a meal.[72] Jesus's Farewell Discourse both defines the precincts of ideal friendship and invites his disciples into that proffered ideal. What better setting for this eternal proposal than a meal—an event shared by friends? However, Jesus knew that the inequality that divided them needed to be remedied, in order that the right relationship of friends, as equals, could be established.

Authentic friendship in the Greco-Roman period was understood as possible only between men of equal rank and status. If that equality was lacking, there were some avenues in classical society by which to bridge it so that a friendship might be enjoyed. Cicero noted in *On Friendship* that the initiative in such situations originated with the person of higher status: "Those who are superior should [both] lower themselves . . . [and] lift up their inferiors."[73] In the foot-washing pericope, Jesus both lowers himself and elevates his disciples. He, who is the superior man, takes on the role of a servant, lowering himself to the status of a slave.[74]

The degree to which Jesus lowers himself is highlighted by the details of the Johannine Jesus just prior to his washing of their feet. The author relates that Jesus first "took off his outer robe and tied a towel around himself" and then "poured water into a basin and began to wash the disciples's feet and to wipe them with the towel that was tied around him" (John 13:4–5). One Pentecostal theologian, John Christopher Thomas, points out that the former made Jesus's attire "reminiscent of the dress of servants depicted in Roman works of art," while the later was a duty "assigned specifically to slaves according to the evidence from antiquity."[75] Thus, the master becomes a servant so that he and his disciples might enjoy the kind of intimate relationship about which he has been speaking and teaching.

The setting of the Last Supper prefigures the eternal dwelling; Jesus spoke of entering "my Father's house" where he is going to prepare a place for them (John 14:2). The washing of the feet of his disciples can be read as Jesus himself preparing them to walk in a new way, on a new path—in

---

72. See D'Arms, "*Convivium*," 308–20.
73. Cicero, *On Friendship*, 20, 72.
74. See Schneiders, "Foot Washing," 76–92.
75. Thomas, *Footwashing*, 59.

Characteristics of "Love" and "Friendship" in the Fourth Gospel

the ways of God.[76] The action itself summons the disciples and prepares them for the events, both natural and supernatural, which lie just ahead of them. They are to join their LORD in his passion, death and resurrection, and through the imparting of the Holy Spirit, in enjoying an intimate relationship with both the Father and the Son together as a blessed and unique community, as well as a specific apostolic task of evangelization.[77] All these events are profoundly connected with Jesus's actions and his final words to them in the subsequent Farewell Discourse of John 13:31–17:26. By far, this Discourse by Jesus is more extensive than any other found in the Fourth Gospel. Johannine scholars have extensively debated the structure, boundaries, and compositional history of the Farewell Discourse.[78] However, our interest is more on how the love-friendship relationship is used in the canonical form of the Farewell Discourse than with the prehistory of the text itself.

In the Fourth Gospel, narrative symbols and motifs are frequently expressed in dualistic terms (light/darkness; above/below). The motif of friendship, likewise, includes references both to what it means to be a friend, and what it means to be a non-friend. By all classical definition of friendship in the Greco-Roman world, Judas is a non-friend; he acts contrary to all that a friend is supposed to be, beginning with his resentment that money was "wasted" on Jesus's feet by Mary of Bethany, as she prepared for him to walk the *via dolorosa*. Rather than being willing to die for his friend, Judas Iscariot initiates the events that lead to Jesus's death. In John 13:21–30, Judas's treachery is revealed, and he is dismissed. Jesus then turns to the vital task of giving his disciples a final word in his urgent, closing instructions.

Jesus's directive to Judas to leave their group situates the intimate discourse that follows as exclusively among true friends. Jesus announces that his time has come, and his disciples respond with declarations of absolute friendship and allegiance: "Peter said to him, 'Lord, why can I not follow you now? I will lay down my life for you'" (John 13:37). By making this claim of absolute loyalty, Peter declares himself to be a true friend of Jesus. Yet, when the crisis ensues, it is not only the Iscariot who falls short. As Jesus predicts to him, Peter fails, too. Not only Peter, but all the apostles

76. See Coloe, "Sources in the Shadows," 77.

77. See Thomas, *Footwashing*, 58.

78. For an overview of the various approaches that have been proposed, particularly in the twentieth century, see Segovia, *Farewell*, 25–27.

run away, when put to the test; only the Beloved Disciple returns and accompanies Jesus to Calvary.

Jesus's response to Peter's declaration of friendship helps to establish the unilateral basis for the intimacy that the followers enjoy with Jesus. Through the act of foot-washing, Jesus lowers himself to the level of his followers, and subsequently, it is also Jesus who raises his disciples through declarations of friendship. He is the one who acts as a true friend and extends the beautiful invitation of friendship to his followers. They, on the other hand, have little or no role in establishing the friendship.[79] However, Peter's declaration of friendship and Jesus's rejection of the veracity of this declaration, set the stage for Jesus's own elucidation of what it means to be a friend.

The friendship between Jesus and his disciples is based on Jesus's ability to be a friend, not on the ability of the disciples themselves to be true friends, but they are given the terms of friendship in an altogether new way, if they can receive it. They receive the ability to be friends by drawing on the power of Jesus's love, working within them. In John 15:1–8, Jesus gives instruction to his disciples about friendship in the symbolism of the vine and the branches. As the branches cannot bear fruit when detached from the vine, so Jesus's disciples/friends cannot function without their relationship with Jesus. This *bildrede* or extended metaphor,[80] as brought out through the image of the vine and branches, discloses the unity that exists between Jesus and his disciples. That unity is entwined in friendship, a friendship that has its archetype in the love of the Father and the Son. The theme of "friendship" follows that of "love" which appears for the first time in v. 9. It marks the whole of the following group of verses until v. 17 and holds it together from the thematic point of view.

The unity of love between the Father and the Son, and the Son and his disciples, is also used to characterize the relationships of the disciples among themselves (John 15:12). Indeed, Jesus's actions and prayers are meant, in part, to facilitate the same type of unity among the disciples that exists between Jesus and the Father.[81] The foundation for Jesus's teaching on the unity of believers has already been laid in the Johannine narrative: "So there shall be one flock, one shepherd" (John 10:16). Their unity is then extended to an even broader set of friends, spanning time and space: "I ask

---

79. See White, *Night*, 94.
80. See Schnackenburg, *John*, 109; Beutler, *John*, 397.
81. See Moloney, *Glory not Dishonor*, 114.

Characteristics of "Love" and "Friendship" in the Fourth Gospel

not only on behalf of these, but also on behalf of those who will believe in me through their word, that they may all be one. As you, Father, are in me and I am in you, may they also be in us, so that the world may believe that you have sent me" (John 17:20–21). This brings out the communion dimension of friendship; that it is both exclusive and yet inclusive of others, an important aspect on which classical friendship also depended. It is also linked with other characteristics, including steadfastness, oneness, and indwelling; the Johannine indwelling language in the Fourth Gospel is a poignant description of the deepest levels of intimacy.

Unity of relationship naturally leads to a sharing of possessions. The Son, who is with God and is God, shares everything with the Father. Remarkably, this perfect friendship is not portrayed as a closed relationship from which others are excluded. The Johannine Jesus explicitly extends the mutuality that he shares with the Father to include his disciples. As the Father had given his words to Jesus, so Jesus shares the word of the Father with his disciples: "the words that you gave to me I have given to them, and they have received them and know in truth that I came from you" (John 17:8). This mutuality knows no bounds! As God, Jesus himself shares in the Father's distinctive and unique glory (as recorded by Isaiah 42:8; 48:11), and he even shares that glory with his disciples: "the glory which you have given me, I have given them" (John 17:22); in this sublime gift of his own glory, Jesus unites them with himself and so with God.[82]

This mutuality between the Son and his disciples also includes perfect transparency or "frankness of speech" (*parrhēsía*) which characterizes an ideal friendship. Earlier in the Gospel, this familiar friendship terminology is used to describe the intimacy between the Father and the Son (John 5:19); in John 15, where the climax of the treatment of friendship reaches its zenith, the Johannine Jesus grants the same intimacy to his followers: "I have called you friends, because I have made known to you everything that I have heard from my Father" (John 15:15). In John 16:25, Jesus goes on to promise them that "the hour is coming when I shall no longer speak to you in figures but tell you plainly of the Father."

Despite the endowment of transcendent and sublime gifts, the distinction between Jesus and his disciples remains. Even though he has invited and granted them friendship, he does so only if they would use it well among themselves. The friendship between Jesus and the disciples is expressed in conditional terms: "You are my friends if you do what I

---

82. See Smith, *John*, 122.

command you" (John 15:14). Thus, the disciples are friends of Jesus by virtue of his command. In this verse, biblical and classical material is brought together. The implementation of what Jesus has "commanded" (*entéllomai*) the disciples remains in the language of Deuteronomy. In Deuteronomy, the word *entéllomai* is regularly used of Moses vis-à-vis the Israelites. The thought of friendship with God is found chiefly in writings of Hellenistic Judaism, beginning with the book of Wisdom (7:13—14:27) up to Philo of Alexandria. A precedent is given by the description of Abraham as "friend of God" in 2 Chronicles 20:7 and Isaiah 41:8.[83] Yet, Jesus still has the authority to command them, and while obedience is a component of friendship between Jesus and his disciples, their friendship cannot be reduced solely to a relationship of obedience. If they abide in his love, that friendship sustains their willingness to respond to God in keeping his commandments: "If you love me, you will keep my commandments" (John 14:15).

The mutual responsibilities of Jesus and his disciples are consistent with the patronage approach, known as the "patron system" of the classical world, in which a powerful benefactor defends his dependents; in turn, the dependents have their own responsibility. Jesus gives them the Paraclete (John 14:16); loves them and reveals himself to them (John 14:21); reveals the Father to them (John 15:15); protects them (John 17:12); comes with the Father to abide within them (John 16:23); and gives them whatever they ask for in his name (John 16:24).

Yet, within the context of the entire Fourth Gospel, and the Farewell Discourse in particular, there are striking clues which point beyond mere patronage to a relationship of the most intimate nature.[84] The disciples are three times called friends by the Johannine Jesus.[85] They do not decide on their own to be friends of Jesus; he calls them first to be his friends—and to value friendship in a mysterious and altogether new way: originating in God through Jesus.

The disciples are friends of Jesus because they have fulfilled his word. Thus, their status originates not in self-assignation but from responding to a divine gift and transcendent calling. To highlight the intensity of such an intimate love, Brown opts to translate *phílōn* in John 15:13 as "those

---

83. See Beutler, *John*, 406.

84. See Furnish, *The Love Command*, 141.

85. In a complement of advantage or favor: *hypèr tōn phílōn autoû* (John 15:13); in the nominal clause: *hymeîs phíloi moú este* (John 15:14); and in a complement of denomination: *hymâs dè eírēka phílous* (John 15:15).

he loves" and *phílous* in John 15:15 as "my beloved" because, he contends: "The English word 'friend' does not capture this relationship of love (for we have lost the feeling that 'friend' is related to the Anglo-Saxon verb *frëon*, 'to love')."[86] Those who are loved by Jesus and know it respond with the desire to do as they are required: to keep his commandments. However, friendship with Jesus does not dissolve the distinction between divine and human. Disciples may well be friends of Jesus, abiding in his love, but they remain disciples, nevertheless, and followers of the one who is both source and model of their love. Indeed, proof or evidence of the friendship is linked to the lifestyle of the disciples being aligned with the teaching of the Master; the status of friend is inextricably linked to a manner of living that honors the LORD and that supernaturally flows from being loved by Jesus.

The new status that Jesus's disciples enjoy cannot be taken casually; it is more than a redefining of what it means to serve him as Lord. At Jesus's word, friendship becomes a new creation altogether. Even as the institution of the Eucharist originates with Jesus's words at the Last Supper, so it can be said that the "love of friendship" is instituted by Jesus himself as it had not been known since prelapsarian Eden. Obedience is certainly required, but this obedience is rooted in the shared holy knowledge of friends who have been given spiritual sight, rather than in the blind compliance of servants. Indeed, friendship is seen in the revelation of Jesus himself to his disciples. They are not kept in the dark, but given access to understanding and insight, so that the allegiance they render is a free allegiance, both intelligent and perceptive.

Here, friendship has the elements of reciprocity and responsibility, with an added dimension of "being chosen," selected to be friends. This is more than a fortuitous group bonding; it describes a new way of being in community: "The followers of Jesus are particularly being called to exhibit friendship as an expression of *who they are* in the matrix of connected relationships, with God and with each other."[87]

The Fourth Gospel gives friendship an explicitly central place and is recreated in a new dimension. Jesus's relationship with John the Baptist, Mary, Martha, Lazarus, and the Beloved Disciple provides a starting point for understanding what friendship with Jesus and with others entails. He responds to his friends' request for help, though not always as they may have expected (John 11:6). He raises Lazarus from the dead, even though he

---

86. Brown, *John*, 664.
87. Summers, *Friendship*, 23.

had every reason to believe that this act would lead to his own death. John 11:6 thus serves as a vivid example of Jesus's willingness to lay down his life for his friends. "Since the raising of Lazarus is the final offence which sets in motion the plot to kill Jesus—and he was well aware that it would be (John 11:7–8. 16)—Jesus actually lays down his life for a friend by returning to bring life to Lazarus."[88]

Similarly, Jesus's willingness to share personal information with the Beloved Disciple (John 13:26) reveals the ideal nature of their friendship. These relationships portrayed in the Johannine Jesus shed light on how the eternal *Logos* made flesh relates to his own. However, the densest concentration of material used to describe the mutual relationship between Jesus and his followers is found in the Last Supper scene of John 13:1—17:26.

While at first glance the foot-washing pericope may appear to supply little more than background information for the more important discourse that follows, when read in light of Greco-Roman notions of ideal friendship, this scene, which is unique to the Gospel of John, takes on new significance. As Culpepper has noted, the Fourth Gospel, "Achieves its most subtle effects . . . through its implicit commentary, that is, the devices and passages in which the author communicates with the reader by implication and indirection."[89]

During the Last Supper, the Johannine author lays out his description of Jesus's friendship with his disciples. He records that Jesus explicitly directs his disciples to love one another as he loves them, and he emphasizes that what he is about to say is not something heard before, but an altogether "new commandment." This is more than a fortuitous group bonding; it describes a new way of being in community of friends, with God and with each other. If Jesus's disciples are to be his friends, they are to keep his commandments and abide in his love just as Jesus has kept the commandments of his Father and abides in his love. Thus, friendship with Jesus and the keeping of his commandments are complementary to each other. They, "Exist in a dialectical relationship, both equally necessary in defining the profound relationship between disciples and the one who is their Lord and Friend."[90]

Jesus elaborates on the love command with a contrast between two kinds of relationships. First, there is the relationship between a master and

88. Culpepper, *Anatomy*, 141.
89. Culpepper, *Anatomy*, 233.
90. Lee, "Friendship," 71.

his slaves, in which commands are given and obeyed simply on the basis of the master's authority and backed by force. While Jesus is "master and teacher" (John 13:14), he does not issue the love command in the context of a master-slave relationship but in the context of friendship. Friends do good things for each other because of the friendly affection between them. The disciples are to love one another because this is what Jesus, their friend, has done for them and asked of them. The reason why they are no longer considered "servants/slaves" but "friends" hinges on the lengthy communication by which Jesus shares with them intimate knowledge given to him by the Father, and, implicitly, they have been willing to receive it. This knowledge was previously available only to him, but he now intends to share it—in unity and reciprocal love—with his intimate friends. Through this conversation, Jesus elevates the status of his followers and incorporates them into the relationship between him and the Father. The very fact that the disciples have come to know Jesus is a gift of divine love: "It was not you who chose me, but I who chose you" (John 15:16). Jesus earlier said, "No one can come to me unless the Father who sent me draw him" (John 6:44). The Father works to bring people to believe in Jesus so that they might receive eternal life through him (John 6:37–39; 17:6–9). Faith, by which people come to know Jesus, is a free, underserved gift of divine love, which people must receive and embrace.

The divine choosing of Jesus's disciples brings a commission: "Go and bear fruit that will remain" (John 15:16). The fruit that the Father seeks from the vine's branches is that they "love one another" (John 15:17). The communion of the disciples with Jesus enables them to produce works of love (John 15:4–5). Their mission now is no longer an answer to a call from the master but a direct share in the same mission of Jesus emanating from the very love and obedience, which he himself lives out in his relationship with the Father.[91] They are his friends, connected with him by virtue of his word and enabled to produce fruit. Their prayers will be heard. This, they can receive Jesus's renewed command with confidence. In their fulfilling of his commandment, Jesus will not leave them on their own. Accordingly, disciples who pray to the Father in Jesus's name pray in communion with Jesus in his perfect, loving obedience to the Father's will. They ask the Father to accomplish his plan in the world and their lives and, if they are

---

91. See Malina and Rohrbaugh, *Social-Science Commentary*, 235–36.

ready to obey the Father and yield to his will, the Father will give them this request (John 15:16).[92]

In the light of the present text, it is sometimes thought that what we have here is a "sectarian ethic" in which the love command of Jesus in confined to the community of friends to the exclusion of the neighbor and, *a fortiori*, the enemy. More recent scholarship is skeptical of this criticism. An opening of the Johannine love command beyond the boundaries of the community is also visible in John 13:34–35. There it says, in v. 35: "By this everyone will know that you are my disciples, if you have love for one another." Thus, the love lived out in the community of friends is to be the mark of the disciples and also act as an advertisement to those outside (cf. John 17:21). In this way, the narrow circle of the community of friends is broken open and the vista opened to all who are called to salvation in Christ.[93]

The next chapter turns to Thomas Aquinas, one of the towering Western scholastic theologians. Through his exegesis of the Fourth Gospel, his synthesis of the Christian tradition, and his ability to rearticulate Christian theology through Aristotelian philosophy, he uniquely defines Christian love, *caritas*, fully and in every respect as friendship, *amicitia*.

---

92. See Martin and Wright IV, *John*, 259–60.
93. See Beutler, *John*, 407.

Chapter 3

Caritas as "*Amicitia* with God" in Thomas Aquinas

SAINT THOMAS AQUINAS MADE a stunning and brilliant theological move. By equating *caritas* with *amicitia*,[1] more clearly and resoundingly than any who came before him, Aquinas depicts friendship as the finality, the *telos* of the Christian life. Moreover, by implication, he makes friendship the interpretative principle for moral theology as a whole. In this sense, Aquinas is deepening the tradition and can be considered as a high point for the theology of friendship. In fact, Carmichael calls him the "greatest theoretician" of friendship.[2]

Paul J. Wadell has noted and discussed the significance of Aquinas's theology of friendship. He sees friendship as the interpretative key to the understanding of Aquinas's whole moral project. Wadell even goes as far as to say that, "If one understands what Thomas means by charity as friendship with God and how that functions as something of a metaphor for the Christian moral life, then not only will his account of the virtues be better appreciated, but it will also be clear why what he says about the virtues cannot be separated from what he says about the passions and the Gifts."[3]

Aquinas was familiar with the Fathers of the Church in their interpretation of Greco-Roman understanding of friendship in the light of

---

1. As he does for example at *ST* II–II.23.1.
2. Carmichael, *Friendship*, 101.
3. Wadell, *Friends of God*, 1.

the testimony of a reflective faith, namely, Holy Scripture. Their theological method was essentially experiential, historical and hermeneutical—a method that persisted in the monastic tradition.[4] This method is also reflected in medieval theological accounts of friendship, the chief example being the English Cistercian monk Aelred of Rievaulx's treatise, *Spiritual Friendship*. Commenting on Aelred's work, Hallier claims that Aelred's theology of friendship is the result of his own struggle for holiness in his monastic vocation, most particularly in his tireless activities as abbot and spiritual father of the burgeoning community in Rievaulx.[5]

While the early Cistercians flourished in the wild valley, the cathedral schools and nascent universities of Europe in the twelfth century saw the development of the new style of argued philosophical theology: scholasticism. The scholastic method still relied on Holy Scripture, and it leaned heavily on earlier theologians and philosophers. However, it tended to be more strictly conceptual, systematic and even speculative.[6] These characteristics are reflected both in the ways scholastic theologians interpreted Holy Scripture, as well as in their style and method of writing. Whereas the monastic method of writing, in general, tends to be more biblical, literary, aesthetically self-aware, and even poetic at times, the scholastic method is invariably dialectical, logical, technical, and abstract. The scholastic method was to instill scientific knowledge through definition, division, as demonstration, or demonstrative proof. The main difference between the monastic and the scholastic method lay in, "The differences between the two states of life: the state of Christian life in the world and the state of Christian life in the religious life."[7] According to another critic, the scholastic method *per se* was in fact, "The attempt of the intellect to discover and articulate the whole range of truth discoverable in, or hinted at, in the

---

4. See Fiorenza and Galvin, *Systematic Theology*, 20.

5. See Hallier, *Monastic Theology*, 52–53.

6. There is a profound divergence between monastic and scholastic reading (*lectio*) of the Scripture. While in both the activity of reading the Holy Scripture is holy, *sacra, divina*, the accent is put on two different aspects of the same activity; the orientation differs, and, consequently, so does the procedure. The scholastic *lectio* takes the direction of the *quaestio* and *disputatio*. The reader put questions to the text and then questions himself on the subject matter: *quaeri solet*. The monastic *lectio* is oriented toward the *meditatio* and the *oratio*. See Leclercq, *Love of Learning*, 72.

7. Leclercq, *Love of Learning*, 196.

seminal works of Christianity."[8] This theological method is also reflected in Aquinas's treatment of friendship.

The gradual development of the twelfth century schools into universities coincided with the maturation of theology as an academic discipline, indeed, as the Queen of Sciences. At the medieval university, instruction developed from the "reading" to the practice of the "disputation" of questions. This development provided the context as well as the means for the emergence of the theological *summas* with their diverse "articles."[9] Like other theologians before him, Aquinas makes use of the sources available to him. Yet, as it should be, his primary text for the teaching of theology was indeed the Holy Scripture; in fact, the discipline was called *sacra doctrina*. Aquinas was content with the Vulgate translation which he owned (The Vulgate is the Latin version of the Bible). In general, scholastic theologians showed a thorough familiarity with the biblical text from beginning to end. That is because it was a time when books were rare and cumbersome; thus, one had to memorize not just passages and chapters but whole books![10]

Together with Holy Scripture, Aquinas relies heavily on the collected works of both the Latin and Greek Fathers of the Church. In the latter case, the works at Aquinas's disposal increased substantially during his lifetime, especially through the translating activities of William of Moerbeke. In addition, by the early 1260s, Aquinas had discovered translations of the *acta* and *gesta* of the early Church councils.[11] Of particular importance to his understanding of "love" and *caritas*—and therefore, at least by extension, of *amicitia*—was Aquinas's familiarity with the mystical theological work of Pseudo-Dionysius, translated from the Greek several centuries earlier by John Scotus Erigena.[12]

In general, Aquinas often surpassed his contemporaries in the breadth and depth of his patristic reading: Aquinas "read everything and everyone, distilling from the vast wealth of sources what is most true and good."[13] Aquinas's genius is especially evident in his ability to simplify, synthesize, and bring things together in a cohesive whole. Another exceptional fact is that, unlike his theological predecessors, Aquinas was also deeply

---

8. Southern, *Making of the Middle Ages*, 191.
9. Cf. Chenu, *Toward Understanding Saint Thomas*.
10. See Smalley, *Study*; Evans, *Language and Logic*; Brown et al., "Texts and Versions."
11. See Weisheipl, *Friar Thomas*, 164–65.
12. See Weisheipl, *Friar Thomas*, 173–74.
13. Lefler, *Theologizing Friendship*, 97.

conversant with the great medieval Islamic scholars, Avicenna and Averroes, as well as with the works of the medieval Jewish thinker, Moses ben-Maimon.[14]

Aquinas also cultivates a thorough familiarity with the writings of the saintly thinkers of the preceding centuries, including Saint Anselm, Abelard, Hugh of Saint Victor, and Saint Bernard of Clairvaux. He was also familiar with the thought of his contemporaries; not least of these being his own master, Saint Albert the Great, and the gifted Franciscan, Saint Bonaventure. Interestingly, however, he never refers to Aelred's *Spiritual Friendship*, and he mentions Cicero's treatment on friendship only once.[15] Torrell offers a plausible explanation for Aquinas's lack of familiarity, explicit or otherwise, with Aelred's *Spiritual Friendship*. According to Torrell: "Thomas may not have known the latter figure, owing to the shift in interest by the widespread introduction of Aristotle in the thirteenth century."[16]

Indeed, Aquinas relies extensively on the works of Aristotle. He comments on Aristotle's major works. Beyond the commentaries themselves, Aristotelian philosophy is evident throughout Aquinas's theological enterprise. Nevertheless, this does not mean that Aquinas identified as an Aristotelian or that he tried to defend Aristotle's philosophy at any cost. In fact, as Joseph Pieper observed, we often "find Thomas giving us ever new shades of the fundamental Aristotelian position."[17] In developing his understanding of *caritas*, Aquinas not only relied on, but transformed, Aristotle's understanding of friendship, as Guy Mansini notes: "One of St. Thomas' most successful theological innovations was to identify the charity poured forth into our hearts through the Holy Spirit (Rom. 5:5), the love by which we are children of God (1 John 3:1), with friendship, the mutual benevolence of the virtuous, flowering in intimacy, as discussed by Aristotle in Books 8 and 9 of the *NE*."[18]

From the outset it should be noted that, in the Thomistic corpus, one finds no theological treatise specifically devoted to the subject of friendship. This does not imply, however, that Aquinas considers friendship as trivial. On the contrary, the theological category of friendship is present in most of Aquinas's major theological works. (This would be analogous to

---

14. See Torrell, *Aquinas*, 267–308.
15. See Aquinas, *ST* II–II.29.3; noted in Carmichael, *Friendship*, 105.
16. Torrell, *Aquinas*, 277.
17. Pieper, *Guide*, 43–44.
18. Mansini, "*Similitudo, Communicatio*," 1.

what we find in the Fourth Gospel: what at first might not have appeared to be a major theological theme, friendship is constantly present, either implicitly or explicitly, throughout the narrative and it appears in crucial moments in the life of the Johannine Jesus.)

There are five major works in which friendship constitutes a significant category in Aquinas's corpus: (1) in *Liber Super Ethicorum Aristotelis* (*Eth.*); (2) in *Librum Beati Dionysii De Divinis Nominibus* (*DDN*); (3) in Super *Evangelium S. Ioannis Lectura* (*Ioannis*), especially his commentary on Christ's Farewell Discourse during the Last Supper at John 15:13–17; (4) in *Summa Contra Gentiles* (*SCG*) and (5) in *Summa Theologiae* (*ST*).

In *Eth.*, Aquinas maintains a strictly philosophical perspective, carefully confining his treatment of friendship to the natural level, withdrawing entirely from matters of divine revelation.[19] On the other hand, in *DDN*, the discussion on "love" and "friendship" goes beyond the natural realm. Most of Aquinas's original insights on the subject of friendship make their first appearance in this work and are often cited to support his arguments in his later discussion in the *ST*.

In *Ioannis*, Aquinas focuses on Jesus's explicit references to friendship during the Last Supper in John 15:13–17. His interpretation of these verses is treated below, and so a comment suffices here. In his commentary of John 15, Aquinas recognizes the parallel between the communication of secrets as a sign of friendship and Jesus's renaming his disciples as "friends," on the basis of his disclosure to them of what he heard from the Father.

Friendship does not feature as an explicit theme in the *SCG*. However, in *SCG* III.95.5, while discussing the relationship between the immutability of God's providence and the value of prayer, Aquinas recalls the classical notion of friendship as characterized by lover and beloved both willing the same thing. Immediately after, Aquinas explicitly says that "on the basis of friendship God grants the wishes of those who are holy."[20] Later on, Aquinas explains that it is when Jesus reveals what he heard from the Father that he makes the disciples his friends. In our case, Aquinas concludes, we

---

19. There is a long-running debate over whether Aquinas's commentaries on Aristotle in general, and his commentary on the *NE* in particular, ought to be classified as philosophical or theological works. See Owens and Gauthier, "Aquinas as Aristotle Commentator," 213–38; Jordan, "Thomas Aquinas's Disclaimers in the Aristotelian Commentaries," 99–112.

20. Aquinas, *SCG* III.96.5.

receive the revelation of the divine mystery through the Holy Spirit who makes us lovers of God.[21]

Aquinas's most condensed and refined theological treatment of friendship is found in his *opus magnum*, the *ST*.[22] Apart from the "Introduction" and the "Supplement," the *ST* consists of four parts: *Prima Pars* (the First Part), *Prima Secundae* (the First Part of the Second Part), *Secunda Secundae* (the Second Part of the Second Part) and *Tertia Pars* (the Third Part). Each part of the *ST* is divided into *Quaestiones* (Questions). Each "Question" is then divided into *Articulis* (Articles). Each "Article" is preceded by objections, followed by an authoritative statement and replies to the objections. Broadly speaking, the *ST* follows what has generally been termed as *exitus-reditus*—literally the "coming out, going back"—scheme.[23] Commenting on the structure of the *ST* Nicholas Lash writes that:

> We might almost say that, for Aquinas, the 'soundness' of his 'educational method' depended upon the extent to which the movement of his exposition reflected the rhythm of God's own act and movement: that self-movement 'outwards' from the divine simplicity to the utterance of the Work and breathing of the Gift which God is, to the "overflowing" of God's goodness in work of his creation (*Prima pars*); the 'return' to God along that one way of the world's healing which is Christ (*Tertia pars*); and, because there lies across this movement the shadow of the mystery of sin, we find, between his treatment of the whence and whither, the "outgoing" and "return" of creaturely existence, the drama of conversion, of sin and virtue, of rejection or acceptance of God's grace (*Secunda pars*). And this by way of explanation of who in a

---

21. See Aquinas, *SCG* IV.21.4. Phrases almost identical to this recur several more times in *SCG* IV.21.5.8; IV.22.3–4. In comparing these phrases, one notes that Aquinas uses "friends" (*amici*) and "lovers" (*amatores*) of God synonymously. Lefler notes that, though the reference here is to John 15:15, the stress is not so much on Jesus's own action as on the Holy Spirit's agency in "establishing us as friends of God." Lefler, *Theologizing Friendship*, 119.

22. Aquinas took seven years to compose the *ST*, right down to his last year, and which nevertheless remains unfinished. Josef Pieper corrects the general misunderstanding that the reason which snatched the pen from Aquinas's hand was his early death. On the contrary, Pieper insists, Aquinas refrained from writing after a revelation he experienced on December 6, 1273, when he was returning to his cell from the celebration of the Mass. See Pieper, *Guide*, 158.

23. See Nichols, *Discovering Aquinas*, 10.

summary of Christian theology, Christ can make a central appearance only towards the end.[24]

In the *Prima Pars*, Aquinas describes God in Trinitarian terms and identifies him as the fount or source of all existence. Then, Aquinas considers all variety in creation, first that of the pure minds, the angels, followed by the natural order as a whole, and, finally, the place of the human being, created in the image and after the likeness of God, in this whole system of world order.

The *Prima Secundae* contemplates, in general terms, the movement of man to God. It begins by an account of human happiness which, according to Aquinas, is the purpose of morality. Thanks to the doctrines of creation and redemption, however, the content of such happiness must be re-described so as to include—indeed, center on—the beatific vision of God.[25] Here Aquinas also gives an account of the basic emotional drives of human nature and how these, like mind and will, are distorted by sin.

The *Secunda Secundae* considers what might be called "a phenomenology—reflective description—of the Christian life, a life informed by charity and articulating itself in both practical goodness and contemplation."[26] Here the theological virtue of *caritas* is developed as being expressed in the relationship of *amicitia*. This makes charity—and therefore friendship—the heart of the human-divine relationship (which is really what theology as *sacra doctrina* is about) and, therefore, of the theology of the Christian life (moral theology).

In the *Tertia Pars*, Aquinas shows what actually makes possible the return of rational creatures to God. Having spoken of the human being's origin and goal, Aquinas makes clear the path that connects them, and this he identifies as Christ, the pathway to God. The *ST*, therefore, has a clear and systematic structure. However, to reproduce an adequate structure, particularly an outline, one cannot write the titles of its three parts under each other. Rather, as Pieper suggests: "We must . . . arrange them in a circular diagram, in a ring returning back upon itself: the outpouring of reality out of the divine Source, which by necessity contains within its initial stages the state of being on the way back to the same Source, with the

---

24. Lash, *Beginning*, 141–42.
25. See Nichols, *Discovering Aquinas*, 10.
26. Nichols, *Discovering Aquinas*, 11.

creator who in Christ has become one with the creation revealing Himself as the way of this return.²⁷

It is in the *Prima Secundae*, after identifying *amor* (love) as the first of the affective emotions, at *ST* I-II.25.2, that Aquinas briefly introduces the notion of *amicitia* (friendship). He introduces it within the context of his exposition of *amor* and its prominent position among the emotions, or passions, of the soul.²⁸ Here Aquinas discusses the important question "whether love may be divided into love of friendship and love of desire."²⁹ The distinction between the loves of friendship and desire leads Aquinas to consider the important question of whether *similitudo* (similarity/likeness) causes love or rivalry.³⁰ Then, at *ST* I-II.28.1-3, further terms crucial for a thorough understanding of *amor* are discussed, namely, *unio* (union), *mutua inhaesio* (mutual indwelling) and *extasis* (ecstasy/transport). Then, in Question 23 and proceeding through Question 27 of the *Secunda Secundae*, Aquinas offers a sustained discussion on the theological virtue of *caritas*, for which the point of departure is a definition of *caritas* in terms of *amicitia*, at *ST* II-II.23.1.³¹ Aquinas invites anyone who does not agree with his definition to consider John 15:15: "No longer do I call you servants . . . but I have called you friends." We can thus turn to the record of his lectures on the Gospel of John, made by his friend and secretary Reginald, to hear him expounding John 15:13-17, the scriptural heart of his teaching on friendship in the context of man's relationship with God, namely, *caritas*.³²

AQUINAS'S EXEGESIS OF JOHN 15:13-17

The numerous biblical commentaries of Thomas Aquinas express his passion for the Word of God. Contrary to his philosophical and theological contributions, however, modern scholars do not refer to them frequently. Some of this relegating of Aquinas's work as irrelevant, which was took place in the "progressive" seminaries of the 1960s through 1990s, has begun to reverse, and the "Angelic Doctor" is once again teaching current seminarians in many places, but one still often hears, dismissively, that the work

27. Pieper, *Guide*, 101-2.
28. See Aquinas, *ST* I-II.26.3.
29. Aquinas, *ST* I-II.26.4.
30. See Aquinas, *ST* I-II.27.3.
31. See Lefler, *Theologizing Friendship*, 103.
32. See Carmichael, *Friendship*, 109.

of Thomas Aquinas is dated, or "medieval." In fact, Aquinas has no equal in any century for erudition and education.[33] His methods of investigating the "literal sense"[34] of a text as well as "multiple spiritual senses"[35] without distinguishing them, are sometimes considered as naïve and pre-critical, as they do not correspond to contemporary, post-modern scholarship.[36] Aquinas connects the literal sense as the basis for the spiritual sense. Although he makes many distinctions, Thomas did not separate his analysis into discrete categories for academic discussion and pastoral application. Rather, he considered study as a spiral that embraced and connected prayer to apostolic preaching, teaching, and writing; it was a way of discerning truth. Accordingly, interpreting the Bible and questioning it were integral and preliminary to teaching and preaching.[37]

In the encyclical *Divino Afflante Spiritu*, Pius XII writes that "in Scripture divine things are presented to us in the manner which is common use amongst men."[38] The Bible, the encyclical continues, is the Word of God written in human words and, so, this manner of speaking in various ages to various people must be carefully studied with all the auxiliary available sciences. However, the Pope argues, even after all this has been fulfilled, there is still "the theological doctrine" contained in the biblical books.[39] And these would be the spiritual senses: allegorical, tropological and anagogical. In the first volume of *Jesus of Nazareth*, Pope Benedict XVI also urges readers to go beyond the strictly historical readings of Holy Scripture;

---

33. His studies at Naples, Paris and Cologne provided him with diverse contributions of theologians and philosophers for interpreting scriptural texts. He was familiar with Conciliar and Papal decrees, the Greek and Latin Fathers (the *sancti Doctores*), the *Sentences* of Peter Lombard, Plato, Aristotle and Boethius. He read only the Latin or Vulgate edition of the Bible since the philological study with comparative languages began a century after his death. See Pazdan, "Aquinas," 465–66. For a thorough investigation on the history of medieval exegesis, see de Lubac, *Medieval Exegesis*.

34. The "literal sense" of Scripture refers to the sacred message intended by the human and divine author. It is the reconstruction of authorial intention that is discovered through the Historical-Critical Method.

35. The "spiritual sense" of Scripture is the enlarged reality intended by person, place, or thing signified in the literal sense. The "spiritual sense" includes three levels of reality: the biblical text, the paschal mystery and the present circumstances of life in the Spirit.

36. See Steinmetz, "Superiority," 74–82.

37. See Pazdan, "Aquinas," 470.

38. Pius XII, *Divino Afflante Spiritu*, par. 37.

39. Pius XII, *Divino Afflante Spiritu*, par. 24.

he reiterated that one must read the Word of God theologically.[40] It is in the light of this theological sense of interpreting the Bible, so much expounded by patristic and medieval commentators, that Aquinas's exegesis of John 15:13–17 should be read.

John 15 unfolds with the imagery of the vine and the branches. This imagery expresses the dynamic life of Jesus, the Father and the disciples in mutual knowing and abiding. According to Aquinas's division of chapter 15, the verses under consideration fall under two pericopes: vv. 9–13 and vv. 14–17.[41] At the beginning of his commentary on John 15, Aquinas informs his audience that "in this talk our Lord wants to comfort his disciples" about his imminent suffering and death as well as "the troubles which would come upon them."[42]

Commenting on vv. 9–13 Aquinas indicates how the disciples are to abide in Jesus's love. They are to love their neighbor, based on Jesus's example.[43] These verses serve as an overture to his reflections about friendship, beginning from v. 13: "Greater love has no man than this that a man lay down his life for his friends." To the objection that laying down one's life for one's enemies is considered to be a sign of a greater love, Aquinas states: "Christ did not lay down his life for his enemies so that they would remain his enemies, but to make them his friends."[44] He also notes that "laying down one's life for one's friends" is a sign of the greatest love, "because there are four lovable things to be put in order: God, our soul, our neighbor, and our body. We should love God more than ourselves and our neighbor, so that for the sake of God we ought to give ourselves, body and soul, and to our neighbor."[45]

Commenting on v. 14—"You are my friends if you do what I command you"—Aquinas then notes that, previously, Jesus had urged the

---

40. See Benedict XVI, foreword to *Jesus of Nazareth*, xi–xxiv.

41. Aquinas divides John 15 into five pericopes: vv. 1–8; 9–13; 14–17; 18–21; 22–27. It is of importance to follow the divisions of the text in the context made by Saint Thomas himself. Since "order" and "division" are such important elements in the scholastic method, these must be continuously related to the whole, whether it be a collection of chapters, an individual chapter, part of a chapter, a parable, narrative, pericope, or sentence. See Weisheipl, introduction to *Commentary on the Gospel of St. John*.

42. Aquinas, *Ioannis* 15.1.1978.

43. See Aquinas, *Ioannis* 15.3.2010.

44. Aquinas, *Ioannis* 15.2.2009.

45. Aquinas, *Ioannis* 15.2.2009. Aquinas expounds more on this in the *ST* II-II.25–27, where he speaks about the order and the priorities of charity.

disciples to love one another, but now he is speaking and teaching them about their friendship with him, exclusively, and not with others.[46] For Aquinas "friendship can be understood in two ways: either because one loves or is loved"; likewise, "if you do what I command you," would mean that a friend, who is like a "guardian of one's soul," will guard or keep God's commandments. Moreover, God confers grace and helps those who he loves to keep the commandments. Aquinas makes it clear that it "is not they [the disciples] who first loved God, but God makes them lovers by loving them." For Aquinas, the keeping of commandments "is not the cause of divine friendship but the sign that both God loves us and that we love God..."[47]

The sign of Jesus's friendship for his disciples is in fact the heart of John 15: "No longer do I call you servants, for the servant does not know what his master is doing; but I have called you friends, for all that I have heard from my Father I have made know to you" (v. 15). Indeed, Aquinas affirms that Jesus's sign of friendship for the disciples is first highlighted when he excludes what appears to be in opposition to friendship, namely, servitude.[48] When Jesus says to the disciples: "No longer do I call you servants," it is like saying that although they were formerly servants under the law, now they are free under grace. Or as St Paul's writes in Romans 8:15, "You have received the Spirit of adoption." Secondly, it is affirmed when Jesus mentions the sign of true friendship, namely, the revelation or communication of knowledge.[49] The state of true friendship brings to perfection and charity what was before only an inclination to perfection, prompted by something less that fair love.

---

46. See Aquinas, *Ioannis* 15.3.2011.

47. Aquinas, *Ioannis* 15.3.2012.

48. See Aquinas, *Ioannis* 15.3.2014. In line with Augustine, here Aquinas also notes that servitude is created by fear. He explains that there are two kinds of fear: servile fear, which charity casts out (cf. 1 John 4:18), and filial fear, which is generated by charity, since one fears losing the person he loves. It is with filial fear that all the just are servants and sons of God. On the other hand, servile fear comes from fear of punishment and is contrary to love. It is with reference to this kind of servitude that Jesus is talking about when in John 15:15 he says: "I no longer call you slaves/servants."

49. There is a subtle difference between "freeman" and "freedman," which comes to us from antiquity. In Roman law, a "freedman" was one who had legally been released from being a slave, whereas a "freeman" was one who had never been a slave at all. The implication is stunning: Jesus, being a "freeman" paid the price of freedom to make his people "freedmen and freedwomen," since before God, all were under enslavement to sin. See, https://en.wikipedia.org/wiki/Freedman.

A freedman, Aquinas comments, is his own motivator. Freed by the sacrificial love of Christ, man moves and acts on his own authority. On the contrary, a slave/servant is someone who is not. This would imply that there is a difference between the acts of a slave still in bondage and a freedman, for a slave acts when another prods or induces him, whereas a freedman acts for his own sake and by himself. On the contrary, the servant/slave does not act for the sake of himself, as "charity does not seek its own, but the interest of Jesus and the salvation of one's neighbor."[50] If until now the disciples were servants/slaves, it is because they were inclined by charity, albeit an imperfect charity, as slaves could love a good master, but still remain in slavery. For Aquinas "the disciples were servants, but it was a good servitude springing from love."[51] In Roman law, after a slave had been freed by what was known as "manumission," he became known as a *libertus* with civic duties and rights; in relationship to the former owner, however, the *libertus* was known by the hand (*manus*) that had freed him, and the former owner was known as the *patronus*, or patron, to the *libertus*. Thus, by extension of this Roman law that was in force at the time of Christ, while the disciples, who had been freed (from sin) by Jesus, yet they were to remain "free servants" (*libertus*) of Jesus, who became their equal in law, yet still their *patronus* in love. They were able to be called to be his friends, and free to act out of love—not just respond to the prodding of the law in order to be compelled to the good. As Aquinas notes, the disciples "were moved by their own will, inclined by love."[52]

Aquinas emphasizes the point that a sign of friendship is the mutual exchange of self. Aquinas contends, "A friend reveals the secrets of his heart to his friends . . . Now God reveals his secrets to us by letting us share in his Wisdom: 'In every generation she [Wisdom] passes into holy souls and makes them friends of God and prophets' [Wisdom 7:27]."[53] According to Aquinas, what Jesus shares with his disciples is the knowledge of his essence that he hears from the Father.[54] Citing Gregory,[55] Aquinas claims

50. Aquinas, *Ioannis* 15.3.2014.
51. Aquinas, *Ioannis* 15.3.2014.
52. Aquinas, *Ioannis* 15.3.2014.
53. Aquinas, *Ioannis* 15.3.2016.
54. See Aquinas, *Ioannis* 15.3.2017.
55. The identity of Gregory is unclear. Apart from Gregory, Aquinas cites also Chrysostom and Augustine. For Chrysostom, "all that I have heard" means all that I have heard which you ought to hear, but not absolutely all things (cf. John 16:12), whereas for Augustine, what Jesus would say to the disciples was so certain that he used the past

that: "All the things he has made known to his servants are the joys of interior love and the feasts of our heavenly fatherland, which he excites in our minds every day by the breath of his love. For as long as we love the sublime heavenly things we have heard, we already know we love, because the love itself is knowledge."[56]

In John 15:16a—"You did not choose me, but I chose you"—Aquinas sees a beautiful description of the cause of friendship:

> It is the usual practice for each one of us to say that he or she is the cause of friendship ... Our Lord rejects this ... He [says]: Whoever has been called to this sublime friendship should not attribute the cause of this friendship to himself, but to me, who chose him or her as a friend ... So, I have chosen you by predestining you from all eternity, and by calling you to the faith during your lifetime.[57]

Being chosen for friendship with Jesus is just the beginning. In John 15:16b, Jesus continues, "and [I] appointed you that you should go and bear fruit and that your fruit should abide; so that whatever you ask the Father in my name, he may give it to you." Aquinas interprets this verse as to go to travel "over the whole world to convert the whole world to the faith ... [which] is the fruit of conversion ... [so that] the faithful would be led into eternal life and their spiritual flourish."[58] In other words, it would imply that one should go, in the sense, to "progress from virtue to virtue."[59] The friends of Jesus were chosen to receive not only some vague nonentity, but to be given what was needed for specific needs, namely, "all that they ask for"; beyond this specialized endowment, the friends of Jesus were to be offered "someone," as well, namely, "the Spirit."[60]

The effect of Jesus's friendship on his disciples/friends is given in John 15:17 when Jesus says: "These things I command you so that you will love one another." According to Aquinas, what Jesus is saying to the disciples/

---

tense instead of the future, so that the meaning becomes, "all that I have heard from my Father I have made known to you, that is, I will make known with that fullness of which the Apostle says: 'Then I shall understand fully, even as I have been fully understood' (1 Corinthians 13:12)."

56. Aquinas, *Ioannis* 15.3.2018. The citation is attributed to Gregory, *Homiliae in Evangelista XXVII*.

57. Aquinas, *Ioannis* 15.3.2019, 2014.

58. Aquinas, *Ioannis* 15.3.2027.

59. Aquinas, *Ioannis* 15.3.2027.

60. Aquinas, *Ioannis* 15.3.2028.

friends are divine imperatives in his words that should lead them to love one another. In the cause-and-effect terms of friendship, what Jesus initiated—namely friendship with his disciples—is to lead to friendship among themselves as well, and not divisiveness. In this way, Aquinas is emphasizing the communal or ecclesial aspect of friendship. The disciples/friends of Jesus are called to fellowship (*koinonía/societas*) with Jesus; indeed, they are invited to commune with the divine!

They are also called to invite others to believe in Jesus and the Father so that they, too, may share the divine life.[61] Friendship with God is only possible because of divine initiative. Jesus's calling of his disciples to participate in his offer of friendship allows the possibility of a certain "equality" with God.[62] The basis of friendship with God is God's grace through the Holy Spirit. This aspect of Aquinas's thought is beautifully treated by Professor William Young, who describes the human-divine relationship as being that of "derivative equality," in which the knowledge of secrets, necessary to the friendship between Jesus and his disciples, is evidenced.[63] In this case, Young notes, it is the Holy Spirit who makes known the hidden things of God and draws the friends into relationship with him.

CARITAS AS "FRIENDSHIP WITH GOD" IN THE SUMMA THEOLOGIAE

Aquinas's most thorough treatment of friendship is said to begin with his description of *amor* (love) as the first of the affective emotions, or passions, at *ST* I–II.25.2. Here he defines *amor* as "a favourable attitude to some good, such a sense of its attractiveness." In the first Article of the pivotal question that follows, Aquinas then demonstrates that man is capable and can love that which is good for him, including God himself. Aquinas also argues that for every basic kind of appetite there is a corresponding kind

---

61. See Pazdan, "Aquinas," 476–77.

62. It is important to parallel any talk of "equality" with the caveat of God's radical otherness. There is no sense in Aquinas of God's otherness being diluted as a result of friendship with humanity—in this sense, the "distance" between God and humanity is never reduced. Aquinas roots his notion of "equality" with God in a discussion of condign (appropriate or deserved) merit and congruent (compatible) merit, in which the proportional nature of congruent merit would render any "equality" with God impossible. However, through divine providence, grace and free will, condign merit allows a basis for friendship with God. See Summers, *Friendship*, 88.

63. See Young, *Politics*, 110–11.

of love. To the natural appetite, even if the subject is not necessarily aware of it, corresponds a natural love; to the sensitive appetite a sensitive love, and to the intellectual—or rational appetite (the "will")—an intellectual or rational love.[64] Then, Aquinas qualifies what calling *amor* an emotion or a passion means. He argues that it is so "in the strict sense when seated in the affective *orexis*, in an extended sense when seated in the will."[65]

In *ST* I–II.26.3 Aquinas distinguishes the four terms for "love" the meanings of which are very much alike, but still not interchangeable: *amor*, *dilectio*, *caritas* and *amicitia*. Of the three, *amor* has the broadest reference; *dilectio* is described as *amor* that involves *electio* (choice) and is said to reside only in the will, and so is confined to rational creatures. *Dilectio*, then, is intellectual or rational love. While carefully keeping his definition of *caritas* for the Questions dealing with the theological virtues in the *Secunda Secundae*, Aquinas is content to describe it as "a certain perfection of *amor*," inasmuch as it recognizes "that the object loved is highly prized."[66] Here the term *amicitia* is introduced for the first time. In coming to describe *amicitia*, Aquinas is content to include only an important citation from Aristotle, saying that it "is a disposition" (*amicitia est habitus*).[67] By citing Aristotle, Aquinas highlights the fact that *amicitia*, unlike *amor* and *dilectio*, does not fall under the category of passion. It is a habit, and therefore, it is dispositional. This makes *amicitia* a virtue, just like *caritas*.

ST I–II.26.4 deals with the question whether it is fitting to divide "love" into *amorem amicitiae* (love of friendship) and *amorem concupiscentiae* (love of desire). Aquinas demonstrates that these two modes of loving, rightly directed, are complementary and integral to one another. The whole argument hinges on Aquinas's close reading of Aristotle's saying in the Rhetoric that "love consists in wanting good things for someone."[68] Then, love must move both towards the good that one wishes for one's friend and simultaneously to the friend in his own person. Love for the person to whom one wishes the good is *amorem amicitiae*, while the love towards the good that one wishes for one's friend is *amorem concupiscentiae*:

> The object of love-of-friendship is love for its own sake, and in the primary sense of "love"; the object of love-of-desire is loved for the

64. Aquinas, *ST* I–II.26.1.
65. Aquinas, *ST* I–II.26.2.
66. Aquinas, *ST* I–II.26.3.
67. Cf. Aristotle, *NE*, 1157b28.
68. Aristotle, *Rhetoric*, 2.4.1380b35.

sake of something other than itself, and not in the primary sense of "love" . . . that love which consists in wanting good things for someone is love in the primary sense (*amor simpliciter*), and that which consists in loving a thing in so far as it contributes to someone else's welfare, is love in the secondary sense (*amor secundum quid*).[69]

Friendship comprehends both "love of friendship" directed to the friend himself and "love of desire" directed to the good things the person wishes for the friend as the means for the friend's fulfilment. The only necessary thing in the "love of friendship" is that the object for which one wishes the good must be a rational being—whether a human, angelic or divine person. Thus, it is not possible for a person to love irrational creatures, such as wine, with this "love of friendship" because the latter cannot share "in the *communicatio* of rational life on which 'all friendship is based,' nor are they endowed with the capacity to share the communication of eternal beatitude."[70] When a person loves another with a "love of friendship," the person inevitably wishes the other good things, whether material or spiritual. As Gallagher puts it, "one cannot speak of loving someone with a 'love of friendship' without implying the presence of love for what is good for that person."[71]

"Love of desire" is morally ambivalent because the intention with which one desires things may be good or evil, selfish or unselfish. Friendship is truly present just to the degree that one truly wishes the friend some good. In friendships based on usefulness or pleasure, a person wishes some good things for one's friend; and in this respect the term "friendship" is justified. But since the good the person wishes for the friend is further directed to one's own good, to the extent that they are connected with "love of desire," these kinds of friendships fall short of perfect friendship.[72]

The distinction between "love of friendship" and "love of desire" allows Aquinas a straight solution to the question: "Is similarity a cause of love?"[73] Aquinas states that both actual and potential *similitudo* (similarity/likeness) cause love, the former "love of friendship" whereas the latter "love of concupiscence." For Aquinas, actual likeness is when two things, or people,

---

69. Aquinas, *ST* I–II.26.4.
70. Carmichael, *Friendship*, 116; cf. Aquinas, *ST* I–II.26.4.
71. Gallagher, "Desire for Beatitude and Love of Friendship," 14.
72. See Aquinas, *ST* I–II.26.4 ad 3.
73. Aquinas, *ST* I–II.27.3.

possess the same qualities—such as humanity, ethnic background or racial similarities. On the other hand, potential likeness is when one thing has in potentiality what another actually possesses. Thus, the poor man loves money. Potential likeness gives rise to friendships based on convenience or pleasure. In convenience and pleasure friendships, the lover does not love for the beloved's sake, but for the sake of the qualities he possesses, be it material or spiritual, one which the lover wishes for his own perfection.

All love, Aquinas suggests, proceeds from some apprehension of unity between lover and beloved. When one loves with "love of concupiscence," one apprehends some object, such as food, as pertaining to one's own well-being. On the other hand, when one loves with the "love of friendship," the lover renders the other a reflection of the self. As Aquinas points out, "When one has love-of-friendship for a person, one wants good things for him as one does for oneself," thereby showing, Aquinas continues, that he "looks on him as another self, wishing him well in the same way as one does oneself."[74] Aquinas invokes Aristotle's description of a friend as an "other self",[75] and that of Augustine as "half of my soul",[76] to be, as Lefler notes, the "fundamental explanatory principle of a genuine friendship love."[77] *Unitas* (union) between persons, however, actually means "togetherness," and not the merging into one.[78] A friend, therefore, is like a mirror of the self and becomes the means by which one's character and habits become observable.

Aquinas then treats two other important effects of love: *mutua inhaesio* (mutual indwelling), discussed at *ST* I–II.28.2, and *extasis* (ecstasy/transport), treated at *ST* I–II.28.3. On how *mutua inhaesio* is an effect of love, Aquinas quotes 1 John 4:16: "He who abides in love abides in God, and God abides in him." The beloved can be understood as inhering or dwelling in the beloved and the beloved in the lover. "Indwelling," with respect to one's intellect, happens through knowledge and thought, the beloved "inhering" or "dwelling" in the lover's mind and heart and the lover reciprocally seeking to enter the inmost depths of the one who is loved. With respect to the appetitive power, or will, the beloved indwells in the

---

74. Aquinas, *ST* I–II.28.1.
75. Aristotle, *NE*, 1169a31–b6.
76. Augustine, *Confessions*, 4.6.32.
77. Lefler, *Theologizing Friendship*, 110.
78. Gallagher appeals to the notion of an "extension of self-love" to articulate Aquinas's understanding of the "love of friendship." See Gallagher, "Desire for Beatitude and Love of Friendship," 20–34.

lover within their affection through delight. In "love of concupiscence" the lover tries to possess the beloved perfectly by penetrating into his very soul. But in "love of friendship," friends dwell in one another in the sense of identifying with each other as "another self," looking to each other's good or ill fortune as their own, enjoying the other's good fortune or suffering the other's misfortune as their own. Thus, it is only in "love of friendship" that *mutua inhaesio* is indeed always present.[79]

At *ST* I–II.28.3 Aquinas proceeds to explain how *extasis*[80] is an effect of love. By referring to Dionysius, who claims that even "God himself suffered ecstasy because of love";[81] and by his conviction that "all love is in some sort a copy or share of the divine love," Aquinas concludes that, "it would seem that love does produce ecstasy or transport."[82] In "love of concupiscence," although the person does "go out" to find something he wants, the movement finally returns to himself and, so, the ecstasy is said to be *secundum quid* (of a qualified or secondary sense). On the other hand, in "love of friendship," the "going out" from oneself is said to be *simpliciter* (simple, or in a primary sense), insofar as the lover desires and does good things to the beloved, "exercising thought and care about his friend's interests for his friend's sake."[83]

In the *Secunda Secundae*, Aquinas studies friendship in the context of man's relationship with God. By stating, at *ST* II.65.5, that "charity signifies not only love of God, but also a certain friendship with him," a friendship "which consists in a certain familiar colloquy with him" which is "begun here in this life by grace, but will be perfected in the future life by glory," Aquinas might be implying that one truly loves God when one has learned to be the friend of God. In claiming that to love God is to have a certain friendship with him, Aquinas ascends to sublime heights of moral understanding; he "uncovers the most mystical side of his vision of the moral life."[84] For Aquinas, *caritas*, "this friendship with God, is the love with

---

79. See Aquinas, *ST* I–II.28.2 ad 3.

80. Aquinas's *extasis* is not a Latin word, but a transliteration of the Greek *ékstasis*. It implies two meanings: (1) a being-put-out-of-one's-proper-place, and (2) a being-put-out-of-one's-mind. In this article Aquinas is speaking of (2), but assuming that the links with (1) is more than purely verbal. This may be better brought out in English by the term "transport" than "ecstasy".

81. Dionysius, *De Divinis Nominibus* IV, 16. PG 3, 713.

82. Aquinas, *ST* I–II.28.3.

83. Aquinas, *ST* I–II.28.3.

84. Wadell, *Friendship and the Moral Life*, 120.

which the Christian life begins, the love by which it is sustained, and the love in which it is eternally perfected."[85] Charity is not just any kind of love; it is, specifically, the "love of friendship."[86] The "love of friendship" is essentially spiritual and, thus, may well serve to explain the optimum relation that unites man to God.

For Aquinas, it is self-evident that *caritas* is the center and the epitome of the Christian life. However, the understanding that *caritas* is a sort of friendship is anything "but" self-evident because of the unique and peerless relationship: i.e., the friend is God.[87] How can *caritas* be identified as "friendship with God?" This and other questions are discussed in Aquinas's comprehensive treatment on the theological virtue of *caritas* in the *Secunda Secundae* (II–II.23–46), considered by many the key to the whole *ST*.[88]

Aquinas commences his discussion on *caritas* immediately upon asking whether it is a kind of friendship.[89] His answer is in the affirmative and he invites anyone who does not agree to consider the quotation that offers the highest authority in John 15:15: "No longer will I call you servants but my friends." Then, Aquinas proceeds with an argument from his interpretation of Aristotle and explains:

> Not all love has the character of friendship, but that only which goes with well wishing, namely when we so love another as to will what is good for him. For if what we will is our own good, as when we love wine or a horse or the like, it is a love not of friendship but of desire.[90]

Benevolence is not only an absence of malice or merely wishing the friend well. It is a way of being that actively works for the well-being of the friend. The motivation and the focus of the friendship is not the pleasure or usefulness one receives from the friendship, but the happiness of the friend himself. One recognizes that the joy of the friendship comes in being able to do what is good for the friend one loves. Thus, it is through friendship that one discovers this reality: actively working for the good of the friend is one's happiness, not only because the lover loves the beloved, but because the good the lover seeks for the beloved is also the good the

85. Wadell, *Friendship and the Moral Life*, 120–21.
86. Wadell, *Friendship and the Moral Life*, 130.
87. See Schönborn, *Happiness, God and Man*, 32.
88. See Schönborn, *Happiness, God and Man*, 31.
89. See Aquinas, *ST* II–II.23.1.
90. Aquinas, *ST* II–II.23.1.

lover wants for himself. Put another way, it is because the beloved loves what the lover does, there is nothing the lover wants except to offer the beloved the good which the beloved brings to him. Benevolence, then, not only includes working to ensure that no harm comes to the beloved, but what enables this work is not the good thing itself but the person who is loved. As stated above, in "love of friendship," the love on which friendship is based, the good desired is not the good for its own sake but for whom it is wanted.[91] The love which characterizes friendship is a love which toils wholeheartedly for the good of the other, because what the lover loves and sees as his good is the good of his beloved. In this light, friendship is nothing other than, "mutual devotion to the good of the other because it is a good both share."[92] It is the activity where each actively works for the other's well-being. Applied to *caritas*, where the friend is God, benevolence would imply that "we seek God's good for God's sake."[93] This important point in Aquinas's logic is highlighted by Summers who claims that "*caritas* and *amicitia* are both oriented outward, to the other."[94]

While benevolence is necessary for friendship, it is not sufficient. It is a requited and mutual love that transforms benevolence into friendship. It is a love in which the person is aware that the well-wishing one offers to the other is returned. As Aquinas notes when he outlines the qualities of friendship: "Yet goodwill alone is not enough for friendship, for this requires a mutual loving; it is only with a friend that a friend is friendly."[95] And "such reciprocal good will is based on something in common."[96] In friendship, the common element is the good which friends desire for each other. Friendship exists only when each person is aware that the good desired for the other is also the good the other wishes for him. Unless each friend sees for the other this shared good, this good both want for each other, friendship

---

91. See Aquinas, *ST* I–II.26.4.
92. Wadell, *Friendship and the Moral Life*, 132.
93. Wadell, *Friendship and the Moral Life*, 132.
94. Summers, *Friendship*, 90.
95. Aquinas, *ST* II–II.23.1.
96. Aquinas, *ST* II–II.23.3. Here "in common" translates the Latin *communicatio/societas* and the Greek *koinonía*. The Greek *koinonía* is enriched with theological overtones in the New Testament. The NRSV has retained it in many passages where it occurs. In other, terms such as "taking part in," "partnership," "participation," "share," are used. In any case the general idea is plain enough: men must share something, whether in humanity, or in kinship, citizenship, or shared enterprise, if there is to be friendship. See Carmichael, *Friendship*, 110–11.

cannot occur. Friendship, thus, can only occur when one's gift of love is recognized by the other, embraced by him and is reciprocated. In this case, friendship becomes what Aquinas describes as a certain society of lover and beloved in love, a kind of a minute community.[97] Through friendship, through this miniature community, love and good habits/virtues are exchanged. In this way, friendship would qualify as a virtue; it constitutes a way of life, a special way of being a self.[98] The good in which a person sees himself completed is not something one can offer to himself; it is only something one can receive from a friend whose love continually offers it.

In the case of "friendship with God, which is charity",[99] the commonality is a participation or a sharing in God's happiness. As Aquinas comments:

> Now there is a sharing of man with God by his sharing his happiness with us, and it is on this that friendship is based. St Paul refers to it, God is faithful by whom you were called into the fellowship of his Son [1 Cor 1:9]. Now the love which is based on this sort of fellowship is charity. Accordingly, it is clear that charity is a friendship of man and God.[100]

If every friendship is the sharing, or the communion, we have with others based upon the good shared by the friendship, charity is the communication we have with God based upon happiness of God, from which the friendship begins. In charity the good we share with God is a dynamic participation in the shared life of God. It is known by a living communication with God where we are continually transformed by the Holy Spirit. Charity is a gift of God and is returned by the one who loves God. The gift offered and received is charity's activity, charity's life. God seeks to communicate his love with humanity. Yet, God's gift of friendship to humanity is not mutual giving and receiving to fulfil a need on the part of God.[101] Rather, "it is the free sharing in the life of God (sending out and receiving

---

97. See Johann, *The Meaning of Love*, 46–47.
98. See Wadell, *Friendship and the Moral Life*, 133.
99. Aquinas, *ST* I–II.65.5.
100. Aquinas, *ST* II–II.23.1.
101. Aquinas is clear that God, as creator, has no need of the creature in the sense of being deficient without their love. However, he is also clear that the creature's love is unique. There is completeness in God, a unity of being, and action, so that nothing can be added to God's beatitude. See Aquinas, *ST* I–II.3.2; Summers, *Friendship*, 91.

back of divine love) whereby the Christian is incorporated into that life."[102] Therefore, human beings already have now a real, albeit imperfect, fellowship/friendship with God that "will be made perfect in heaven."[103] It is precisely on the basis of this gift of God's self-communication that friendship between humanity and God can be established. Cardinal Schönborn notes that the entire *ST* can, in fact, be summarized in the expression: *"fundari amicitiam.* God wills 'to establish a friendship' with his creature."[104] Schönborn describes the whole path of human and Christian life as a process of establishing friendship with God, and he concludes that, "the whole ethics of interpersonal communication among men is summarized in the one expression: establishing friendship."[105]

But if *caritas* demands that we ought to love all people, friendship seems to contradict this evangelical command since one cannot be a friend with all people. Here Aquinas proves the possibility of loving one's enemy. To the extent that we love God, we also love those whom God loves. Aquinas explains that when we love a friend, we love everything about him, "be they children, servants or anyone connected with him at all, even if they hurt or hate us."[106] Thus "the friendship of caritas extends even to our enemies, for we love them for the sake of God who is the principal in our loving."[107] The same holds also with regards to love for sinners. Even though a friendship of true worth is between persons of virtue, the love that God has for sinners suffices to regard sinners also as our friends, and thus to love them with the "love of friendship" for God's sake.[108]

In *ST* II-II.23.2, Aquinas clarifies the position of Peter Lombard who holds that *caritas* "is not something created in the soul but the Holy Spirit himself dwelling there (*De Virtutibus* I. I)," or put differently, that the movement of *caritas* comes from the Holy Spirit unmediated by any habit. If such were the case, Aquinas counter argues, the active principle in *caritas* would then be the Holy Spirit moving the soul directly. Aquinas makes it clear that this would impoverish the greatness of *caritas* because it would destroy the person's free will. In such a case, loving would not depend on

---

102. Summers, *Friendship*, 91.
103. Aquinas, *ST* II-II.23.1 ad 1.
104. Schönborn, *Happiness, God and Man*, 34-35.
105. Schönborn, *Happiness, God and Man*, 35.
106. Aquinas, *ST* II-II.23.1 ad 2.
107. Aquinas, *ST* II-II.23.1 ad 2.
108. See Aquinas, *ST* II-II.23.1 ad 3.

the person's will, and so, love itself would not be love and, by implication, would not be friendship, "if it were not also, on the part of man, a genuine, human act (that is, voluntary and rational)."[109] Through the grace of the Holy Spirit, then, there must be an inner supernatural habit, created by God, "superadded" to our natural powers and informing the person's will, inclining it to perform freely the act of *caritas*.[110] However, inasmuch as "[t]he divine essence itself is *caritas*," the love with which we formally love our neighbor "is a sharing in the divine charity;"[111] it "joins the soul to God by justifying it."[112] In effect, *caritas* makes us "connatural" with God and makes it possible for us really to love God and to be united with him in friendship; *caritas* thus "makes us 'deiform,' restoring our likeness to God."[113] The entire meaning of human life, in effect, "consists in realizing the likeness of God in friendship with God."[114] The purpose of the Christian moral life "is for us to become for God who God has always been for us, a friend who seeks our good and wishes our perfect happiness."[115] Aquinas encapsulates this in the following phrase: "The ultimate end of things is to become like God."[116]

Becoming in the likeness of God does not entail "becoming God"; nor does it mean that there is no longer any difference between God and oneself. H. D. Simonin speaks of the relationship between God and humanity as an "ontological similitude,"[117] a "similitude of being revealed in the capacity for friendship-love."[118] Through *caritas*, one becomes like and not identical to God. It is precisely the "otherness" between God and humanity that bestows the possibility of friendship, since one cannot be a friend of oneself. Speaking in friendship terms, Wadell writes that in *caritas* we become "another self to God . . . the more we become like God, the more we become someone other than God, namely, ourselves. In becoming godly, in being formed in the goodness of God, we become our most

---

109. Schönborn, *Happiness, God and Man*, 37.
110. Aquinas, *ST* II-II.23.1 ad 3.
111. Aquinas, *ST* II-II.23.2 ad 1.
112. Aquinas, *ST* II-II.23.2 ad 3.
113. Carmichael, *Friendship*, 111.
114. Schönborn, *Happiness, God and Man*, 35.
115. Wadell, *Friendship and the Moral Life*, 138.
116. Aquinas, *SCG* III.1.3.19.
117. Simonin, "Autour De La Solution Thomiste," 265–66.
118. Summers, *Friendship*, 91.

genuine selves."[119] This is the beauty and, at the same time, the paradox of the friendship between God and humanity: as one's friendship with God grows, likeness with God increases because one comes to love what God loves, one makes God's good his own. But, at the same time, one becomes more unlike God because one becomes more his own genuine self.[120]

At *ST* II-II.24, Aquinas discusses the subject, or the seat of *caritas*, saying that since divine goodness can only be recognized by the intellect, the subject of *caritas* is our will. Here Aquinas elaborates that *caritas*, "our friendship for God arising from our sharing in eternal happiness," is "infused by the Holy Spirit, who is the love of the Father and the Son; our participation in this love . . . is creaturely (*creata*) charity itself."[121] The friendship of *caritas*, by which we embark on our journey to God, is imperfect in our bodily life, but will be perfect in the next when our "whole heart is always actually intent on God."[122]

Nevertheless, there is an indefinite potential spiritual growth of *caritas* in our bodily life because *caritas* is a movement towards God, our ultimate end. Such a growth is marked by three stages: beginning, progressing and perfection.[123] *Caritas* increases not by way of being extended to more and more acts of charity, but by way of being made more intense in the acts. But equally the same, *caritas* can diminish and even be destroyed when "one makes creatures its end."[124] While repentance is always possible, if one continuously chooses sin in preference to friendship for and with God, the "habitual" characteristic of *caritas* would be lost.[125]

According to Aquinas, friendship ought to be directed toward specific objects. Gallagher notes that "for Thomas the moral life is essentially a matter of relationships among persons."[126] These persons are the objects of friendship for Aquinas and lead to a practical outworking of his ethic. Following Augustine, Aquinas claims that there are four objects with whom

---

119. Wadell, *Friendship and the Moral Life*, 139.

120. Indeed, Gallagher terms "the paradox of *amor amicitiae*" the fact that "the motion to overcome otherness, the affective union, does not merely leave the ontological otherness intact but actually depends upon it. I can love the other as myself only if the other is not myself." Gallagher, "Desire for Beatitude," 26.

121. Aquinas, *ST* II-II.24.1.

122. Aquinas, *ST* II-II.24.8.

123. See Aquinas, *ST* II-II.24.9.

124. Aquinas, *ST* II-II.24.10.

125. See Aquinas, *ST* II-II.24.10–12.

126. Gallagher, "The Will and Its Acts (Ia IIae, qq. 6–17)," 84.

Caritas as "Amicitia with God" in Thomas Aquinas

man can be friends: God, self, neighbors and bodies.[127] Aquinas discusses these within the context of hierarchy that places a priority on God and then works in decreasing priority toward self, neighbors, and bodies. Within his discussion of neighbors, he creates a second level of priority which moves in concentric circles from the closest to the self and outward to enemies and sinners.

Friendship with God serves as the basis for all friendship just as God serves as the ground of all being and of perfect happiness/goodness. In Mark 12:30 we read that God is to be loved with all our heart, and with all our soul, and with all our might.[128] This means that, "as St Bernard notes (*De Diligendo Deum I*. PL 182, 974), the measure of our love for God is without measure and the more we love [God], the better we love."[129] By applying Aristotelian metaphysics, Aquinas suggests that God is the *principium* (principle/cause) of *caritas* from which the *communicatione* (sharing/communication) of divine friendship flows.[130] On the basis of divine communication—the ultimate form of communication being the incarnation of Christ—friendship is possible between God and man. As the cause of *beatitudinis* (eternal happiness/beatitude) God is to be loved more than we love ourselves and our neighbor, who participates with us in it.[131] In view of Aquinas's use of John 15 as his authoritative statement for the possibility of friendship with God, one needs to stress that, for Aquinas, it is God who bestows friendship upon humanity apart from the actions of humanity.[132] Bauerschmidt clarifies, "Here it should be understood that the charity Aquinas is speaking of is a theological virtue, which means that it is instilled in us by God's grace. As 1 John 4:19 says, 'We love because he first loved us.' The initiative is always on God's part. Nothing we do wins God's friendship; it is a gift freely bestowed."[133]

Furthermore, our *similitudo* (likeness) to God also prompts us to love God first, as, "our likeness to God precedes and is the cause of the likeness

---

127. See Aquinas, *ST* II–II.25.12; 26.1; cf. Augustine, *On Christian Doctrine*, I.22; Song of Songs 2:4.

128. See Deuteronomy 6:5; 10:12.

129. Aquinas, *ST* II–II.27.6.

130. See Aquinas, *ST* II–II.26.1.

131. See Aquinas, *ST* II–II.26.2–3.

132. Aquinas drives this point in *Ioannis* where, with reference to John 15:14, he writes that "keeping the commandments is not the cause of divine friendship but the sign, the sign both that God loves us and that we love God." Aquinas, *Ioannis* 15.3.2012.

133. Bauerschmidt, *Holy Teaching*, 154.

we bear our neighbor."[134] Although the will to enjoy God is to love him with "love of concupiscence," in reality what predominates is "love of friendship," because in itself God's "good is greater than any we can derive by enjoying it."[135] God is not only the cause of *caritas*, but he is also the principle object of *caritas*; and, so, in friendship with God, we love God for his own sake.[136] God is the originator of all that is and belongs to no one else: "as the final, formal and efficient cause of all creation, God is capable of being loved without further reference to any other being."[137]

The second part of Jesus's commandment of love in Mark 12:31 is that the neighbor/friend is to be loved "as yourself."[138] This would imply that, after God, "a man ought in charity to love himself more than his neighbor."[139] The "I" that reflexively loves my "self" is said to be my will, which evidently has reflexive power since a person can freely "will [oneself] to will."[140] By "self" here Aquinas does not mean the corporal but the spiritual nature of the human person.[141] Although there is in Aquinas an ontological priority of self-love that appears as the primordial form and root of the love of neighbor (*forma et radix amicitiae*), Aquinas does not intend to diminish the biblical commandment of love nor to give any allowance to egoism.[142] By his analysis on the ontological priority of self-love over the love of neighbor, Aquinas intends to explain how the "as yourself" of the biblical command of love is to be understood. After recalling again that *caritas* is a kind of friendship with God, Aquinas observes that, strictly speaking, a person cannot be said to be one's own friend, inasmuch as friendship implies a certain *unionem* (union) with reference to God.[143] And, since *unitas* (unity) is the metaphysical principle of *unionem*, a person's *unitas* to oneself is greater than his *unionem* with any other. One has with the self

---

134. Aquinas, *ST* II–II.26.2 ad 2.
135. Aquinas, *ST* II–II.26.3.
136. See Aquinas, *ST* II–II.27.3.
137. Lefler, *Theologizing Friendship*, 116.
138. Cf. Leviticus 19:18. In the Vulgate translation, from which Aquinas quotes, it reads "love your friend (*amicus*) as yourself."
139. Aquinas, *ST* II–II.26.4.
140. Aquinas, *ST* II–II.25.2; see Carmichael, *Friendship*, 118.
141. See Aquinas, *ST* II–II.25.7; 26.4.
142. See Aquinas, *ST* II–II.27.4.
143. See Aquinas, *ST* II–II.26.4.

not an existential friendship, but something more than friendship.[144] Thus, self-love becomes, "the model and root of friendship; for our friendship for others consists precisely in the fact that our attitude to them is the same as to ourselves."[145] As Schockenhoff notes:

> For Thomas, the primacy of self-love over love of neighbor . . . is not a statement of normative ethics. He simply describes the natural weight of the human will, which is inscribed in it as an ontologically fundamental direction. In a specific way, the human will also stands under the fundamental law of all creaturely being according to which being-one is prior to becoming-one (*unitas est potior unione*).[146]

Indeed, the priority with which self-love precedes "love of neighbor" stands from the fact that *unitas* is stronger than *unionem*; the fact that a person participates directly in the divine good "is more powerful reason for loving than the fact that another is associated with him in this participation."[147]

Loving oneself can wrongly result in the gratifying of one's lower "sensible" nature.[148] But in friendship with God, that is *caritas*, one loves and seeks to perfect one's rational nature.[149] The priority of self-love over neighbor-love also implies that, one may not, even when attempting to free a neighbor from sin, commit such an evil that prevents one's own participation in the eternal happiness/beatitude.[150] However, as far as the neighbor's soul is concerned, the neighbor ought to be loved more than our own body.[151]

In the Thomistic synthesis of friendship, the natural extension of friendship with God is friendship with one's neighbors. Friendship for and with God indeed leads the person to friendship with the neighbor, where he is commanded to love every person as his neighbor.[152] Since there is in charity only one foundation and one motive, namely, man's friendship with

144. See Aquinas, *ST* II–II.25.4.
145. Aquinas, *ST* II–II.25.4.
146. Schockenhoff, "Charity," 253.
147. Aquinas, *ST* II–II.26.4.
148. Cf. 2 Timothy 3:1–2.
149. See Aquinas, *ST* II–II.25.4.
150. See Aquinas, *ST* II–II.26.4.
151. See Aquinas, *ST* II–II.26.5.
152. See Aquinas, *ST* II–II.25.6.

God as the cause of all good things,[153] "love of God" and "love of neighbor" are in effect one and the same virtue,[154] despite their distinct acts and objects.[155] Thus, just as "self-love" proceeds from the "love of God," so our charitable love for our neighbor is an expression of our love for God, who destines human beings to a friendship with him. In *caritas*, thus, the neighbor is loved for God's sake. Specifically, "what we ought to love in him [the neighbor] is that he be in God."[156]

Seen in this way, love entails not just the love for one's own good, or the good of another, but a common movement toward God; because humans are united with God as their highest good, they also become worth of each other's love.[157] As Aquinas explains, "It is then with the same love of charity that we love all our neighbors, seeing them in relation to the one common good, which is God."[158] Aquinas reconciles the apparent contradiction between the universality of the biblical command to love all people and the particularity of friendship by saying that we are not required to do specific acts "towards every man individually, as being something physical impossible."[159] And this principle, Aquinas contends, applies to every neighbor, including our enemies and sinners, insofar as they are friends or potential friends of God.[160] Aquinas's discussion does not entirely solve the paradox of loving one's enemies who do not reciprocate the "love of friendship," but the reciprocity of friendship from God replaces, at least in part, the mutuality lacking from enemies and sinners. Thus, being friends with all people is grounded strongly in one's friendship with God and all of creation's contingent nature in him. Specifically, with regards to one's enemies who are also generally his neighbors, Aquinas says that it is not required that one makes particular actions of love toward them; yet, one is required to be ready to love them and to offer them friendship "if real necessity arise."[161] Apart from that, Aquinas continues, it belongs to the

---

153. See Aquinas, *ST* II–II.23.1 ad 2.
154. See Aquinas, *ST* II–II.23.5; 23.5 ad 5.
155. See Aquinas, *ST* II–II.44.2 ad 4.
156. Aquinas, *ST* II–II.25.1.
157. See Aquinas, *ST* II–II.25.1 ad 2; Schockenhoff, "Charity," 252.
158. Aquinas, *ST* II–II.25.8.
159. Aquinas, *ST* II–II.25.8.
160. See Aquinas, *ST* II–II.23.1.
161. Aquinas, *ST* II–II.28.8.

Caritas as "Amicitia with God" in Thomas Aquinas

perfection of *caritas* "to do this actually and to love one's enemy for God's sake."[162]

The final object of friendship noted by Aquinas in his hierarchy of *caritas* is friendship with one's own body. Based on Aquinas's previous distinction regarding love for one's spiritual self over one's corporeal self, one can see his logic to address love for one's body. According to Aquinas, one's own body is to be loved with the same love of *caritas* because it receives with one's spiritual self the divine happiness "by a kind of overflow."[163] Our body is to be used for the service of God. We ought to love it, "Though not the taint of sin and the corruption that punishment brings it; on the contrary, charity should make us long for an end to these."[164]

In response to Jesus's statement in John 15:13 concerning the love of a man laying down his life for his friends, Aquinas contends, "The care of his own body is the intimate charge of every man, but not the care of his neighbor's, except in a particular case. Consequently, charity does not oblige us to sacrifice our own body for our neighbor's safety, except where we are bound to provide for it. All the same, freely to offer oneself in such a case is an act of the highest charity."[165] In this reply, Aquinas offers a supererogatory act as an example of love for one's neighbor, but he does not obligate anyone to perform this act. He simply considers it to be the perfection of charity.

After discussing the proper order and priorities of *caritas* in ST II–II.26 and further clarifying some other characteristics and acts of charity in *ST* II–II.27, Aquinas then devotes six Questions to discuss all the partial virtues connected with *caritas*, namely, joy, peace, mercy, kindness, almsgiving, and fraternal correction,[166] and another ten to discuss their opposed vices, namely, hatred, boredom, envy, discord, contentiousness, schism, war, quarrel, and riotousness, as well as irksomeness.[167] These virtues give the contours of what it is like to live as a Christian and what characteristics to embrace.

This chapter showed how Aquinas uses friendship as the outworking of the greatest of the virtues, namely, *caritas*. Aquinas defines *caritas* as "friendship with God." In order to substantiate his definition, it is no

---

162. Aquinas, *ST* II–II.25.8.
163. Aquinas, *ST* II–II.25.12.
164. Aquinas, *ST* II–II.25.5.
165. Aquinas, *ST* II–II.26.2.
166. See Aquinas, *ST* II.II.28–32.
167. See Aquinas, *ST* II–II.34–43.

surprise that he cites Jesus's statement in John 15:15: "I do not call you servants any longer . . . I have called you friends." By nature, human beings are nothing more than servants, but notwithstanding the asymmetrical difference between God and humanity, through divine communication, the gifts of the Holy Spirit and *caritas*, human beings become the children and friends of God. Aquinas is clear that humanity's friendship with God does not impinge upon God's sovereignty, in the sense of God being incomplete without it. Indeed, Aquinas is clear that the very act of friendship with God is a divine act rather than a human one.

Friendship with God is God's gift which brings about the final *telos* meant for all human beings and the highest fulfilment of their longing for definitive community with God.[168] To be God's friend is to love God as the principle of eternal happiness and to love the neighbor in a certain way: it is to love God and neighbor with "love of friendship," the same love with which God loves. "Love of friendship" is "the moral determinant of the relationship to each and every other human being."[169] This "love of friendship" is not exclusive; it is exercised openly towards all. We are so created to find our happiness in friendship with God, and in that friendship, we are to love our neighbor as "our self." For Aquinas, man's path to God is thus thought of not simply as a preparation for the reception of future happiness after our bodily life, but rather as a "growth process of a happiness already realized initially in moral acts, which will lead from its now imperfect shape to eschatological perfection."[170] As a result, community and ethics are intricately related in the thought of Saint Thomas Aquinas, but just as with other issues, friendship with God serves as the ultimate purpose for their existence and the goal for human acts within the context of such relationships.

The virtue of *caritas,* as "friendship with God," touches eternity and the divine. Friendship is an exchange of self, which, in a certain sense, is analogous to Trinitarian kenotic love. It must develop and become more and more actual in the life of each person by living a life of virtue. The practice of virtue is completed and perfected by the seven gifts of the Holy Spirit.[171] The gifts of the Holy Spirit reach their highest perfection in the gift of wisdom, the gift associated with the theological virtue of *caritas*.[172] It

---

168. See Schockenhoff, "Charity," 245.
169. McEvoy, "The other as oneself," 31.
170. Schockenhoff, "Charity," 245.
171. See Catechism, III.1.1831.
172. See Aquinas, *ST* II–II.45.

inspires the person to reflect contemplatively on the divine mysteries, enjoys thinking about them, and directs the human mind to judge all things according to their right principles. With the gift of wisdom, the person experiences the goodness of joy. We are thus called to go beyond justice in our relationship with the neighbor. Aided by the gift of wisdom, we are called to love the neighbor with the same charitable love of God and, thus, with "love of friendship," and be in friendship with him. A study of the Thomistic understanding of friendship can indeed be helpful for ethical discussion in the contemporary context, which is the subject of the next chapter.

Chapter 4

Friendship in the Process of Renewal of the Theology of the Christian Life

SCHOLASTIC THEOLOGY SYSTEMATIZED THE achievements of the Fathers—scriptural hermeneutics, dogma, moral theology and spiritual theology—by both distinguishing between these dimensions and at the same time relating the disciplines to one another. Moral Theology emphasized the law, but even more, it accentuated the formation of the character through the virtues and the gifts of the Holy Spirit in the life of grace. However, from the late medieval period and after the crisis of Nominalism, the emphasis on virtues and on formation of the character could not withstand the trials in daily life. Nominalism challenged the traditional understanding of morality centered on the fulfilment of ends, such as Aquinas's morality of happiness. Moral theology was becoming more concerned with strict obligations imposed on all the faithful; it was becoming a matter of drawing up detailed manuals for the training of confessors in their task of hearing confessions. The emphasis of these manuals was more on the law, sin and the judgement of conscience. Their approach was more than intertwined with dogma and spiritual theology. The result of this deductive approach was that morality, "[s]eemed more aimed at natural human ends, cut off from the sense of the moral life as part of the Christian response to God."[1] The moral theology of the manuals gave rise to what Pinckaers calls "morality of obligation" (such as the moralities of duties, imperatives,

---

1. O'Keefe, *Becoming Good, Becoming Holy*, 14.

Friendship in the Process of Renewal of the Theology of the Christian Life

norms, etc.).[2] Obedience to law encroached upon charity and the virtues; and as a consequence the theme of friendship was lost. The theological virtues were effectively deported "into the now specialized realm of mystical theology," largely reserved for the special elite corps of Christians from among the priests and the religious.[3] The dichotomy between moral and spiritual theology obscured the interconnection of both moral and spiritual dimensions of the Christian life. Servais Pinckaers highlights the reason as to why the disjunction between ethical and spiritual or mystical theology was deeply problematic:

> The preoccupation of Christian mysticism has always been love, its growth, and the different stages leading to its perfection, as well as its most concrete manifestations. Unfortunately, mysticism has been excluded from Christian ethics, as if it were intended only for the elite and as if morality could forgo this dimension without cutting itself off from the very strength and dynamism of charity.[4]

With some few exceptions, this situation in the church and its moral thought in general lasted up to the Second Vatican Council.[5]

THE CALL FOR THE RENEWAL OF MORAL THEOLOGY IN VCII AND ITS AFTERMATH

Attempts for revising moral theology were initiated even before the event of Vatican Council II, with the work of moral theologians including (amongst others) Bernard Häring and Fritz Tillmann. Tillmann was the expositor of a theological tradition which had its origins among the Catholic theologians of Tübingen in the nineteenth and early twentieth centuries. He was deeply concerned with developing a theology which would mediate a spirituality that could nourish the lives of Christian men and women. His was not a deductive system, but rather an inductive one which attempted to detail the requirements of the following of Christ on the basis of what Christians know and experience about God through revelation. The most distinctive feature of Tillmann's theology was "his attempt to establish all

---

2. See Pinckaers, *Sources*, 14–22.
3. Carmichael, *Friendship*, 127.
4. Pinckaers, *Sources*, 32.
5. See Cloutier and Mattison III, "The Resurgence of Virtue," 228.

of his theology in direct relation to scriptural themes."[6] In their distinctive way, these so called "revisionists,"[7] proposed alternatives to the neo-Thomist and neo-scholastic manuals of moral theology and engaged themselves in retrieving from the tradition to renew and revitalize moral theology, which in their opinion was focusing too much on particular sins and on the sacrament of penance.[8] Their aim was twofold: to ground moral theology more on the sources of Holy Scripture and the Christian tradition, and for moral theology to feed more from dogmatic, spiritual and pastoral theology, incorporating virtue into a relational-anthropological vision.[9]

Even before Vatican Council II took place, one could see this change taking place, mainly in Bernard Häring, who was considered by many to have been the new Alphonsus Liguori and the father of contemporary moral theology. There is a significant shift in the title of his two seminal works, from his three-volume pre-conciliar work, *The Law of Christ*[10] to his three-volume post-conciliar work *Free and Faithful in Christ*.[11] Häring's work attempts "to develop positions on specific [moral] topics in relation to a theology of morality, not to law."[12] He replaces the concept of "nature" with that of "personhood" as "the primary category by which moral agents are depicted."[13]

A central role in the theology of Häring is the notion of responsibility, qualified as "an expression of creative freedom and fidelity."[14] The notion of faithfulness refers to the kind of responsibility that Christians have both to God and to neighbor. The creative aspect of responsibility is the consequence of Häring's conviction that moral theology should never be reduced to mere observance of precepts and laws; rather it is a vision that leads one through its own inner dynamisms and cultivates a sense of Christ's presence. Hence, "In loyalty and fidelity the Christian community must search

6. Gallagher, *Time Past, Time Future*, 166.

7. "The 'revisionists' are those who accepted that the moral theology of the manuals was far from adequate and began the task of reconstructing moral theology on the basis of Scripture and tradition, rather than on natural and canon laws." Mealey, *The Identity of Christian Morality*, 8n27.

8. See Mealey, *The Identity of Christian Morality*, 1–12.

9. See Harrington and Keenan, *Jesus and Virtue Ethics*, 7.

10. Häring, *The Law of Christ*, 3 vols.

11. Häring, *Free and Faithful in Christ*, 3 vols.

12. Gallagher, *Time Past, Time Future*, 204.

13. Gallagher, *Time Past, Time Future*, 205.

14. Häring, *Free and Faithful in Christ*, 59.

Friendship in the Process of Renewal of the Theology of the Christian Life

out those ways of living that are responsive to the invitation of Christ."[15] What is revolutionary about Häring's approach is not that he invented a new vision of moral theology, but that he continuously recalls this inner dynamism of moral theology.

Vatican Council's II call for renewal of moral theology is seen clearly in the oft-quoted injunction in the Decree on the Training of Priests, *Optatam Totius* (*OT*):

> Special care should be given to the perfecting of moral theology. Its scientific presentation should draw more fully on the teaching of Holy Scripture and should throw light upon the exalted vocation of the faithful in Christ and their obligation to bring forth charity for the life of the world.[16]

The renewal that *OT* sought for moral theology requires, "Retrieval from the sources of Scripture and Tradition through exhaustive and comprehensive research of classical theological texts and their interpretation in their proper cultural context, as well as the thorough study of the history of development of moral theology itself vis-à-vis cultural transitions."[17]

A less explicit call for renewal of moral theology in Vatican Council II can also be noticed in the Pastoral Constitution on the Church in the Modern World, *Gaudium et Spes* (*GS*). With the intention to read "the signs of the times" and with an approach of "dialogue," the Constitution aims to transform the Church's understanding of its relationship to the world.[18] It also indicates the course for a personalistic approach in moral theology.[19]

The call for the renewal of moral theology in *OT*, the approach of dialogue that characterizes the Pastoral Constitution *GS*, and indeed the whole ecclesial event of Vatican Council II, was interpreted by many as the Church's readiness to change its teaching on particular moral issues, rather than its understanding and praxis of moral theology per se.[20] However, a few years after Vatican Council II issued its call for the renewal of moral theology, the crisis that had been building for several centuries—whether moral theology should be predominantly about analyzing moral acts or rather to form moral agents—erupted fully with the promulgation of Pope

15. Gallagher, *Time Past, Time Future*, 206.
16. Vatican II, *Opatatam Totius*, par. 16.
17. Delicata, "The renewal of moral theology," 139–40.
18. Vatican II, *Gaudium et Spes*, par. 7.
19. See Kennedy, "Paths of Reception," 115–45.
20. See Mealey, *Identity of Christian Morality*, 18.

Saint Paul VI's encyclical *Humanae Vitae* (*HV*). "Revisionists" argued that, while Vatican Council II was indicating the course for a personalistic approach to contemporary moral questions, the teaching of *HV* was based on a physicalist or biological interpretation of natural law.[21] The position of *HV* on one particular case—the means of artificial contraception—has provoked so many reactions that they have, "Become progressively more far-reaching in their implications, even to the point of calling into question the very principles underlying traditional Catholic moral theology."[22] Mahoney suggests that one important reason as to why such a papal directive provoked so much public dissent is the manner in which the encyclical seems to differ from the reconciliatory spirit of the Second Vatican Council.[23]

A major attempt for the renewal of moral theology after Vatican Council II was the so-called "Proportionalism,"[24] a "teleological"[25] system of moral analysis that is opposed to a morality of obligation.[26] Proportionalism "developed, in part, out of several reconsiderations of the principle of double effect."[27] In his essay, "The Hermeneutic Function of the Principle of Double Effect," Peter Knauer went so far as to argue that the principle of double effect "provides the criterion for every moral judgement."[28] The principle of double effect was initially utilized mostly to deal with difficult cases and therefore for a limited specific range of moral situations; however, proportionalism "understood proportionate reason to be relevant to every moral decision."[29] What makes proportionalism such an important factor is

---

21. See Mahoney, *Making of Moral Theology*, 301.

22. Pinckaers, *Morality*, 46.

23. See Mahoney, *Making of Moral Theology*; cited in Gallagher, *Time Past, Time Future*, 223.

24. "Proportionalism" is hardly a term that so-called proportionalists embraced for themselves. See Keenan, *A History of Catholic Moral Theology*, 157.

25. In Greek, *telos* means end; hence the name "teleology" or "teleological ethics".

26. See Pinckaers, *Morality*, 54.

27. Gallagher, *Time Past, Time Future*, 246. The principle of double effect aims to provide specific guidelines for determining circumstances when, "A person may licitly perform an action that he foresees will produce a good and a bad effect provided that four conditions are verified at one and the same time: 1) that the action in itself from its very object be good or at least indifferent; 2) that the good effect and not the evil effect be intended; 3) that the good effect be not produced by means of the evil effect; 4) that there be a proportionately grave reason for permitting the evil effect." Mangan, "An Historical Analysis of the Principle of Double Effect," 43.

28. Knauer, "The Hermeneutic Function," 133.

29. Gallagher, *Time Past, Time Future*, 247.

that it presented itself, "Not just as an element within a moral theory or as a tool of casuistry such as the principles of double effect and totality had been ... but rather ... as [being] in itself a consistent alternative moral theory."[30]

Proportionalism employs moral judgment in the comparing or balancing of the good and evil effects that an action causes in a given situation in relation to the technical, rather than final end pursued. It maintains that no act, "[a]part from acts immediately directed against God or direct involvement in the sin of another, is immoral and sinful by its very nature. The morality of the act must be assessed in relation to its circumstances and end as well."[31]

While proportionalism may be listed among the "teleological" systems of moral analysis, and so a moral theory that opposed moralities of obligations and duties and, therefore, one which favors the reappreciation of the virtues and the importance of friendship in the Christian life, it threatens the Church's teaching on "intrinsically evil acts."[32] The Church's position on "intrinsically evil acts" is presented most clearly in *Veritatis Splendor* (*VS*), the encyclical that Pope Saint John Paul II wrote, at least in part, to safeguard against consequentialist thought in moral theology. Yet, while the truth that some acts are intrinsically evil must be safeguarded, the very notion of "intrinsically evil acts" assumes a morality that focuses more on the analysis of acts and considers less the flourishing of the moral subject. Thus, *VS* also tries to reorient moral theology to its true center: the moral subject who seeks the greater good. The exegesis of the pericope of the rich young man not only introduces the encyclical, but grounds its theological meaning for the renewal of moral theology. As Servais Pinckaers argues, the terminology of intrinsically evil acts emerges in the sixteenth century in the context of a Nominalist moral theology. Aquinas himself, whose moral theology is realist, and therefore grounded in the final human end, reflects on the "nature" of moral acts in view of the subject's ultimate finality. In this regard, he concludes that certain acts are "*per se mala*," because they contradict the law of reason as the order of human flourishing. Aquinas, however,

---

30. Gallagher, *Time Past, Time Future*, 247.

31. Gallagher, *Time Past, Time Future*, 247. On the understanding of the morality of the act, see Pinckaers, "Revisionist Understandings of Actions in the Wake of Vatican II," 236–72.

32. Intrinsically evil acts (*intrinsice mala*) are those acts that by their very nature (*ex objecto*) are immoral, independently of any circumstance or situation such as murder, contraception, the sexual sins against nature (*contra naturam*), rape, incest and fornication.

doesn't use the terminology "intrinsically evil acts," since for Aquinas, what is "intrinsic" to the moral action, what makes an action properly "moral" is the actor's intentionality, with the external action being the "matter" of the truly moral act. Pinckaers adds:

> St Thomas did not believe the distinction between *finis operis* and *finis operantis* necessary for the analysis of the composite parts of morality . . . The end being the proper object of the will, all finality, even external, is led to the voluntary finality and integrated with it when it is taken up in the voluntary action. But later on, a new concept of morality and of action will lead interpreters of St Thomas to consider this separation essential to moral finality.[33]

This is further explained by Martin Rhonheimer who, following Aquinas, defines "moral objects as objects of human actions that are acts of deliberate will."[34]

Even though proportionalism was initially a reaction against the neo-Thomist and neo-scholastic manualists' rigid reliance on the law (understood as being a once and for all articulation of moral truth), it still ended up focusing mostly on particular acts rather than on persons. As James Keenan puts it: "In trying to establish a method for moral judgment as an alternative to the moral manuals, proportionalism was simply the logic of the moral manuals without the overriding absolute norms."[35]

The Magisterium of the Church responded by condemning this methodology, deeming it "Consequentialist."[36] However, the specific moral theologians were not condemned, in the encyclical *VS* promulgated in 1993, a year after the publication of the *Catechism of the Catholic Church* (CCC). The CCC re-establishes the close unity between the moral and the spiritual dimension of the Christian vocation. It provides an overall, well-ordered teaching of Christian doctrine in its entirety, a presentation augmented by constant references to the biblical texts, the Church Fathers, medieval theologians (particularly Saint Thomas Aquinas), modern theologians, and recent documents of the Catholic Church. In "Part Three" the CCC presents the Christian (moral) life as a "Life in Christ."

VS attempts to replicate the approach of the CCC. A main concern of *VS* that it aimed to address was, "The lack of harmony between

---

33. Pinckaers, "A Historical Perspective on Intrinsically Evil Acts," 210.
34. Rhonheimer, "Moral Object," 455.
35. Keenan, *History of Catholic Moral*, 158.
36. See Cessario, *Introduction to Moral Theology*, 31–34.

Friendship in the Process of Renewal of the Theology of the Christian Life

the traditional response of the Church and certain theological positions, encountered even in Seminaries and in Faculties of Theology," [37] and specially to treat the question of "intrinsically evil acts." Another concern was to "renew the weakened link between Catholic moral teaching and the Gospel,"[38] as a result of which the traditionalist (manualist) positions featured strongly on issues of Christian moral life. By taking the question the rich young man makes to Jesus in Mt 19:16—"What good must I do to attain eternal life?"—as its point of departure, *VS* reaffirms the inadequacy of a completely autonomous moral judgement, for "only God can answer the question about what is good, because he is the Good itself."[39] At the same time, however, it is not satisfied to just defend traditionalist positions, proposing a profound renewal of moral theology and offering as one of the main paths a return to the Gospel and to the person of Jesus Christ as its chief source.[40]

Since the promulgation of the CCC and *VS* in particular, the renewal of moral theology has also turned to rediscover and renew the original insights of Thomas Aquinas's ethics and his emphasis on virtue, initiated even before the publication of these documents. In the United States, the revival of virtue ethics was initiated with the works of professors like Stanley Hauerwas[41] and Alasdair MacIntyre in his *After Virtue*, as well as by people like the Belgian-born Dominican theologian Servais Pinckaers.

Indeed, Pinckaers was one of the pioneers who worked for a renewal in the understanding of morality as a whole—a renewal in which virtue, alongside the New Law of the Gospel and grace, stands at the root and center of the entire Christian moral life. In his own attempt to rediscover the insights of Aquinas, Pinckaers emphasizes that since virtue is the departing point for Aquinas's whole moral teaching, it must regain its rightful place in contemporary Thomist interpretations. Pinackaers also insisted, "[o]n the primacy of charity-friendship and of freedom of excellence as an efficacious moral-spiritual motivator and the center of Christian vocation to beatitude, though not without faith, knowledge, natural law, and

---

37. Pinckaers, "An Encyclical for the Future," 13.
38. Pinckaers, "An Encyclical for the Future," 13.
39. John Paul II, *Veritatis Splendor*, par. 9.
40. Pinckaers, "An Encyclical for the Future," 13–14.
41. See Hauerwas, *Character and the Christian Life*; *Community of Character*; *Peaceable kingdom*; and *Toward a Constructive Christian Social Ethic*.

the prudent judgement giving from charity."[42] While the amount of explicit attention to technical examination of virtue in Pinckaers's masterpiece, *The Sources of Christian Ethics*, is somewhat limited, it sets clear pathways for future work on virtue.[43] Furthermore, by presenting the practical necessity of virtue in the Christian life, Pinckaers is also able to carefully re-establish the principle motivator of all human action which is a natural and primordial desire for happiness. Pinckaers reminds us: "For St. Thomas, in the mainstream tradition of Aristotle and the Fathers of the Church, the question of happiness is incontestably the first consideration in Christian moral theology. It is natural to everyone. It points to the question of our last end, which presupposes a certain amount of reflection."[44] It is this reflection, which Pinckaers insists is not "extrinsic" to human action, which orders our actions ultimately to our final end, namely, communion with God through ultimate beatitude.[45]

If moral theologians like Pinckaers cleared the way and laid the groundwork for a full-blown contemporary ethic of virtue, it remained for others, including Jean Porter and Martin Rhonheimer, to sustain the effort for the retrieval of such an ethic in Catholic moral theology. In her book, *The Recovery of Virtue*, Porter clearly and persuasively demonstrates the teleological coherence of Aquinas's ethics and develops a carefully nuanced interpretation of his description of the human good. She also sets out the inter-relationality of natural law and virtue in Thomistic ethics, a topic on which she continues to elaborate in her later work, *Nature as Reason*.[46] There Porter takes a comprehensive approach to moral theology where virtue features prominently. She advances the discussion of virtue with more technical precision.[47] One of Porter's main contributions in *Nature as Reason* is precisely her ability to summarize the distinct, yet close connections, between virtue and natural law, and nature and grace. As she argues:

> A Thomistic account of the natural law takes its teleological focus from an account of happiness, understood as the practice of the

---

42. Titus, "Servais Pinckaers and the Renewal of Moral Theology," 60.

43. See Cloutier and Mattison III, "The Resurgence of Virtue in Recent Moral Theology," 238.

44. Pinckaers, *Sources*, 6.

45. Pinckaers, *Sources*, 12.

46. Porter, *Nature as Reason: A Thomistic Theory of Natural Law*.

47. See Cloutier and Mattison III, "The Resurgence of Virtue in Recent Moral Theology," 244.

virtues. This section clarifies and develops that claim by showing that the relevant conception of happiness is to be identified with the practice of the infused virtues, including faith, hope, and charity as well as the infused cardinal virtues. Thus, the theory of natural law being presented is tethered to an ideal of terrestrial happiness, but the terrestrial happiness in question is directly oriented toward a still more complete form of happiness, which it anticipates in ways we cannot now grasp.[48]

Therefore, for Porter, a key vehicle for working out the relationship of nature and grace is infused cardinal virtues. Her Thomistic articulation of the role of the infused cardinal virtues offers a way to connect the topics of practical reasoning and nature/grace quite explicitly.[49]

Like Porter, Martin Rhonheimer situates moral theology in what he calls "classical" virtue ethics.[50] Perhaps the main contribution of Rhonheimer to a virtue-centered approach to morality is his detailed explanation of human intentional action from the perspective of the acting person, including discussion of how a person's ultimate *telos* functions in relations to more proximate ones.[51] Rhonheimer continues to offer a comprehensive virtue-centered approach to morality and develops extensively the themes that mark the revival of virtue in moral theology, including moral virtues, happiness, practical reasoning and the object of action. There are, of course, many other contemporary discussions in moral theology that can be identified here and that demonstrate the various attempts of renewing moral theology. The examples given above, however, show that fifty years on, the task of renewing moral theology is still an ongoing process.[52]

---

48. Porter, *Nature as Reason*, 396.

49. See Cloutier and Mattison III, "The Resurgence of Virtue in Recent Moral Theology," 246.

50. Rhonheimer, *The Perspective of Morality*, 15.

51. See Rhonheimer, "Perspective," 195–249.

52. Other important contributions to the revival of virtue in contemporary moral theology include, Keenan, *A History of Catholic Moral Theology in the Twentieth Century*; Cessario, *The Moral Virtues and Theological Ethics*; Mattison III, *Introducing Moral Theology*; and Schockenhoff, "Charity," 244–58.

FRIENDSHIP IN A PERSONALISTIC APPROACH TO MORAL THEOLOGY

After the Second Vatican Council, there were crucial attempts for renewing moral theology in its fundamental aspect. Foremost among these attempts, one finds the turn to the resurgence of virtue, the relation between moral reflection and the communion ecclesiology reflected in the Council, and a new person-in-relationship, known as "personalism." A personalistic approach to moral theology is inspired by personalism, a philosophical thought that focuses on the reality of personhood, be it human, angelic or divine.[53] Reason and experience are the foundations of "personalism," which itself focuses on the categorical distinction between persons and all other non-personal beings. From an historical point of view, however, personalism has nearly always been accompanied by biblical theism and insights drawn from revelation.[54] The many strands of personalistic thought arose as a reaction to the dominant dehumanizing forces of determinism and materialism in the nineteenth century, and particularly against collectivism on the one hand and individualism on the other.

Personalism can also be applied to other disciplines, including "theological personalism," and its inversion, namely, "personalistic theology." In the twentieth century, personalistic thought was gradually integrated into the philosophical and the theological works of various Catholic authors, including Jacques Maritain (*The Person and the Common Good*), Étienne Gilson (*L'esprit de la philosophie medieval*), Robert Spaemann (*Personen: Verisuche über de Unterschied zwischen "etwas" und "jemand*), Karol Wojtyla (*Love and Responsibility*), and Hans Urs von Balthasar (*On the Concept of Person*). Gilson traces theological personalism back to the mediaeval period when he observes that Thomas Aquinas saw the uniqueness of human persons among other beings by virtue of their reason and their self-mastery.[55] On the same line of thought, Karol Wojtyla, later Saint John Paul II, forms the essentials of his personalistic theology grounded in Thomas Aquinas. Although Aquinas was unfamiliar with the problem of personalism, Wojtyla contends, one can speak of "Thomistic personalism," a moral theory which focuses on the singularity, irreducibility and subjectivity of

---

53. See von Balthasar, "On the Concept of Person," 24.
54. See Williams, "What is Thomistic Personalism?," 164.
55. See Gilson, *L'esprit de la philosophie medieval*, 195–215; cf. Aquinas, *ST* I.29.1.

Friendship in the Process of Renewal of the Theology of the Christian Life

personhood.[56] Hans Urs von Balthasar wrote so much on the concept of personhood. He notes: "Few words have as many layers of meaning as *person*. On the surface it means just any human being, any countable individual. Its deeper senses, however, point to the individual's uniqueness which cannot be interchanged and therefore cannot be counted."[57] The subjectivity of the person forms the basis of the moral life, through which the person is the author of his own actions (self-determination). The person's power of self-determination then explains the non-transferability of personhood.

At the heart of personalistic moral theology lies the dignity of the human person.[58] The dignity of the human person requires that human persons are never to be treated merely as a means but as ends in themselves.[59] Human persons are likewise to be loved for their own sake. This affirmation echoes Aquinas's treatise on *caritas* which is friendship with God. In the *ST* Aquinas explains that man is to be loved with "love of friendship:" "that which is loved with the 'love of friendship' is love simply and for itself."[60] To love with "love of friendship" is also to affirm the subjectivity and irreducibility of the human person. Likewise, to make friends is to find out each other's value, to enjoy the company of the other and to wish and work for the flourishing of the other. Therefore, one may state that a proper theology of friendship can be in harmony with a moral theology centered on the human person and also may contribute to it.

Since personalism insists on the value and on the flourishing of the human person, paradoxically, at times it might be viewed, as giving too much emphasis to the individual, and in this, as being incompatible with the Christian emphasis on justice and the common good.[61] While it is specifically contemporary Catholic social thought that foregrounds the common good, it also plays an important role in the thought of Thomas Aquinas, when he speaks of the common good as the proper end of the

---

56. See Wojtyla, "Thomistic Personalism," 165–75.

57. Von Balthasar, "On the Concept of Person," 18.

58. Von Balthasar claims that "if one distinguishes between *individual* and *person* (and we should for the sake of clarity), then a special dignity is ascribed to the person, which the individual as such does not possess. We see this in the animal kingdom where there are many individuals but not persons." Von Balthasar, "On the Concept of Person," 18.

59. Wojtyla designated this maxim the "pesonalistic principle" or "personalistic norm". Wojtyla, *Love and Responsibility*, 21–44.

60. Aquinas, *ST* II.26.4.

61. See Porter, "The Common Good in Thomas Aquinas," 94–120.

political rule and of God as common good of all creation.[62] Aquinas reconciles the individual and the communal good by claiming that the good of the individual is always to be found in the community. Jean Porter expressed a similar reflection: "The highest natural good of the individual consists in participation in a just society."[63] And it is here where friendship can relate, and indeed contribute, to a more personalistic approach in moral reflection.

In friendship, "The good of each is truly the other's good and so, in seeking the good of the friend, one's own good is achieved. But this self-fulfillment involves no subversive seeking of self; it is simply the by-product of the friend's happiness."[64] Friendship is not an excuse for turning one's back upon most of the world, but can be a model for the way every human person might be appreciated.[65] In friendship the friend becomes what Karl Barth suggests: "a model of the neighbor."[66] Friendship, thus, provides the context for a just society and upholds that the person's happiness and self-fulfillment is only to be found within a community. As Saint John Henry Newman puts it: "The best preparation for loving the world at large, and loving it duly and wisely, is to cultivate an intimate friendship and affection towards those who are immediately about us."[67] This idea of happiness and self-fulfillment brings together the concepts of community and action. Aquinas recognizes that moral action takes place in the context of relationship and community and that the "love of friendship" serves as a basis from which to perform moral actions.[68] A personalistic approach to moral theology rightly understood—as in friendship—is what constitutes the flourishing of the human person; it is not self-gratification but reciprocal self-gift and love. Given the incommunicability of the human person, no doctrine of love suffices if it sees "the neighbor" in merely abstract and generalized terms. Self-gift and love need to be specifically directed to actual persons, just as God's love for each human person is partial and concrete since, "It singles out the particular . . . from the general mass of humanity and gives its contemplative 'attention' to the particular person who is at this moment

---

62. See Aquinas, *ST* II–II.58.7.
63. Porter, *Recovery*, 51.
64. Schneiders, *Written that you may believe*, 194.
65. See Oppenheimer, *The Hope of Happiness*, 118–21.
66. Barth, *Ethics*, 189.
67. Newman, "Love of Relations and Friends," Sermon 5.
68. See Aquinas, *ST* I–II.4.8; Gallagher, "The Will and Its Acts," 84.

in front of it."[69] Schneiders sees in Jesus's command to love one's friends unto death in John 15:13 a potential of friendship for the enrichment of the human person—"to die that a friend might live is to live in a transcendent way."[70] According to her, while it may be heroic to die for another, "It is only genuine service if the other is truly another self, a friend, for in this case the gift of one's life is experienced as an enrichment rather than as an impoverishment of oneself."[71]

A central category in personalistic moral theology is indeed the person's call to communion/friendship. As Pope John Paul II said during a General Audience on 24 November 1999, the human person is "a 'being for others' in interpersonal communion." Although our call to interpersonal communion, or friendship, is a natural inclination, its deepest explanation is found only in our heart, in our spiritual nature, particularly by virtue of our being created in the image and after the likeness of God, who is himself a community of persons (*communio personarum*).[72] Friendship is a gratuitous, reciprocal divine gift, an undeserved and unmerited privilege of souls whose self-possession enables them to offer themselves to the others, as Maritain contends: "Personality, in its essence, requires a dialogue in which souls really communicate."[73] Seen in this perspective, therefore, friendship can perfectly relate to the current attempt for moral theology to become more focused on the person because in friendship personhood is preserved as it is transcended. Martin D'Arcy also highlights the relation between friendship and personhood. D'Arcy notes that when Christianity awakens a "new reverence for personality and the glory which it possesses it awakens a new appreciation for friendship."[74] On the other hand, a moral theology that claims to be person-centered, but ignores friendship, would remain incomplete.

---

69. Carmichael, *Friendship*, 175.
70. Schneiders, *Written that you may believe*, 194.
71. Schneiders, *Written that you may believe*, 194.
72. See Williams, "What is Thomistic Personalism?," 195.
73. Maritain, *The Person and the Common Good*, 40.
74. D'Arcy, *The Mind and Heart of Love*, 153.

FRIENDSHIP AND CHARACTER FORMATION IN VIRTUE

Virtue plays an important role in the history of Catholic moral theology, especially in the ascetical tradition, and in the patristic and the medieval periods.[75] As elaborated above, virtue is the key organizing principle in Thomas Aquinas's treatment of morality in the *Secunda Pars* of the *ST*.[76] This prominence receded, even if it did not disappear completely, after Nominalism and a more deontological turn in the late Middle Ages and in Modernity. After Vatican Council II called for renewal in moral theology, virtue is once again becoming increasingly central in recent Catholic moral theology.[77]

A virtue-centered morality differs in many ways from a typical modern moral theory based on precepts and laws "not simply by adding a focus on character, but by challenging the whole pattern of looking at the Christian moral life implied by standard theories of evaluation centered on either (Kantian) rules or (utilitarian) consequences."[78] It focuses on human identity and what the human is called to become, rather than on what to do when faced with specific moral dilemmas. In line with the theology of the *imago Dei*, a morality focusing on character formation in virtue attempts to resurge the kind of synthesis that Thomas Aquinas succeeds to adopt between the virtues and the natural law written on human hearts. According to the theology of the *imago Dei*, human beings are created in the image of God and are called to embark on a never-ending process of transformation into his likeness. Likewise, a morality centered on character formation in virtue sees the Christian (moral) life as a journey towards perfection, authentic self-realization, and ultimately beatitude—even amidst difficulties encountered in a world marred by sin and suffering.[79]

---

75. See Cloutier and Mattison III, "The Resurgence of Virtue in Recent Moral Theology," 228.

76. Porter attempts to provide a reconstruction of Thomas Aquinas's theology of virtue in order, she writes, "to restore a basis for common conversation in the field of Christian ethics." Porter, *The Recovery of Virtue*, 16.

77. See Cloutier and Mattison III, "The Resurgence of Virtue in Recent Moral Theology," 230.

78. Cloutier and Mattison III, "The Resurgence of Virtue in Recent Moral Theology," 230–31.

79. See Pieper, *Four Cardinal Virtues*.

Friendship in the Process of Renewal of the Theology of the Christian Life

Following Augustine and the tradition, Thomas Aquinas defines virtue as a good operative habit.[80] Virtues belong to the inner part of the human person, are expressed in concrete actions, mature and help in the formation of the character. Persons are not born with a ready-made collection of virtues; these are acquired through the repetitive practice of good deeds that become habitual. Neither do persons learn the practice of virtues by themselves; they acquire them from imitating the early examples they find in their family, their community, and their social environment. The Christian tradition speaks also of the "infused" or "supernatural" virtues, which are given in the power of the Holy Spirit who makes us more inclined to act in conformity to God's action and being of love.

The learning and practice of virtues correspond to man's natural inclination to life in society. Yet, the true reason is to be found in man's spiritual nature of reason and personhood. Pinckaers attributes the deepest foundation for man's inclination to life in society to man's "need for friendship, affection, or love."[81] Now, since as Aristotle's claims, friendship is "a virtue or implies a virtue",[82] it is a natural inclination and reflects the best of human nature. This makes of friendship a foundational category of human nature. But as Aquinas contends, friendship is also *caritas*,[83] that is, an infused theological virtue. Friendship, therefore, understood as excellence in human relations and excellence in spiritual life, can also be understood as a foundational category for the Christian moral and spiritual life.

According to Pinckaers, friendship as a virtue, "clearly transcends the order of material usefulness."[84] For him, it is within the theme of friendship that the radical relationship of one person to another is intended, so as to fulfil the biblical command to love the neighbor as oneself. Indeed, "because of our spiritual nature, we are inclined to unite with one another in love or friendship. It is a primordial desire, at the source of every community and society."[85]

In friendship, what begins in the natural life of man is perfected supernaturally in Jesus Christ. Indeed, true friendship flows down to man through the incarnation of Jesus Christ. As a result, man is then capable of

---

80. See Aquinas, *ST* I–II.55.3.
81. Pinckaers, *Sources*, 433.
82. Aristotle, *NE* 1155a3–4.
83. Aquinas, *ST* II–II.23.1.
84. Pinckaers, *Sources*, 433.
85. Pinckaers, *Sources*, 433.

expressing true friendship to others and to God himself. The perfecting of friendship begins in this earthly life and is consummated in the afterlife. By opening ourselves to others in friendship we discover who we really are and who we are called to become. As Saint John Henry Newman contends: friendship is a "special *test* of our virtue."[86] Friendship, therefore, unites the "natural" with the "supernatural"; it is rooted in Holy Scripture, theology and spirituality, and can therefore also be understood as contributing to the task of the renewal of moral theology.

FRIENDSHIP IN COMMUNION ECCLESIOLOGY

Friendship also has the potential to help moral theology become more deeply integrated into the ecclesiology of communion called for by Vatican Council II and in so doing, even to strengthen unity-in-difference within the Church. Indeed, the ecclesiology of communion is the central and fundamental idea of the documents of Vatican Council II.[87] In Christianity, various expressions are used to describe the identity of the Church; some of these include: the People of God, the mystical Body of Christ, the Temple of the Holy Spirit, the Communion of Saints, and the Bride of Christ. Yet, the Church may also be described as a "Community of Friends". This possibility is offered and enabled by the ongoing promise of John 15:15. Jürgen Moltman notes that Jesus calls his disciples into "the new life of friendship" in John 15:15 because he [Jesus] considers friendship as "the highest form of love," that which "leads to actually risking one's life to protect a friend."[88] Moltmann contends that it is Jesus's love for his disciples "to the end" (John 13:1) that makes it possible for the disciples to "[r]emain in the circle of his friendship . . . keep his commandments and become friends to one another."[89] On the basis of his love for the disciples Jesus commands them to love one another just as he has loved them (see John 15:12). This command is the result of "the abundance of . . . Christological friendship—an intimate, transformative relation that enabled the disciples to receive this new commandment."[90] As argued above, Jesus's love for his

---

86. Newman, *Spiritual Writings*, 43.

87. See Ouellet, "The Ecclesiology of Communion, 50 Years after the Opening of Vatican II."

88. Moltmann, *Church*, 117.

89. Moltmann, *Church*, 117.

90. Gregor, "Friends and Neighbors," 939.

disciples is beautifully depicted when analyzed in terms of friendship. Now, when Jesus calls his disciples friends, he also calls them to be friends with one another. This results in the "community of the disciples" being also a "community of friends" by the power of the Spirit.

The church's potential of being a "Community of Friends" is formed by the communion of the Triune God, who is the ultimate communion of persons (*communio personarum*) in a relationship of perfect love. The French theologian Henri de Lubac stresses this analogy: "The Church is a mysterious extension of the Trinity into time, which not only prepares us for a life of unity but allows us already to participate in it."[91] The Triune nature of God in a relationship of perfect love has implications for the relationality within communion ecclesiology, as Orthodox theologian John Zizioulas reflects:

> There is no other model for the proper relation between communion and otherness either for the Church or for the human being than the trinitarian God. If the Church wants to be faithful to her true self, she must try to mirror the communion and otherness that exists in the Triune God. The same is true of the human beings as the "image of God". What can we learn about communion and otherness from study of the Trinity? First, otherness is constitutive of unity. God is not first One and then Three, but simultaneously One and Three. God's oneness or unity is not safeguarded by the unity of substance, as St. Augustine and other western theologians have argued, but by the *monarchia* of the Father. It is also expressed through the unbreakable *koinonia* (community) that exists between the three Persons, which means that otherness is not a threat to unity, but the *sine qua non* of unity.[92]

The two aspects of interest for friendship in communion ecclesiology in this quotation are: "affirming the implications of Trinitarian unity in the bond of love between the three persons, whilst noting that communion is not threatened by the otherness of those three persons, the unity of divine three is in fact enabled by their otherness. Because, as Vatican Council II teaches, there exists "a certain likeness" between the unity of the Triune God and the unity of "God's sons in truth and love,"[93] by affirming the otherness in the person, friendship enables unity-in-diversity in the ecclesial community.

91. De Lubac, *The Church: Paradox and Mystery*, 49.
92. Zizioulas, "Communion and Otherness."
93. Vatican II, *Gaudium et Spes*, par. 24.

LOVE OF FRIENDSHIP IN THE CHRISTIAN LIFE

As noted previously, Aquinas believes that when one loves with the "love of friendship," the lover renders the other a reflection of the self.[94] What greater unity could the church express than when its members consider the other as a reflection of the self? The unity drawn from friendship within the church serves as a practical expression of the nature of the ecclesial community. Charles Pinches affirms that, "the Christian is a Christian in the Church; in an important way he or she does not know what it means to be a Christian—indeed, cannot be a Christian—apart from the community of friends who together form one another into selves who reflect the image of their God."[95] For this unity to be realized, the ecclesial community needs to be a living witness of friendship in everyday, ordinary life. A Russian Orthodox priest, Pavel Florensky, beautifully writes about this truth of unity:

> *Philía* knows a friend not by his outward pose, not by the dress of heroism, but by his smile, by his quiet talk, by his weaknesses, by how he treats people in ordinary human life, by how he eats and sleeps . . . the true test of a soul's authenticity is through life together, in the love of friends . . .[96]

Friendship "is rooted in the love of God himself and takes on an ecclesial dimension, extending to all in desire and intention."[97] Friendship is ultimately an ecclesial practice giving people a sense of personhood that can be lived in unity without hindering the individuality, the otherness of each person; it plays a responsible role in forming new civilizations based on humanizing love for all.[98] Members of the ecclesial community are indeed called to invite others to friendship with God because "those who love God . . . work hard to see him loved by others."[99] The ecclesial community needs to work not only for the enrichment of its members but also for the perfection of the whole of God's creation. By living together as a "Community of Friends" the church also demonstrates that friendship is providential in that it participates in the divine plan for each person. On the example of Jesus, the "Community of Friends" ought to be a living entity that helps

---

94. See Aquinas, *ST* I–II.28.1.
95. Pinches, "Friendship and Tragedy," 42–43.
96. Florensky, *The Pillar and Ground of the Truth*, 314.
97. Pinckaers, *Sources*, 434.
98. See Moser and Leers, *Moral Theology*, 165.
99. Preca, *The Watch*, 52–53.

Friendship in the Process of Renewal of the Theology of the Christian Life

people complete an arduous journey towards our heavenly Father, the *summum bonum*.

FRIENDSHIP IN PERSONAL, FAMILY, ECONOMIC AND SOCIO-POLITICAL ETHICS: VERY BRIEF CONSIDERATIONS

The task of renewing "fundamental moral theology" also includes a mode of approaching "special moral theology"; this is because friendship, as an important category in the renewal of moral theology in its fundamental aspect, even affects our understanding of particular moral questions relating to personal, economic, socio-political and family ethics.

The kind of friendship that comes to the fore in Thomas Aquinas's exegesis of the Fourth Gospel plays an important role in the pursuit for justice. According to Aquinas, the goal of Jesus's words and deeds during the Last Supper is to bring about *caritas*,[100] and in the perspective of this *caritas*, to establish friendship (*fundari amicitiam*) among his disciples. The circle of friends was to keep growing because Jesus laid down his life for all humanity, even for those who at present are still his enemies.[101] Aquinas defines justice as that virtue which impels us to give to the other that which is due to him.[102] A definite, constant determination to give everyone their due as our equals, "justice is the virtue proper to life in society."[103] The golden rule in Matthew 7:12 suggests that justice is not a private affair; it suggests that human rights are not private property but rather imply reciprocity. What people demand as their right, they must also recognize and respect as the right of others. This sense of justice seeks the equality of all, with no distinction of person or class, no discrimination on grounds of gender, race, or national origin, because human dignity is something that belongs to everyone.

Friendship is the paradigmatic way by which a person comes to know what it means to "give to the other that which is due to him." As Wadell notes: "It is by learning how to seek the good of another in friendship that we gradually acquire the skill to act rightly toward every person with whom we come into contact, respecting their dignity, acknowledging their rights,

---

100. See Aquinas, *ST* II–II.24.2.
101. See Aquinas, *Ioannis* 15.2.2009.
102. See Aquinas, *ST* II–II.58.1.
103. Pinckaers, *Sources*, 434.

and fulfilling the responsibilities toward them."[104] In their living together, Christian friends "engage humanity in partnership to renew the earth and establish justice," creating in it "an attitude of profound friendship toward all."[105]

This implies that justice does not reach its full potential "until it succeeds in creating friendship at various levels of society, ranging from personal and familial friendship to friendship in the political and social spheres."[106] Once friendships are established, persons will no longer speak solely in terms of justice but can live together in freedom, freedom of being other. Aristotle says, "Between friends there is no need for justice, but people who are just still need the quality of friendship; and, indeed, friendliness is considered to be justice in the fullest sense. It is not only a necessary thing but a splendid one."[107]

To be a person implies not simply the right to be different from others but the freedom to be oneself. However, in friendship the person comes to perceive that freedom does not mean freedom "from the other" but freedom "for the other." When friendships among human beings cease, respect for the otherness of people, and for what is not human diminishes. Commenting on the integral and integrating vision of God's creation, Pope Francis explains in *Laudato Si'* that as persons, human beings cannot care for the rest of creation if their "hearts lack tenderness, compassion and concern for their fellow human beings."[108]

Friendships indeed renew and enrich mutual relationships at personal and social levels because friends seek the good of others for the others' sake. A shared vision of the good within a community or a society can only come about if that community is constructed on the basis of the bond of friendship. As MacIntyre contends:

> The application of [a] measure [of human goodness] in a community whose shared aim is the realisation of the human good presupposes . . . a wide range of agreement in that community on goods and virtues, and it is this agreement which makes possible

---

104. Wadell, *Becoming Friends*, 153.

105. Johnson, *She Who Is*, 218.

106. Pinckaers, *Sources*, 434. Contra Gilbert Meilaender who pictures friendship as an exclusive relationship that always represents a potential conflict with the impersonality that justice requires. See Meilaender, *Friendship: A Study in Theological Ethics*, 77.

107. Aristotle, *NE* 1155a24–b8.

108. Francis, *Laudato Si'*, chap. 2 par. 1.

Friendship in the Process of Renewal of the Theology of the Christian Life

> the kind of bond between citizens which, on Aristotle's view, constitutes a polis. That bond is the bond of friendship . . . which enables a shared recognition of and pursuit of a good.[109]

According to MacIntyre, friendship seems to be indispensable for the good life of man within a society or community. For him, there is in fact no possibility of community without the bond of friendship and its shared view for the good. Friendship is, according to MacIntyre, "the foundation of the very project of constructing a [moral] community."[110]

The culture of individualism present in our contemporary western life promotes the need for self-disclosure.[111] Since in friendship the emphasis is always on the other and not on the self, it can help us to constantly look beyond our individual and immediate selfish desires. Todd May sees in what he calls "deep friendship"—a relationship between equals that is characterized by trust—a potential, at least in some of its forms, to undermine what, according to him, is the result of today's dominant individualist, capitalist and neo-liberal economic, political, and social structures. The central principle of neo-liberalism, as May understands it, is that "an unfettered capitalist market is the best and most efficient way for an economy to run."[112] In a capitalist and in a neo-liberal economy, the only stakeholders are the consumer and the businessperson. The consumer is simply a person for whom "buying is a central part of [his] sense of who [he] is," while the businessperson is someone who sees his successful life in terms of a "calculative self-enhancement" while considering consumers a "means for personal gain."[113] According to May, in a capitalist and a neo-liberal economy, both the consumer and the businessperson are selfish: the former aims to gain immediate pleasure by satisfying his immediate desire while the latter works for the future pleasure of being rich. His conclusion is that friendship can provide a training ground for solidarity movements with the potential to undermine the dominance of a capitalist and a neo-liberal modern society.

Then there is "Family Life," so full of experiences and challenges. Pope Francis considers the current experiences and challenges of families in his recent post-synodal Apostolic Exhortation on Love in the Family

---

109. MacIntyre, *After Virtue*, 146.
110. MacIntyre, *After Virtue*, 146–47.
111. See Konstan, *Friendship*, 14–15.
112. May, *Friendship in an Age of Economics*, 4.
113. May, *Friendship in an Age of Economics*, 32, 42.

Amoris Laetitia (*AL*). Particularly, the Pope notes that rampant individualism makes it difficult today for a person to give oneself generously to another.[114] From a theological perspective, these challenges are part the result of sin, which corrupts human will and desires.[115] Because of sin human beings sometimes find themselves choosing things opposed to their true good.[116] God created man as male and female; he created them in his image and after his likeness, with equality and dignity.[117] However, the "Fall of Man" as narrated in the Book of Genesis, overturns this objective order established by God in creation.[118] Human beings assumed the role of their creator. Rather than awaiting the reception of divinity as a divine gift that would have made them like obedient children before their loving God, thus receiving the sharing in divine relationship as God's gift, humanity chose to grasp at divinity.[119] This resulted in a rupture in the relationship between humanity and God, among human beings themselves, and also between human beings and God's entire creation. To attain some perceived good, sinful human beings are inclined to reduce the intrinsic value of others and to seek to dominate them.

Pope Francis reiterates the effects of sin in marital relationships as narrated in the Book of Genesis when he writes that the family has been confronted with sin from the beginning, when the relationship of love turned into domination.[120] Likewise, Lemmons writes:

> Genesis 3:16 is quite explicit that some penalties of Original Sin are gender-specific, affecting even the spousal union of love; "Your desire shall be for your husband, and he shall rule over you." In other words, Original Sin left woman with the desire to close her love in upon her husband and make him the lord, while Original Sin left men with the desire to dominate women. Yielding to either desire is the wellspring of all gender sins—even in today's world.[121]

---

114. See Francis, *AL*, par. 33.

115. By virtue of the Fall as narrated in the Book of Genesis, the powers of human nature are weakened, and human beings are "subject to ignorance, suffering, and the domination of death; and inclined to sin." Catechism, I.2.418.

116. See Romans 7:15.

117. See Genesis 1:26–31.

118. See Genesis 3:1–8.

119. See Catechism, I.2.398.

120. See Francis *AL*, par. 19.

121. Lemmons, "Equality, Gender, and John Paul II," 115.

Domination and unhealthy submission can hinder the enduring union of love and the very realization of successful marriages.[122] Because domination "arises from, expresses, and reinforces inequality,"[123] it is also totally foreign to friendship. Friendship indeed upholds equality and, thus, friendship between spouses, or spousal-friendship, realizes the pure ideal of marriage, and facilitates the growth and the flourishing of the deeper expression of love towards which marriage is ordered, namely, betrothed love.[124]

Spousal-friendship is a special kind of friendship that exists between a man and a woman who commit themselves to love each other in the relationship of marriage. The importance of spousal-friendship in marriage is present in the whole Christian tradition. At times, however, it is overshadowed by the definition of marriage in terms of its end as an institution necessary for society. Such a definition tends to not only widen the scope of the relational, even societal, nature of marriage, but also to eclipse its essential nature as friendship in body and soul, reflecting not only the complete mutual self-giving of Trinitarian love, but the love of Christ for his Church.[125] In marriage, a man and a woman, even as symbol of the *telos* of humanity, are called to pursue growth in virtue toward an ideal of flourishing, not just individually, but together, in body and soul. Augustine acknowledges the importance friendship has in marriage as in any other relationship:

> Friendship perishing, there will be preserved in the mind the bonds neither of marriage, nor of kindreds and relations; because in these also there is assuredly a friendly union of sentiment. Spouse therefore will not be able to love spouse in turn, inasmuch as each believes not the other's love, because the love itself cannot be seen.[126]

Augustine speaks of the three goods of Christian marriage, namely *proles* (the procreation and education of children), *fides* (the fidelity of the spouses), and *sacramentum* (the sacredness and preserving commitment of marriage until death).[127] He also holds, however, that the "very essence of

---

122. "The vocation to marriage is written in the very nature of man and woman as they came from the hand of the Creator." Catechism, II.2.1603.

123. Schneiders, *Written that you may believe*, 194.

124. See Walz, "Marriage," 5–6.

125. See Aquinas, *ST* III.65.3.

126. Augustine, *Concerning Faith of Things Not Seen*, vol. 3.

127. Augustine generally considered procreation as the principal, yet not the sole,

the institution of marriage is a unique kind of loving friendship."[128] Indeed, Augustine classifies marriage as a form of friendship:

> Forasmuch as each man is a part of the human race, and human nature is something social, and has for a great and natural good, the power also of friendship; on this account God willed to create all men out of one, in order that they might be held in their society not only by likeness of kind, but also by bond of kindred. Therefore, the first natural bond of human society is man and wife. Nor did God create these each by himself and then join them together as alien by birth; He created the one out of the other, setting a sign also of the power of the union in the side, whence she was drawn, was formed. For they are joined one to another side by side, who walk together, and look together whither they walk. Then follows the connection of fellowship in children, which is the one alone worthy fruit, not of the union of male and female, but of the sexual intercourse. For it were possible that there should exist in either sex, even without such intercourse, a certain friendly and true union of the one ruling, and the other obeying.[129]

In his discussion of marriage, Aquinas relies heavily both on Augustine and on Aristotle.[130] Aquinas speaks of the three goods of marriage

---

purpose of marriage, part of the reason being the justification of sexual intercourse in marriage. As Augustine puts it, "Propagation of children, therefore, is in fact the primary, natural and legitimate purpose of marriage." Augustine, *On Adulterous Marriages*, 2.12; see Fullam, "Toward a Virtue Ethics of Marriage," 668. Fidelity refers to more than the physical or sexual monogamy of the spouses. As Fullam continues to explain, "it also implies a self-sacrificial concern for the partner's salvation as well." Augustine uses *fides* in both the narrow sense of sexual exclusivity and the broader sense "to indicate wholehearted devotion to one's spouse . . . that hews closer to the framing metaphor of friendship with which Augustine begins his treatise on marriage." Fullam, "Toward a Virtue Ethics of Marriage," 673–75.

128. Burt argues that the sacred aspect of the marital goods is a reflection of the eternal love of God which we will not experience first-hand until we have reached heaven. He writes that, "Marriage is a sacred sign (*sacrametnum*) because the permanent fidelity of the husband and wife reflects the unending love which will exist in its fullness only in the heavenly city." Burt, *Augustine's World*, 85; see Augustine, *On the Good of Marriage*, 32.

129. Augustine, *On the Good of Marriage*, 1.

130. Aquinas's treatment of marriage is found in the *SCG* and in the Supplement to the *ST*. The latter was compiled after Aquinas's death from his *Commentary on the Sentences*, which was written about 1252 to 1256 when Aquinas was 27 to 31 years old. At the end of the *Summa*, therefore, we have some of his earliest thoughts on the subject of marriage. See Fullam, "Toward a Virtue Ethics of Marriage," 677.

identified by Augustine, but his main concern is to define the nature of marriage itself. Aquinas describes marriage first and foremost as a kind of partnership: "since by marriage certain persons are directed to one begetting and upbringing of children, and again to one *vita domestica*, it is clear that in matrimony there is a joining."[131]

Aquinas recognizes the importance of friendship in marriage. In fact, he argues against the inequality created by polygamy not only on the basis of natural law and indeed, justice, but also on the grounds that marriage is a kind of friendship:

> Besides, friendship consists in an equality. So, if it is not lawful for the wife to have several husbands, since this is contrary to certainty as to offspring, it would not be lawful, on the other hand, for a man to have several wives, for the friendship of wife for husband would not be free, but somewhat servile. And this argument is corroborated by experience, for among husbands having plural wives the wives have a status like that of servants. Furthermore, strong friendship is not possible in regard to many people, as is evident from the Philosopher in Ethics VIII. Therefore, if a wife has but one husband, but the husband has several wives, the friendship will not be equal on both sides. So, the friendship will not be free, but servile in some way.[132]

---

131. Aquinas, *ST* Supplement 44.1.

132. Aquinas, *SCG* III.124.4. In the *ST* Aquinas argues that polygamy only contradicts human nature as reasonable, not as "animalistic." Therefore, in effect polygamy goes against justice and, of course, the gift of grace that is sacramental marriage: "Now marriage has for its principal end the begetting and rearing of children, and this end is competent to man according to his generic nature, wherefore it is common to other animals (see *NE* 8.12), and thus it is that the 'offspring' is assigned as a marriage good. But for its secondary end, as the Philosopher says (see *NE* 8.12), it has, among men alone, the community of works that are a necessity of life, as stated above (*ST* Supplement 41.1). And in reference to this they owe one another 'fidelity' which is one of the goods of marriage. Furthermore, it has another end, as regards marriage between believers, namely the signification of Christ and the Church: and thus the 'sacrament' is said to be a marriage good. Wherefore the first end corresponds to the marriage of man inasmuch as he is an animal: the second, inasmuch as he is a man; the third, inasmuch as he is a believer. Accordingly, plurality of wives neither wholly destroys nor in any way hinders the first end of marriage, since one man is sufficient to get children of several wives, and to rear the children born of them. But though it does not wholly destroy the second end, it hinders it considerably for there cannot easily be peace in a family where several wives are joined to one husband, since one husband cannot suffice to satisfy the requisitions of several wives, and again because the sharing of several in one occupation is a cause of strife: thus 'potters quarrel with one another' (Aristotle, *Rhetoric* 2.4), and in like manner the several wives of one husband. The third end, it removes altogether, because as

Furthermore, for Aquinas, it is friendship which enables indissolubility in marriage:

> The greater that friendship is, the more solid and long-lasting will [the marriage] be. Now, there seems to be the greatest friendship between husband and wife, for they are united not only in the act of fleshly union, which produces a certain gentle association even among beasts, but also in the partnership of the whole range of domestic activity.[133]

In his encyclical *Casti Connubii*, Pope Pius XI hints at the importance of friendship in marriage when he writes that the mutual perfection of spouses is "the chief reason and purpose of matrimony, provided matrimony be looked at not in the restricted sense as instituted for the proper conception and education of the child, but more widely as the blending of life as a whole and the mutual interchange and sharing thereof."[134]

From the perspective of virtue ethics, the language of *Casti Connubii* on the "mutual perfection" of spouses offers the potential to explore marriage as a friendship of mutual formation in virtue.[135] Friendship between spouses can foster spousal relationship in two ways: first, it affirms the dignity of each spouse and, thus, "excludes the possibility of treating the person as a means to an end and as an object of use;"[136] secondly, it helps to strengthen spousal relationships into enduring ones. When the husband and the wife are also friends to each other, they do not dominate and possess each other because their good is mutual respect and dignity. Commenting on the importance of mutual respect between spouses, Pope Francis contends that when "a couple can come up with a shared and lasting life project, they can love one another and lives as one until death do them

---

Christ is one, so also is the Church one. It is therefore evident from what has been said that plurality of wives is in a way against the law of nature, and in a way not against it." Aquinas, *ST* Supplement 61.1.

133. Aquinas, *SCG* III.123.6.

134. Pius XI, *Casti Connubii*, par. 11.

135. Pope Francis writes that "marriage . . . entails a dynamic process..., one which advances gradually with the progressive integration of the gifts of God." Francis, *AL*, par. 122. For a specific treatment of the sacramental character of Christian marriage in the sense of "one-of-seven," see Rahner, "Marriage as a Sacrament," 351–66; Kasper, "The Sacramental Dignity of Marriage," 340–50; Caffarra, "Marriage as a Reality in the Order of Creation and Marriage as a Sacrament," 166–80; Salzman, "Friendship, Sacrament, and Marriage," 115–24.

136. Wojtyla, *Love and Responsibility*, 30.

part, enjoying and enriching intimacy."[137] Once mutual respect is perceived and becomes the normative response of both husband and wife in relation to each other, then their natural response—pursuing the good of the other for the other's sake—becomes their mutual growth in virtue. In this way, friendship can become the medium for the flourishing of spouses and can facilitate that flourishing through mutual help.[138] The spouses accept the risks of suffering in advance and consider them as opportunities for self-sacrifice and purification on the way to self-transcendence.

The *Catechism of the Catholic Church*, by referring to the encyclical *Familiaris Consortio*, identifies the formational character of marriage:

> Conjugal love involves a totality, in which all the elements of the person enter—appeal of the body and instinct, power of feeling and affectivity, aspiration of the spirit and of will. It aims at a deeply personal unity a unity that, beyond union in one flesh, leads to forming one heart and soul.[139]

Conjugal love is directed to a "deeply personal unity" that leads to the formation of "one heart and soul." One of the effects of friendship is that the person discovers more of himself as he discovers more of the other. By its nature, friendship moves the friend into a deeper union "toward a depth of intimacy in which it is free to express love in vulnerability as is needed in the exchange of deeply personal love."[140] In this way, friendship between spouses can enhance the marital relationship and facilitates the personal unity, a characteristic of conjugal love. Pope Francis forcefully stresses the fact that conjugal love by its very nature defines the partners in a richly encompassing and lasting union,[141] precisely within that "mixture of enjoyment and struggles, tensions and response, pain and relief, satisfactions and longings, annoyances and pleasures" which indeed make up a marriage.[142]

Yet, perhaps a greater potential of friendship in a spousal relationship is that it facilitates the distinctive expression of love in marriage, namely, betrothed love. The decisive character of betrothed love:

---

137. Francis, *AL*, par. 163.
138. See Waltz, "Marriage," 45–52.
139. Catechism, II.2.1643.
140. Walz, "Marriage," 35.
141. See Francis, *AL*, par. 123.
142. Francis, *AL*, par. 126.

> . . . is the giving of one's own person [to another]. The essence of betrothed love is self-giving, the surrender of one's 'I'. This is something different from and more than attraction, desire or even goodwill. These are all ways by which one person goes out towards another, but none of them can take him as far in his quest for the good of another as does betrothed love. 'To give oneself to another' is something more than merely 'desiring what is good' for another—even if as a result of this another 'I' becomes as it were my own, as it does in friendship. Betrothed love is something different from and more than all the forms of love . . . both as it affects the individual subject, the person who loves, and as regards the interpersonal union which it creates. When betrothed love enters into this interpersonal relationship something more than friendship results: two people give themselves to each other.[143]

Authentic love between the husband and the wife cannot be reduced to merely the emotional level, to mere consumption of sympathy or pleasure. It "consists in the thoroughgoing transformation of sympathy into friendship."[144] In friendship the person wills the good for the friend's sake; the person loves the friend for the friend's sake. In betrothed love the spouses, without losing possession of the self, fully surrender the self to another and become the good that is given to the other for the other's own sake.[145] Friendship thus provides the context wherein the spouses are able to express the intimacy of betrothed love. The spouses cannot themselves be the good to each other without first willing the good of the other for the other's own sake. Although betrothed love is distinct and deeper than friendship, it cannot develop in isolation from friendship. As Wojtyla concludes:

> In particular, it is essential that betrothed love should ally itself closely with goodwill and friendship. Without these allies it may find itself in a very dangerous void, and the persons involved in it may feel helpless in face of conditions, internal and external, which they have inadvertently permitted to arise within themselves or between themselves.[146]

Therefore, without friendship in the interpersonal relationship of marriage, love remains mere sympathy and can never be transformed into

143. Wojtyla, *Love and Responsibility*, 96.
144. Wojtyla, *Love and Responsibility*, 93.
145. See Waltz, "Marriage," 53.
146. Wojtyla, *Love and Responsibility*, 100.

betrothed love. It is on this same line of thought that Pope Francis concludes his post-synodal Apostolic Exhortation: "[n]o family drops down from heaven perfectly formed; families need constantly to grow and mature in the ability to love."[147]

---

147. Francis, *AL*, par. 325.

Chapter 5

Conclusion

IT IS BOTH ANCIENT and new—to retrieve confidence in the divine beauty and transcendental character of friendship, as a particular form of Christian love. This retrieval can be accomplished. This book has shown the novelty of the Christian understanding of friendship as it emerged in the Fourth Gospel and how, through scriptural interpretation and theological systematic reflection, it reached its culmination in the synthesis of Thomas Aquinas in the thirteenth century. Then, in order to strengthen the central focus, other writers, philosophers, and theologians were utilized to outline how, in a practical way, a deeper theological appreciation of friendship enriches the life of an authentic Christian and contributes to the continuous renewal of moral theology called for by the Second Vatican Council.

The historical-philosophical study in the first chapter of the understanding of friendship in classical times reveals that, for the ancients, friendship was an essential element in their moral reflection, especially in the pursuit of happiness and human flourishing. The chapter showed how the classical understanding of friendship is appropriated in the Christian tradition, and how "love of friendship" has managed to secure its place as a particular form of Christian love, notwithstanding it being at times overshadowed or absorbed by "love of God and of neighbor." This was especially the case during the late medieval period and, even more, in Modernity, when moral theology started to distance itself from its biblical and patristic roots. This dichotomy resulted in a morality that was concerned with the adherence to laws and precepts rather than with the broader vision of

Conclusion

forming a Christian character through the virtues, the gifts of the Holy Spirit and a life of grace.

The relationships between Jesus and a number of Johannine characters and, especially, the whole group of the disciples during the intimate occasion of the Last Supper, were primarily relationships of love. These relationships are beautifully understood when analyzed in terms of friendship. Having lowered himself by washing the feet of the disciples,[1] thus addressing the problem of inequality, Jesus raises the status of the disciples from "slaves/servants" to "friends."[2] By sharing the knowledge given to him by the Father with the disciples, Jesus incorporates them in the mutual unity that exists between him and the Father. As friends of Jesus, the disciples are called to abide in his love and to love one another in the same way Jesus loves them.[3] They are also called to share in the same mission of Jesus and to keep his commandments.[4] Yet, theirs is not a servile obedience like that between a slave and his master, but one which emanates from the very love of Jesus, which he himself lives out in his relationship with the Father. Through the descent of the Spirit of Jesus, something unimaginable in the classical tradition—relationship between humanity and the divine—becomes a possibility.

Through an exegesis of the Fourth Gospel, together with the heritage of friendship in the Christian tradition and philosophy, in the thirteenth century, Saint Thomas Aquinas defines the theological virtue of *caritas* in terms of *amicitia* of man with God. In the *Summa Theologiae*, Aquinas argues that *caritas*—the ideal relationship that unites humanity to God—can also be explained in terms of *amicitia*. By equating *caritas* with *amicitia*, Aquinas highlights the transcendental character of friendship and makes "love of friendship" the highest expression of love.

"Love of friendship" is essentially a spiritual kind of love, is exercised "[o]penly towards all, without ceasing; with a view to, and in joyful hope of, a reciprocity that . . . [is] personal, universal and eternal."[5] According to Aquinas, human beings are so created to find their ultimate happiness/beatitude in friendship with God, and the "love of neighbor" is incorporated in that friendship. In this way, Aquinas makes friendship the *telos* of the

---

1. See John 13:1–30.
2. John 15:15.
3. See John 15:10. 12.
4. See John 15:14.
5. Carmichael, *Friendship*, 126.

Christian life. Aquinas's consideration of friendship as a foundational piece to his ethical system provides a fundamental cornerstone for the renewal of contemporary Christian ethics.

Chapter 4 shows how the retrieval of a theology of friendship, rooted in Holy Scripture and the Christian tradition, relates to the continuous renewal of the theology of the Christian life (moral theology) called for by the Second Vatican Council. Since friendship upholds the singularity, the subjectivity, the irreducibility and non-transferability of personhood, it is necessary for moral theology to become more person-centered and virtue-centered in the context of communion ecclesiology. It also proposes it as a means of enriching the spiritual and the ethical dimension of the Christian life by showing how one can apply a theology of friendship to the personal, economic, and socio-political spheres, as well as to marriage and family ethics. Friendship understood as an excellence in human relationships and an excellence in spiritual life can therefore be viewed as a foundational category for the Christian moral and spiritual life. Since it also brings together Holy Scripture, theology and spirituality, it can also be understood as contributing to the task of renewal in moral theology, both in its fundamental and practical aspect.

The "love of friendship" discussed in this book is love that sets people free to be and to become in their own individual uniqueness, and which is essentially directed towards, hopes for and invites, reciprocal love and the joy of fulfilment in mutual relationship, yet without possessively demanding it. Such love can exist as an open offer without being reciprocated. However, it is precisely its orientation towards the person of the other and towards mutuality, with goodwill and respectful interest, that distinguishes the "love of friendship" from possessive love on one hand, and an absolutely disinterested (or uninterested) altruism on the other. Having engendered a relationship, this same love remains within it, continually given and received. As Saint John Henry Newman beautifully puts it: "love of friendship" gives "form and direction" to the "love of mankind at large, making it intelligent and discriminating."[6]

When a person loves with "love of friendship" the person desires the good for the friend's own sake and loves the friend for the friend's sake, and thus one acknowledges the dignity of the person. Through the practice of "love of friendship" all persons involved flourish and mature.

---

6. Newman, "Love of Relations and Friends," Sermon 5.

Conclusion

"Love of friendship" is based on the desire to give oneself. But this desire is also a natural inclination reflecting the best of human nature since, according to Aristotle, friendship is a virtue or implies a virtue.[7] Now friendship is also *caritas*.[8] *Caritas* signifies "not only the love of God, but also a certain friendship with him; which implies, besides love, the mutual return of love, together with a certain mutual communion."[9] This communion consists in a certain familiar conversation with God, begun here in this earthly life and perfected in the next life, through glory.[10] Indeed, it is God who reveals what friendship is. In our LORD Jesus Christ, our whole being becomes aligned with the universal loving friendship of God. Unity in such friendship may be considered as sacramental, an icon of the transcendent presence of the Trinitarian God. Friendship with God in prayer relates us with the whole human community and all creation as we look to the joy that Saint Augustine's words express, the eternal "enjoyment of God, and of each other in God."[11]

---

7. See Aristotle, *NE*, 1155a3–4.
8. See Aquinas, *ST* II-II.23.1.
9. Aquinas, *ST* II-II.65.5.
10. See Aquinas, *ST* II-II.65.5.
11. Augustine, *City of God*, 19.17.

Bibliography

Aelred of Rievaulx. *Spiritual Friendship*. Translated by Mary E. Laker. Kalamazoo, MI: Cistercian, 1977.

Ambrose. *On the Duties of the Clergy*. Edited by Philip Schaff and Henry Wace. Vol. 10. Translated by H. de Romestin et al. Buffalo, NY: Christian Literature, 1885. http://www.newadvent.org/fathers/34013.htm.

Anderson, B. W. "Abraham: The Friend of God." *Interpretation* 42 (1988) 353–66.

Aquinas, Thomas. *Commentary on the Gospel of John*. Translated by J. A. Weisheipl and F. R. Larcher. Albany, NY: Magi, 1998. http://dhspriory.org/thomas/SSJohn.htm.

———. *Commentary on the Nicomachean Ethics*. 2 vols. Translated by C. I. Litzinger. Chicago: Henry Regnery, 1964. http://dhspriory.org/thomas/Ethics8.htm#12.

———. *Librum Beati Dionysii De Divinis Nominibus*. Translated by Robert Busa. Turin, 1950. http://www.corpusthomisticum.org/cdnoo.html.

———. *Scriptum Super Sententiis Magistri Petri Lombardi*. Edited by R. P. Maria Faianus Moos. Paris: P. Lethielleux, 1933.

———. *St. John*. Catena Aurea. Vol. 4. Albany, NY: Preserving Christian Publications, 1995.

———. *Summa Contra Gentiles*. Edited by Joseph Kenny. Translated by Vernon J. Bourke et al. New York, NY: Hanover, 1955–1957. http://dhspriory.org/thomas/ContraGentiles.htm.

———. *Summa Theologiae*. Translated by David Bourke. Vol. 56. London: Blackfriars, 1975.

———. *Summa Theologiae*. Translated by Eric D'Arcy. Vol. 19. London: Blackfriars, 1967.

———. *Summa Theologiae*. Translated by R. J. Batten. Vol. 34. London: Blackfriars, 1975.

———. *Summa Theologiae*. Translated by Thomas R. Heath. Vol. 35. London: Blackfriars, 1972.

———. *Summa Theologiae*. Translated by W. D. Hughes. Vol. 23. London: Blackfriars, 1969.

Aristotle. *Nicomachean Ethics*. Translated by David Ross. London: Oxford University Press, 1954.

Augustine. *City of God*. Translated by J. W. C. Wand. London: Oxford University Press, 1963.

———. *Concerning Faith of Things Not Seen*. Edited by Philip Schaff. Translated by C. L. Cornish. Buffalo, NY: Christian Literature, 1887.

Bibliography

———. *Confessions*. Translated by Henry Chadwick. London: Oxford University Press, 1991.

———. *Eighty-Three Different Questions*. Translated by D. L Mosher. Washington, DC: The Catholic University of America Press, 1982.

———. *On Christian Doctrine*. Vol. 2. Edited by Philip Schaff. Translated by James Shaw. Buffalo, NY: Christian Literature, 1887.

———. *On the Good of Marriage*. Vol. 3. Edited by Philip Schaff. Translated by C. L. Cornish. Buffalo, NY: Christian Literature, 1987.

Banham, Gary. "Kantian Friendship." In *Critical Communities and Aesthetic Practices: Dialogues with Tony O'Connor on Society, Art, and Friendship*, edited by F. Halsall et al., 171–80. Manchester: Springer, 2011.

Barr, James. "Words for Love in Biblical Greek." In *The Glory of Christ in the New Testament: Studies in Christology in Memory of George Bradford Caird*, edited by L. D. Hurst and N. T. Wright, 3–18. Oxford: Clarendon, 1987.

Barth, Karl. *Ethics*. Translated by G. W. Bromiley. Edinburgh: T. & T. Clark, 1981.

Bauerschmidt, Fredrick Christian. *Holy Teaching: Introducing the Summa Theologiae of St. Thomas Aquinas*. Grand Rapids: Brazor, 2005.

Benedict XVI. *Jesus of Nazareth: From the Baptism in Jordan to the Transfiguration*, xii–xvii. Vol. 1. New York: Doubleday, 2007.

———. "General Audience" October 8, 2008. http://w2.vatican.va/content/benedict-xvi/en/audiences/2008/documents/hf_ben-xvi_aud_20081008.html.

Bernard, J. H. *A Critical and Exegetical Commentary on the Gospel According to St. John*. Edited by A. H. McNeile. Vol. 2. Edinburgh: T. & T. Clark, 1928.

Beutler, Johannes. *A Commentary on the Gospel of John*. Translated by Michael Tait. Grand Rapids: Eerdmans, 2017.

Blum, Lawrence A. *Friendship, Altruism, and Morality*. London: Routledge & Kegan Paul, 1980.

Bolotin, David. *Plato's Dialogue on Friendship: An Interpretation of the Lysis with a New Translation*. New York: Cornell University Press, 1979.

Brown, Raymond E. *The Gospel According to John: Introduction, Translation, and Notes*. 2 vols. Garden City, NY: Doubleday, 1966–70.

———. *The Gospel According to John, XIII–XXI*. Anchor Bible. London: Geoffrey Chapman, 1971.

Brown, Raymond E. et al. "Texts and Versions." In *The New Jerome Biblical Commentary*, edited by Raymond E. Brown et al., 1083–1112. Bangalore: Theological, 2011.

Burt, Donald X. *Augustine's World: An Introduction to His Speculative Philosophy*. Maryland: University of America Press, 1996.

Caffarra, Carlo. "Marriage as a Reality in the Order of Creation and Marriage as a Sacrament." In *Contemporary Perspectives of Christian Marriage*, edited by Richard Malone and John Connery, 166–80. Chicago: Loyola University Press, 1984.

Carmichael, Liz. *Friendship: Interpreting Christian Love*. London: T. & T. Clark, 2004.

Cassian, John. *The Conferences*. Translated by Boniface Ramsey. New York: Paulist, 2000.

Cessario, Romanus. *Introduction to Moral Theology*. Washington, DC: The Catholic University of America Press, 2001.

———. *The Moral Virtues and Theological Ethics*. Notre Dame, IN: University of Notre Dame Press, 1991.

Charlesworth, James H. *The Beloved Disciple: Whose Witness Validates the Gospel of John?* Valley Forge, PA: Trinity, 1995.

Bibliography

Chenu, Marie D. *Toward Understanding Saint Thomas*. Chicago: Henry Regency, 1964.
Cicero, Marcus Tullius. *On Friendship*. Translated by Benjamin E. Smith. New York: Century, 1906.
Clark, Elisabeth. *Jerome, Chrysostom, and Friends: Essays and Translation*. New York: Mellen, 1979.
Cloutier, David and William C. Mattison III, "The Resurgence of Virtue in Recent Moral Theology." *Journal of Moral Theology* 3 (2014) 228–59.
Coloe, Mary L. "Sources in the Shadows: John 13 and the Johannine Community." In *New Currents through John: A Global Perspective*, edited by F. Lozada Jr. and T. Thatcher, 69–82. Society of Biblical Literature Resources for Biblical Studies 54. Atlanta, GA: Society of Biblical Literature, 2006.
———. "Witness and Friend: Symbolism associated with John the Baptiser." In *Imagery in the Gospel of John*, edited by J. Frey et al., 319–32. WUNT 200. Tübingen: Mohr Siebeck, 2006.
Corley, Jeremy. "Caution, Fidelity, and the Fear of God: Ben Sira's Teaching on Friendship in Sir 6:5–17." *Estudios Biblicos* 24 (1996) 313–40.
Crouse, Robert D. "Love and Friendship in Medieval Theology: Aristotle, St. Augustine, St. Thomas and Dante." In *Christian Friendship*, edited by Susan Harris, 140–41. Charlottetown: St. Peter, 2005.
Culpepper, R. Alan. *Anatomy of the Fourth Gospel: A Study in Literary Design*. Philadelphia: Fortress, 1983.
———. *John, the Son of Zebedee: The Life of a Legend*. Columbia: University of South Carolina Press, 1994.
Culy, Martin M. *Echoes of Friendship in the Gospel of John*. Sheffield: Sheffield Phoenix, 2010.
D'Arcy, Martin. *The Mind and Heart of Love*. London: Collins Fontana, 1962.
D'Arms, John. "The Roman *Convivum* and Equality." In *Sympotica: A Symposium on the Symposion*, edited by O. Murray, 308–20. Oxford: Oxford University Press, 1990.
Delicata, Nadia. "The renewal of moral theology: from confessing sins to forming Christians in the world." In *The Quest for Authenticity and Human Dignity: A Festschrift in honour of Professor George Grima on his 70th birthday*, edited by Emmanuel Agius and Hector Scerri, 135–53. Malta: University of Malta, 2015.
De Lubac, Henri. *Medieval Exegesis: The Four Senses of Scriptures*. 3 vols. Translated by Mark Sebanc and E. M. Macierowski. Grand Rapids: Eerdmans, 1998–2009.
———. *The Church: Paradox and Mystery*. Translated by J. R. Dunne. New York: Alba House, 1969.
Dillon, John M., and Jackson P. Hershbell. *Lamblichus: On the Pythagorean Way of Life. Test, Translation, and Notes*. SBL Texts and Translations 29. Graeco-Roman Religious Series 11. Atlanta: GA, 1991.
Elowsky, Joel C, ed. *John 1–10*. Vol. 4a. Ancient Christian Commentary on Scripture: New Testament. Downers: InterVarsity, 2006.
Esler, Philip F., and Ronald A. Piper. *Lazarus, Mary and Martha: A Social-Scientific and Theological Reading of John*. London: SCM, 2006.
Evans, Gillian R. *The Language and Logic of the Bible: The Earlier Middle Ages*. Cambridge: Cambridge University Press, 1984.
Ferreira, Jamie M. *Love's Grateful Striving: A Commentary on Kierkegaard's Works of Love*. Oxford: Oxford University Press, 2001.

Bibliography

Fiorenza, Francis Schüssler, and John P. Galvin. *Systematic Theology: Roman Catholic Perspective*. Vol. 1. Minneapolis: Fortress, 1991.

Fiske, Adele M. "Cassian and Monastic Friendship." *American Benedictine Review* 12 (1961) 190–205.

———. *Friends and Friendship in the Monastic Tradition*. Mexico: Cuernavaca, 1970.

Fitzgerald, John T. *Greco–Roman Perspectives on Friendship*. Atlanta: Scholars, 1997.

Florensky, Pavel. *The Pillar and Ground of the Truth: An Essay in Orthodox Theodicy in Twelve Letters*. Translated and annotated by Boris Jakin. Princeton: Princeton University Press, 1997.

Francis. *Amoris Laetitia*, Apostolic Exhortation. March 19, 2016. http://w2.vatican.va/content/dam/francesco/pdf/apost_exhortations/documents/papa-francesco_esortazione-ap_20160319_amoris-laetitia_en.pdf.

———. *Laudato Si'*, Encyclical. May 24, 2015. http://w2.vatican.va/content/francesco/en/encyclicals/documents/papa-francesco_20150524_enciclica-laudato-si.html.

———. "Message for the celebration of the World Day of Peace." December 8, 2013. https://w2.vatican.va/content/francesco/en/messages/peace/documents/papa-francesco_20131208_messaggio-xlvii-giornata-mondiale-pace-2014.html.

Fullam, Lisa. "Toward a Virtue Ethics of Marriage: Augustine and Aquinas on Friendship in Marriage." *Theological Studies* 73 (2012) 663–92.

Furnish, Victor Paul. *The Love Command in the New Testament*. Nashville: Abingdon, 1972.

Gallagher, David M. "Desire for Beatitude and Love of Friendship in Thomas Aquinas." *Medieval Studies* 58 (1996) 1–45.

———. "The Will and Its Acts (Ia IIae, qq. 6–17)." In *The Ethics of Aquinas*, edited by Stephen J. Pope, 69–89. Washington, DC: Georgetown University Press, 2002.

Gallagher, John A. *Time Past, Time Future: An Historical Study of Catholic Moral Theology*. Eugene, OR: Wipf & Stock, 1990.

Gignac, Francis T. "The Use of Verbal Variety in the Fourth Gospel." In *Transcending Boundaries: Contemporary Readings of the New Testament: Essays in Honor of Francis J. Moloney* 187, edited by Rekha M. Chennattu and Mary L. Coloe, 193–95. Rome: Salesiano, 2005.

Gilson, Étienne. *L'esprit de la philosophie medieval*. Paris: Librairie philosophiqe J. Vrin, 1932.

Gregor, Brian. "Friends and Neighbors: Kierkegaard and the Possibility of Transformative Friendship." *Revista Portuguesa de Filosofia* 64 (2008) 924–26.

Gregory of Nyssa. *The Life of Moses*. Translated by A. J. Malherbe and E. Ferguson. New York: Paulist, 1978.

Hallier, Amédée. *The Monastic Theology of Aelred of Rievaulx: An Experiential Theology* 2. Translated by Columban Heaney. Spencer, MA: Cistercian, 1969.

Häring, Bernard. *Free and Faithful in Christ: Moral Theology for Clergy and Laity*. 3 vols. Slough: St Paul, 1978–81.

———. *The Law of Christ: Moral Theology for Priests and Laity*. 3 vols. Translated by Edwin G. Kaiser. Westminster: Newman, 1961–65.

Harnach, Adolf. "'Friends' (*hoi philoi*)." In *The Mission and Expansion of Christianity in the First Three Centuries*, translated by J. Moffatt, 419–21. London: Williams & Norgate, 1908.

Harrington, Daniel J. "Sage Advice About Friendship." *The Bible Today* 32 (1994) 79–83.

Bibliography

Harrington, Daniel J., and James F. Keenan. *Jesus and Virtue Ethics: Building Bridges between New Testament Studies and Moral Theology.* Chicago: Sheed & Ward, 2002.

Hauerwas, Stanley. *A community of character: toward a constructive Christian social ethic.* Notre Dame, IN: University of Notre Dame Press, 1981.

———. *The peaceable kingdom: a primer in Christian ethics.* Notre Dame, IN: University of Notre Dame Press, 1983.

Hayden Lemmons, R. Mary. "Equality, Gender, and John Paul II." *Logos* 5 (2002) 111–30.

Hobbes, Thomas. *Leviathan.* Edited by C. B. Macpherson. London: Penguin, 1982.

Irwin, William H. "Fear of God, the Analogy of Friendship, and Ben Sira's Theodicy." *Biblica* 76 (1995) 553–59.

Jacques Maritain Center. "A First Glance at St. Thomas Aquinas." http://maritain.nd.edu/jmc/etext/peep-22.htm.

John Paul II. *Fides et Ratio*, Encyclical. September 14, 1998. http://w2.vatican.va/content/john-paul-ii/en/encyclicals/documents/hf_jp-ii_enc_14091998_fides-et-ratio.html.

———. "General Audience." November 24, 1999. https://w2.vatican.va/content/john-paul-ii/en/audiences/1999/documents/hf_jp-ii_aud_24111999.html.

———. *Veritatis Splendor*, Encyclical. October 6, 1993. http://w2.vatican.va/content/john-paul-ii/en/encyclicals/documents/hf_jp-ii_enc_06081993_veritatis-splendor.html#%24B.

Johnson, Elisabeth. *She Who Is: The Mystery of God in Feminist Theological Discourse.* New York: Crossroad, 1992.

Jordan, Mark D. "Thomas Aquinas' Disclaimers in the Aristotelian Commentaries." In *Philosophy and the God of Abraham: Essays in Memory of James A. Weisheipl* 12, edited by R. James Long, 99–112. Toronto: Pontifical Institute of Medieval Studies, 1991.

Julian of Norwich. *Showings.* Translated by E. Colledge and J. Walsh. New York: Paulist, 1978.

Justin Martyr. *Dialogue with Trypho.* Vol. 1. Edited by Alexander Roberts et al. Translated by Marcus Dods and George Reith. Buffalo, NY: Christian Literature, 1885. http://www.newadvent.org/fathers/01281.htm.

Kant, Immanuel. *Fundamental Principles of the Metaphysics of Morals.* Translated by T. K. Abbot. New York: Appleton, 1938.

———. *Lectures on Ethics.* Translated by Louis Infield. New York: Harper & Row, 1963.

———. *The Doctrine of Virtue: Part II of the Metaphysics of Morals.* Translated by Mary J. Gregor. New York: Harper, 1964.

Kasper, Walter. "The Sacramental Dignity of Marriage." In *Theology of Christian Marriage*, translated by David Smith, 340–50. London: Burns & Oaths, 1980.

Keenan, James F. *A History of Catholic Moral Theology in the Twentieth Century: From Confessing Sins to Liberating Consciences.* London: Continuum, 2010.

———. "Bernard Häring's Influence on American Catholic Moral Theology." *Journal of Moral Theology* 1 (2012) 29–41.

Kennedy, Terence. "Paths of Reception: How *Gaudium et Spes* shaped Fundamental Moral Theology." *Studia Moralia* 42 (2004) 115–45.

Kierkegaard, Søren. *Works of Love.* Edited and translated by Howard V. Hong and Edna Hong. Princeton: Princeton University Press, 1995.

Knauer, Peter. "The Hermeneutic Function of the Principle of Double Effect." *The Natural Law Forum* 12 (1967) 132–62.

Bibliography

Konstan, David. *Friendship in the Classical World*. Cambridge: Cambridge University Press, 1997.

———. "Greek Friendship." *The American Journal of Philology* 117 (1996) 71–94.

Lash, Nicholas. *The Beginning and End of Religion*. Cambridge: Cambridge University Press, 1996.

Leclercq, Jean. *The Love of Learning and the Desire for God: A Study of Monastic Culture*. Translated by Catharine Misrahi. New York, NY: Fordham University Press, 1961.

Lee, Dorothy A. "Friendship, Love and Abiding in the Gospel of John." In *Transcending Boundaries: Contemporary Readings of the New Testament: Essays in Honor of Francis J. Moloney 187*, edited by Rekha M. Chennattu and Mary L. Coloe, 57–74. Rome: Ateneo Salesiano, 2005.

Lefler, Nathan. *Theologizing Friendship: How Amicitia in the Thought of Aelred and Aquinas Inscribes the Scholastic Turn*. Eugene: Pickwick, 2014.

Lewis, Clive S. *The Four Loves*. London: Geoffrey Bles, 1960.

Lienhard, Joseph T. "Friendship, Friends." In *Augustine through the Ages: An Encyclopaedia*, edited by Allan D. Fitzgerald, 372–73. Grand Rapids: Eerdmans, 2009.

MacIntyre, Alasdair. *A Short History of Ethics*. New York: Simon & Schuster, 1996.

———. *After Virtue*. Notre Dame, IN: University of Notre Dame Press, 1981.

Mahoney, John. *The Making of Moral Theology*. Oxford: Clarendon, 1987.

Malina, Bruce J., and Richard L. Rohrbaugh. *Social-Science Commentary on the Gospel of John*. Minneapolis: Fortress, 1998.

Mangan, Joseph T. "An Historical Analysis of the Principle of Double Effect." *Theological Studies* 10 (1949) 41–61.

Mansini, Guy. "*Similitudo, Communicatio*, and the Friendship of Charity in Aquinas." In *Thomistica*, edited by E. Manning, 1–26. Leuven: Peeters, 1995.

Maritain, Jacques. *The Person and the Common Good*. Notre Dame, IN: University of Notre Dame Press, 1985.

Martin, Francis, and William M. Wright IV. *The Gospel of John*. Grand Rapids, MI: Baker, 2015.

Mattison III, William C. *Introducing Moral Theology: True Happiness and the Virtues*. Grand Rapids, MI: Brazos, 2008.

May, Todd. *Friendship in an Age of Economics: Resisting the Forces of Neoliberalism*. Plymouth: Lexington, 2012.

McEvoy, James. "The other as oneself: friendship and love in the thought of St Thomas Aquinas." In *Thomas Aquinas: Approaches to Truth*, edited by James J. McEvoy and Michael Dunne, 16–37. Dublin: Four Courts, 2002.

———. "The Theory of Friendship in the Latin Ages: Hermeneutics, Contextualization and the Transmission and Reception of Ancient Texts and Ideas, from c. AD 350 to c. 1500." In *Friendship in Medieval Europe*, edited by Julian Haseldine, 3–36. Stroud: Sutton, 1999.

McGuire, Brian P. *Friendship and Community: The Monastic Experience 350–1350*. Kalamazoo, MI: Cistercian, 1988.

———. "Looking Back on Friendship: Medieval Experience and Modern Context." *Cistercian Studies* (1986) 123–42.

———. "Love, friendship and sex in the eleventh century: The experience of Anselm." *Studia Theologica* 28 (1974) 111–52.

Bibliography

———. "Monastic Friendship and Toleration in Twelfth-Century Cistercian Life." In *Monks, Hermits and the Ascetic Tradition* 22, edited by W. J. Sheils, 147–60. Oxford: Blackwell, 1985.

———. "The Cistercians and the Transformation of Monastic Friendships." *Analecta Cisterciensia* 37 (1981) 1–63.

McLuhan, Marshall. *The Classical Trivium: The Place of Thomas Nashe in the Learning of His Time*. Edited by W. Terrence Gordon. Corte Madera: Gingko, 2006.

McNamara, Marie Aquinas. *Friends and Friendship for St. Augustine*. New York: Alba, 1964.

Mealey, Ann Marie. *The Identity of Christian Morality*. London: Routledge, 2016.

Meilaender, Gilbert. *Friendship: A Study in Theological Ethics*. Notre Dame, IN: Notre Dame University Press, 1981.

Mews, Constant J., and Neville Chiavaroli. "The Latin West." In *Friendship: A History*, edited by Barbara Caine, 73–110. London: Equinox, 2009.

Mitias, Michael H. *Friendship: A Central Moral Value*. Amsterdam: Rodopi, 2012.

Moloney, Francis J. *Glory not Dishonor: Reading John 13–20 (21)*. Minneapolis: Fortress, 1998.

———. *The Gospel of John*. Sacra Pagina 4. Collegeville, MN: Liturgical, 1998.

Moltmann, Jürgen. *The Church in the Power of the Spirit*. London: SCM, 1997.

Moser, Antônio, and Bernardino Leers. *Moral Theology: Dead Ends and Ways Forward*. Translated by Paul Burns. Turnbridge Wells: Burns & Oates, 1990.

Newman, John H. *A Letter Addressed to His Grace the Duke of Norfolk on Occasion of Mr. Gladstone's Recent Expostulation*. New York: Catholic, 1875.

———. "Love of Relations and Friends," Sermon 5. http://www.newmanreader.org/works/parochial/volume2/sermon5.html.

———. *Spiritual Writings*. Modern Spiritual Writers Series. Maryknoll, NY: Orbis, 2012.

Nichols, Aidan. *Discovering Aquinas: An Introduction to his Life, Works and Influence*. London: Darton, Longman and Todd, 2002.

Nygren, Andres. *Agape and Eros*. Translated by Philips Watson. London: SPCK, 1982.

O'Day, Gail R. "Jesus as Friend in the Gospel of John." In *Transcending Boundaries: Contemporary Readings of the New Testament: Essays in Honor of Francis J. Moloney* 187, edited by Rekha M. Chennattu and Mary L. Coloe, 75–92. Rome: Salesiano, 2005.

O'Grady, John F. "The Role of the Beloved Disciple." *Biblical Theological Bulletin* 9 (1979) 58–65.

O'Keefe, Mark. *Becoming Good, Becoming Holy: On the Relationship of Christian Ethics and Spirituality*. Eugene, OR: Wipf & Stock, 2005.

O'Neil, Edward N. "Plutarch on Friendship." In *Greco-Roman Perspectives on Friendship*, edited by John T. Fitzgerald, 105–22. Atlanta: Scholars, 1997.

Oppenheimer, Helen. *The Hope of Happiness: A Sketch for a Christian Humanism*. London: SPCK, 1983.

Ouellet, Marc. "The Ecclesiology of Communion, 50 Years after the Opening of Vatican II." https://adoremus.org/2012/09/15/The-Ecclesiology-of-Communion-50-Years-after-the-Opening-of-Vatican-Council-II/.

Owens, Joseph, and R. A. Gauthier. "Aquinas as Aristotle Commentator." In *St. Thomas Aquinas 1274–1974 Commemorative Studies*, vol. 1, 213–38. Toronto: Pontifical Institute of Medieval Studies, 1974.

Bibliography

Pazdan, Mary M. "Thomas Aquinas and Contemporary Biblical Interpreters: 'I Call You Friends' (John 15:15)." *New Blackfriars* 86 (2005) 465–77.

Pieper, Josef. *Guide to Thomas Aquinas*. Translated by Richard and Clara Winston. Scranton: Pantheon, 1962.

———. *The Four Cardinal Virtues: Prudence, Justice, Fortitude, Temperance*. Notre Dame, IN: University of Notre Dame Press, 1966.

Pinches, Charles. "Friendship and Tragedy: The Fragilities of Goodness." *First Things* 3 (1990) 38–45.

Pinckaers, Servais. "A Historical Perspective on Intrinsically Evil Acts." In *The Pinckaers Reader: Renewing Thomistic Moral Theology*, edited by John Berkman and Craig Titus, 185–235. Washington, DC: The Catholic University of America Press.

———. "An Encyclical for the Future: *Veritatis splendor*." In *Veritatis splendor and the Renewal of Moral Theology*, edited by J. A DiNoia and Romanus Cessario, 11–71. Princeton: Scepter, 1999.

———. *Morality: The Catholic View*. Translated by Michael Sherwin. Notre Dame, IN: St. Augustine, 2001.

———. "Revisionist Understandings of Actions in the Wake of Vatican II." In *The Pinckaers Reader: Renewing Thomistic Moral Theology*, edited by John Berkman and Craig Titus, 236–272. Washington, DC: The Catholic University of America Press, 2005.

———. *The Sources of Christian Ethics*. Translated by M. T. Noble. Edinburgh: T. & T. Clark, 1995.

Pius XI. *Casti Connubii*, Encyclical. December 31, 1930. https://w2.vatican.va/content/pius-xi/en/encyclicals/documents/hf_p-xi_enc_19301231_casti-connubii.html.

Pius XII. *Divino afflante Spiritu*, Encyclical. September 30, 1943. http://w2.vatican.va/content/pius-xii/en/encyclicals/documents/hf_p-xii_enc_30091943_divino-afflante-spiritu.html.

Plato. *Lysis*. Edited by E. Hamilton and H. Cairns. Translated by J. Wright. Princeton: Princeton University Press, 1961.

———. *Phaedo*. Edited by David Gallop. Translated by Clarendon Press. Oxford: Oxford University Press, 2009.

———. *The Symposium*. Translated by Christopher Gill. London: Penguin, 2003.

Popkes, Enno Edzard. *Die Theologie der Liebe Gottes in den johanneischen Schriften: Studien zur Semantik der Liebe und zum Motivkreis des Dualismus*, Wissenschaftliche Untersuchungen zum Neuen Testament II 197. Tübingen: Mohr Siebeck, 2005.

Porter, Jean. "*De Ordine Caritatis*: Charity, Friendship, and Justice in Thomas Aquinas's *Summa Theologiae*." *Thomist* 53 (1989) 197–213.

———. "The Common Good in Thomas Aquinas." In *In Search of the Common God*, edited by Dennis McCann and Patrick D. Miller, 94–120. New York, NY: T. & T. Clark, 2005.

———. *The Recovery of Virtue: The Relevance of Aquinas for Christian Ethics*. Louisville, KY: Westminster/John Knox, 1990.

Preca, George. *The Watch: Prayer Book for SDC Members*. Malta: Veritas, 1998.

Puthenkandathil, Eldho. *Philos: A Designation for the Jesus–Disciple Relationship: An Exegetico-Theological Investigation of the Term in the Fourth Gospel*. New York: Peter Lang, 1993.

Quast, Kevin. *Peter and The Beloved Disciple: Figures for a Community in Crisis*. JSNT 32. Sheffield: JSOT, 1989.

Bibliography

Rahner, Karl. "Marriage as a Sacrament." In *Theological Investigations*, vol. 10, translated by David Bourke, 199–221. New York, NY: Herder and Herder, 1973.

Reumann, John. "Philippians, Especially chapter 4, as a 'Letter of Friendship': Observations on a Checkered History of Scholarship." In *Friendship, Flattery, and Frankness of Speech: Studies on Friendship in the New Testament World*, edited by J. T. Fitzgerald, 83-106. Leiden: E. J. Brill, 1996.

Rhonheimer, Martin. "The Moral Object of Human Acts and the Role of Reason According to Aquinas: A Restatement and Defense of My View." *Josephinum Journal of Theology* 18 (2011) 454–506.

———. "The Perspective of the Acting Person and the Nature of Practical Reason: The 'Object of the Human Act' in Thomistic Anthropology and Action." In *The Perspective of the Acting Person: Essays in the Renewal of Thomistic Moral Philosophy*, edited by William F. Murphy Jr., 195–249. Washington, DC: The Catholic University of America Press, 2008.

Salzman, Todd A. "Friendship, Sacrament, and Marriage: The Distinction between Christian Marital Friendship and Non-Christian Marital Friendship." In *Marriage in the Catholic Tradition: Scripture, Tradition and Experience*, edited by Todd A. Salzmann et al., 115–24. New York, NY: Crossroad, 2004.

Schnackenburg, Rudolf. *The Gospel According to St John*. Vol. 3. Translated by Devin Smith et al. New York, NY: Crossroad, 1982.

Schneiders, Sandra M. "The Foot Washing (John 13: 1–20): An Experiment in Hermeneutics." *Catholic Biblical Quarterly* 43 (1981) 76–92.

———. *Written That You May Believe: Encountering Jesus in the Fourth Gospel*. New York, NY: Herder & Herder, 2003.

Schockenhoff, Eberhard. "The Theological Virtue of Charity (IIa IIae, qq.23–26)." In *The Ethics of Aquinas*, edited by Stephen J. Pope, 244–58. Washington, DC: Georgetown University Press, 2002.

Schönborn, Christopher. *Happiness, God and Man*. San Francisco: Ignatius, 2010.

Schwartz, Daniel. *Aquinas on Friendship*. Oxford: Oxford University Press, 2007.

Segovia, Fernando F. *The Farewell of the Word: The Johannine Call to Abide*. Minneapolis: Fortress, 1991.

Seneca, Lucius Annaeus. *Letters from a Stoic: All Three Volumes*. Translated by Richard Mott Gummere. Morrisville: Enhanced, 2015.

Shepherd, D. "'Do You Love Me?' A Narrative-Critical Reappraisal of ἀγαπάω and φιλέω in John 21:15–17." *Journal of Biblical Literature* 129 (2010) 777–92.

Siebeck, Mohr. *The Resurrection of Jesus in the Gospel of John*. WUNT 222. Edited by Craig R. Koester and Reimund Bieringer. Tübingen: Mohr Siebeck, 2008.

Simonin, H. D. "Autour De La Solution Thomiste Du Probleme De L'Amor." *Archives d'Historie Doctrinale et Litteraire du Moyen Age* 6 (1931) 265–66.

Smalley, Beryl. *The Study of the Bible in the Middle Ages*. Oxford: Blackwell, 1952.

Smith, Dennis E., and Michael E. Williams, eds. *The Storyteller's Companion to the Bible: John*. Nashville: Abingdon, 1996.

Smith, Dwight Moody. *John*. Nashville: Abingdon, 1999.

———. *The Theology of the Gospel of John*. Cambridge: Cambridge University Press, 1995.

Southern, Richard W. *The Making of the Middle Ages*. New Haven: Yale University Press, 1983.

Spaemann, Robert. *Personen: Versuche über den Unterschied zwischen "etwas" und "jemand."* Stuttgart: Klett-Cotta, 1996.

Bibliography

Steinmetz, David C. "The Superiority of Pre-Critical Exegesis." *Ex Auditu* 1 (1985) 74–82.

Stevick, Daniel B. *Jesus and His Own: A Commentary on John 13–17*. Grand Rapids: Eerdmans, 2011.

Summers, Steve. *Friendship: Exploring its Implications for the Church in Postmodernity*. Ecclesiological Investigations 7. London: T. & T. Clark, 2009.

Taylor, Charles. *A Secular Age*. Cambridge: Harvard University Press, 2007.

Taylor, Jeremy. "A Discourse of the Nature and Offices of Friendship, in a letter to the most ingenious and excellent M. K. P." In *Taylor, Whole Works*, vol. 1, edited by R. Heber and C. P. Eden, 71–98. London: Brown, Green and Longmans, 1847.

Teresa of Avila. *Complete Works*. Vol. 1. Edited and translated by E. A. Peers. London: Sheed and Ward, 1946.

Thorne, Gary. "Friendship: The End of Marriage." In *Human Sexuality and the Nuptial Mystery*, edited by Roy R. Jeal, 45–64. Eugene, OR: Wipf and Stock, 2010.

Titus, Steven Craig. "Servais Pinckaers and the Renewal of Moral Theology." *Journal of Moral Theology* 1 (2012) 43–68.

Torrell, Jean-Pierre. *Saint Thomas Aquinas*. 2 vols. Translated by Robert Royal. Washington, DC: The Catholic University of America Press, 1996–2003.

Tracy, Theodore. "Perfect Friendship in Aristotle's 'Nicomachean Ethics.'" *Illinois Classical Studies* 4 (1979) 65–75.

———. *Physiological Theory and the Doctrine of Mean in Plato and Aristotle*. Berlin: Mouton de Gruyter, 2014.

Tull, Patricia K. "Jonathan's Gift of Friendship." *Interpretation* 58 (2004) 130–43.

Van Impe, Stijn. "Kant on Friendship." *International Journal of Art & Sciences* 4 (2011) 127–39.

Van Tilborg, Sjef. *Imaginative Love in John*. Biblical Interpretation 47. Leiden: E. J. Brill, 1993.

Varghese, Johns. *The Imagery of Love in the Gospel of John*. Rome: Gregorian & Biblical, 2009.

Vatican II Council. *Gaudium et Spes*, Pastoral Constitution. In *Vatican Council II: The Conciliar and Post Conciliar Documents*, edited by Austin Flannery, 794–891. Bombay: St Paul, 1992.

———. *Optatam Totius*, Decree. In *Vatican Council II: The Conciliar and Post Conciliar Documents*, edited by Austin Flannery, 627–41. Bombay: St Paul, 1992.

———. *Sacrosanctum Concilium*, Constitution. In *Vatican Council II: The Conciliar and Post Conciliar Documents*, edited by Austin Flannery, 21–261. Bombay: St Paul, 1992.

Vernon, Mark. *The Philosophy of Friendship*. London: Palgrave, 2005.

Von Balthasar, Hans Urs. "On the Concept of Person." *Communio: International Catholic Review* 13 (1986): 18–26.

Wadell, Paul J. *Becoming Friends: Worship, Justice, and the Practice of Christian Friendship*. Grand Rapids: Brazos, 2002.

———. *Friends of God: Virtues and Gifts in Aquinas*. New York, NY: Peter Lang, 1991.

———. *Friendship and the Moral Life*. Notre Dame, IN: University of Notre Dame Press, 1989.

———. "The Role of Charity in the Moral Theology of Thomas Aquinas." In *Aquinas and Empowerment: Classical Ethics for Ordinary Lives*, edited by G. Simon Harak, 134–69. Washington, DC: Georgetown University Press, 1996.

Walz, Gabriel. "Marriage: Passion, Friendship & Vocation." MA diss., University of St. Thomas, 2015.

Bibliography

Weisheipl, James. Introduction to *Friar Thomas D' Aquino: His Life, Thought, and Works.* Washington, DC: The Catholic University of America Press, 1974.

Wennemann, Daryl J. "The Role of Love in the Thought of Kant and Kierkegaard." https://www.bu.edu/wcp/Papers/Reli/ReliWen.htm.

Westcott, B. F. *The Gospel according to Saint John: The Authorised Version with Introduction and Notes.* Grand Rapids: Eerdmans, 1950.

White, Caroline. *Christian Friendship in the Fourth Century.* Cambridge: CUP, 1992.

White, Reginald E. O. *The Night He was Betrayed: Bible Studies in Our Lord's Preparation for his Passion.* Grand Rapids: Eerdmans, 1982.

Williams, Thomas D. "What is Thomistic Personalism?" *Alpha Omega* 7 (2004) 163–97.

Witherington, Ben. *John's Wisdom: A Commentary on the Fourth Gospel.* Vol. 3. Louisville, KY: Westminster and John Knox, 1995.

Wojtyla, Karol. *Love and Responsibility.* New York: Farrar, 1995.

———. *The Acting Person.* Dodrecht: D. Reidel, 1979.

———. "Thomistic Personalism." In *Person and Community: Selected Essays*, vol. 4, edited by Andrew N. Woznicki and translated by Theresa Sandok, 165–75. New York: Peter Lang, 1993.

Young, William W. *The Politics of Praise: Naming God and Friendship in Aquinas and Derrida.* Aldershot: Ashgate, 2007.

Zizioulas, John D. "Communion and Otherness." Orthodox Peace Fellowship's Occasional Paper 19. Summer 1994. http://incommunion.org/articles/previous-issues/older-issues/communion-and-otherness.

Index

Aelred of Rievaulx, xiv, 18, 28–31, 46, 78, 80
agapē. *See* love
Ambrose, Saint, 20
amicitia as friendship, 4, 14, 27–29, 31, 45–46, 50, 76–77, 79, 83–84, 90, 96, 139
amor. *See* love
Aquinas, Thomas. *See* Thomas Aquinas, Saint
Aristotle, 4, 7–14, 24, 40–41, 49–50, 80–81, 85, 91, 93, 95, 116, 123, 128, 132–33, 141
Augustine, Saint, xiv, 4, 18, 20–25, 46, 87–88, 93, 100–101, 123, 125, 131–33, 141

Balthasar, Hans Urs von, 118–19
Barth, Karl, 120
Beloved Disciple (disciple whom Jesus loved), 48–49, 55–57, 62–67, 70, 74
Benedict, Saint, 28
Benedict XVI, Pope, 85
Bernard of Clairvaux, Saint, 28, 80, 101

caritas. *See* love
Cassian, Saint John, 20, 27
Catechism (of the Catholic Church), 2, 106, 114–15, 130–31, 135
Christian ethics. *See* moral theology
Chrysostom, Saint John, 20, 88

Cicero, 8, 15–19, 24, 28–29, 50–51, 68, 80
Clement of Alexandria, Saint, 19
communion, 6, 14, 18n43, 23, 71, 75–76, 97, 116, 118, 121, 124–25, 140–41
conversion, xi, 21–22, 82, 89

de Lubac, Henri, 85, 125
dilectio. *See* love
Dionysius (pseudo-), 79, 94

Enlightenment, 34–35
Epicurus, 14
equality, 10, 13, 17, 20, 27, 35, 37–38, 53, 58, 68, 90, 127, 130–31, 133
erōs. *See* love
Eucharist, 73
eudaimonia. *See* happiness

Fathers of the Church, 18, 46, 77, 79, 116
Francis, Pope, 128–30, 134–35, 137
free will, 90n62, 98
freedom, 1, 87n49, 110, 128
 of excellence, 115
friendship with God, xiv–xv, 2, 32–33, 47, 51, 72, 77, 90, 94–95, 97–106, 119, 126, 139, 141

God as Holy Trinity, 22–23, 125
grace, x, xiv, xvi, 3–4, 21, 23, 31–32, 56, 82, 87, 90, 94, 99, 101, 108, 115–17, 133n132, 139
Gregory of Nyssa, Saint, 20

Index

happiness, 2, 7, 9, 11, 14–15, 17–18, 35–38, 83, 95, 97, 99–101, 103, 105–6, 108, 116–17, 120, 138–39
Häring, Bernard, 109–11
Hauerwas, Stanley, 115
Hesiod, 5
holiness, 4, 33, 78
Holy Spirit, xvi, 21–23, 69, 80, 82, 90, 97–98, 100, 106, 108, 123–24, 139
Homer, 5
Humanae Vitae, 112

imago Dei, 22, 122
Imitation of Christ, 32–33
Incarnation, 3, 53, 101, 123
inclination
    natural, 40–41, 121, 123, 141
    to perfection, 37, 87
intention, x, 6, 41, 61, 85, 92, 111, 126

John Paul II, Saint, 113, 115, 118, 121
John the Baptist, Saint, 49, 55–56, 74
Jonathan and David, 51, 65
Julian of Norwich, 32
justice, virtue of, x, 10, 13, 25, 38, 107, 119, 127–28, 133
Justin Martyr, Saint, 19

Kant, Immanuel, 35–38
Kierkegaard, Søren, 35–42, 47
koinonia, 13–14, 90, 96n96, 125

Lazarus, Saint, 56–61, 74
Lewis, C. S., 44–45, 47
Lombard, Peter. *See* Peter Lombard
love as
    agapē, xiv, 4, 20, 33, 39, 42–45
    amor, 84, 90–92, 100n120
    caritas, xiv–xv, 4, 14, 16, 29, 31, 39, 42, 45–46, 76–77, 79–80, 83–84, 91, 94–96, 98–106, 119, 123, 127, 139, 141
    dilectio, 91
    erōs, xiv–xv, 44
    philía, xv, 4–6, 9–10, 13, 39, 42–45, 52–53, 126
    storgē, 44

Magisterium (of the Church), 4
manuals of moral theology, 110
marriage, 13, 47, 131–36, 140
Martha, Saint, 57, 59, 60–61, 74
Mary Magdalene, Saint, 65
Mary of Bethany, Saint, 57, 59–61, 69, 74
modernity, 6, 33, 122, 138
monasticism, 26, 30, 46
moral act, 106, 111, 113–14
moral life, 11, 33, 77, 94, 99–100, 108, 114–15, 119, 122
moral theology, x, xv, 32, 47, 77, 83, 108–13, 115–19, 121–22, 124, 127, 138, 140
mutuality, x, 58, 68, 71, 104, 140

natural law, 14, 112, 115–17, 122, 133
nature (essence), xi, xvi, 4, 6, 11–15, 17–19, 21, 34–35, 44, 46, 57, 59, 66, 68, 72, 74, 83, 88, 90n62, 99, 102–4, 106, 110, 113, 116–17, 121, 123, 125–26, 130–36, 141
neighbor, x, xiv, 24–26, 28, 30, 37, 39–42, 76, 86, 88, 99, 101–7, 110, 120, 123, 138–39
Newman, Saint John Henry, xiv, 18–20, 120, 124, 140
nominalism, 108, 122
norms, 109, 114
Nygren, Andres, xiv–xv

obligation (to "the other"), 5, 36
Origen, 20, 49, 53

passion (s), 2, 77, 84, 90–91
Paul VI, Saint, 112
peace, x, 13, 105, 133
penance, sacrament of, 110
perfection, xvi, 30, 37, 46, 87, 91, 93, 100, 105–6, 109, 122, 126, 134
Peter Lombard, 31, 85, 98
philía. See love
Philo of Alexandria, 72
Pinckaers, Servais, 108–9, 112–16, 123
Pius XI, Pope, 134
Pius XII, Pope, 85
Plato, 5, 7, 29, 85

Index

pleasure
friendships based on, 9–12, 14–15, 18–19, 24, 50, 92–93, 95, 129, 135–36
Plutarch, 50
precepts, 36, 47, 110, 122, 138
proportionalism, 112–14
prudence, virtue of, 36
Pythagoras, 6

responsibility (for "the other"), 57, 64, 67, 72–73, 110
revisionists, 110, 112
Ruth and Naomi, 51

scholasticism, 31, 78
selfish (possessive), xiv, 40–41, 92, 129
Seneca, 8, 15, 51
Stoics, 15
storgē. *See* love
suffering, 58, 86, 94, 122, 130, 135

temperance, virtue of, 6, 10
Ten Commandments, 32
Teresa of Avila, Saint, 32
Thomas Aquinas, Saint, xiv–xv, 4, 14, 31–33, 41, 46, 49, 76–77, 79–102, 104–6, 108, 113–16, 118–20, 122–23, 126–27, 132–34, 138–40
Trent, Council of, 31–32

unity, 20, 23–24, 36, 58, 68, 70–71, 75, 93, 97, 102, 114, 124–26, 135, 139, 141
utility
friendships based on, 9–10, 35, 50

Vatican, Second Council of, x, xv, 17–18, 109–12, 118, 122, 124–25, 138, 140
Veritatis Splendor, 113
virtue
as excellence, xiv–xv, 4, 10–12, 14–18, 20, 22–24, 29, 36, 39–40n125, 46, 50, 77, 82–84, 89, 91, 95, 97, 101, 104–6, 108–10, 113, 115–18, 122–23, 127–28, 131, 134–35, 139–41
friendships based on, 16, 20, 49–50, 56, 98
vocation, 78, 111, 114–15, 131

wisdom, 1, 10, 16, 51, 88, 106–7

www.ingramcontent.com/pod-product-compliance
Lightning Source LLC
Chambersburg PA
CBHW062003180426
43198CB00036B/2169